John N. Macomb

Report of the Exploring Expedition from Santa Fé, New Mexico,

to the junction of the Grand and Green rivers of the great Colorado of the West, in

1859

John N. Macomb

Report of the Exploring Expedition from Santa Fé, New Mexico,
to the junction of the Grand and Green rivers of the great Colorado of the West, in 1859

ISBN/EAN: 9783337218706

Printed in Europe, USA, Canada, Australia, Japan

Cover: Foto ©Andreas Hilbeck / pixelio.de

More available books at **www.hansebooks.com**

ENGINEER DEPARTMENT, U. S. ARMY.

REPORT

OF THE

EXPLORING EXPEDITION

FROM SANTA FÉ, NEW MEXICO, TO THE JUNCTION OF THE GRAND AND
GREEN RIVERS OF THE GREAT COLORADO OF THE WEST,

IN 1859,

UNDER THE COMMAND OF

CAPT. J. N. MACOMB,
CORPS OF TOPOGRAPHICAL ENGINEERS
(NOW COLONEL OF ENGINEERS);

WITH

GEOLOGICAL REPORT

BY

PROF. J. S. NEWBERRY,
GEOLOGIST OF THE EXPEDITION.

WASHINGTON:
GOVERNMENT PRINTING OFFICE.
1876.

OFFICE OF THE CHIEF OF ENGINEERS,
Washington, D. C., June 28, 1875.

SIR: When Major Macomb, of the Topographical Engineers (now colonel of engineers), made his report of an important exploration in New Mexico, in 1859, he was unable to furnish the report on the geology of that region, owing to the fact that Dr. J. S. Newberry, the geologist who accompanied him, was then actively employed in his duties on the Sanitary Commission in the West.

Colonel Macomb has recently transmitted to this Office Dr. Newberry's report, with its twenty-two illustrations; and I have respectfully to recommend that it be printed at the Government Printing-Office, and that 1,500 copies be furnished for the use of the Engineer Department upon the usual requisition; also, that this Office be authorized to procure the necessary copies of the illustrations.

Very respectfully, your obedient servant,

A. A. HUMPHREYS,
Brig. Gen., Chief of Engineers.

Hon. WILLIAM W. BELKNAP,
Secretary of War.

Approved:
By order of the Secretary of War:

H. T. CROSBY,
Chief Clerk.

JUNE 28, 1875.

CONTENTS.

LETTER OF TRANSMITTAL.

GENERAL REPORT.

Report of November 1, 1860.
Report of November 27, 1861.

GEOLOGICAL REPORT.

PREFATORY NOTE.

LETTER OF TRANSMITTAL.

CHAPTER I.

GEOLOGY OF THE ROUTE BETWEEN ST. LOUIS AND SANTA FÉ.

General geological sketch—Independence to Dragoon Creek—Carboniferous strata—Character of coal and Coal Measures of Kansas—Due to what causes—Coal-plants of Kansas—Molluscous fossils—Dragoon Creek to Cottonwood Creek—Permo-Carboniferous and Permian strata—Difficulty of separating these formations—Cottonwood Creek to Walnut Creek—Gypsum formation—Its parallelism—Walnut Creek to Pawnee Fork—Lower Cretaceous rocks—Sand-stones with impressions of leaves—Pawnee Fork to Cimarron—Tertiary strata—Arkansas basin—Its relation to that of White River—Cimarron to Enchanted Spring—Jurassic ? rocks—Enchanted Spring to Cottonwood Spring—Lower Cretaceous and Tertiary beds—Cottonwood Spring to Canadian—Trap buttes and mesas near Raton Mountains—Cretaceous rocks of the Canadian—Table-lands skirting the Rocky Mountains—Canadian to Las Vegas—Trap plateau at Burgwin's Spring—Cretaceous strata at Fort Union and Las Vegas.

CHAPTER II.

GEOLOGY OF THE VICINITY OF SANTA FÉ.

Santa Fé Mountains—Granite—General geological features, its character and contained minerals—Relations of the Santa Fé mountains—Placer Mountains—Cretaceous and Triassic rocks—Cretaceous lignite converted into anthracite by an outburst of trap—Gold of the Placer Mountains—Copper—Iron—The Cerrillos—Gold—Silver—Lead—Copper—Iron—Turquoise—Ancient Chalchuitl mines—The Sandia Mountain—The Valles—Stratified rocks—Carboniferous formations—Santa Fé section—Section at Pecos Village—Permo-Carboniferous beds—Gypsum formation—Section at San José—Fossil plants—Cretaceous formation—Subdivisions of the system—Yellow sandstones of Cañon Blanco—Cretaceous—Sections at Galisteo and Pope's Well—Tertiary beds of fresh-water origin.

CHAPTER III.

GENERAL VIEW OF THE GEOLOGY OF THE COUNTRY BORDERING THE UPPER COLORADO.

Bird's-eye view of the Colorado plateau and its surroundings—Mountain-chains by which the plateau is encircled—Rocky Mountain system—Its extent and general structure—Different features which it presents on different parallels—Different ranges of the Rocky Mountains, probably not of the same age—Rocky Mountain region has suffered alternations of elevation and depression—The Cretaceous epoch an era of subsidence—The Tertiary, of elevation—Mogollon Mountains—Probably not a distinct system—Mountains of the Lower Colorado a part of the Sierra Nevada system—Relation of the Sierra Nevada to the Rocky Mountains—Cerbat Mountains—Wasatch Mountains—San Francisco group—Recent volcanic phenomena of the Great Central Plateau—Mount Taylor—Sierra Tucano—Sierras Abajo, La Sal, &c.—Structure of the Colorado plateau—Devonian and Silurian rocks of the Great Cañon—Carboniferous formation—Triassic and Cretaceous rocks—Similarity of structure of the valleys of the Little Colorado, San Juan, Grand, and Green Rivers—High mesas of Navajo country and Upper San Juan.

CHAPTER IV.

GEOLOGY OF THE ROUTE FROM SANTA FÉ TO THE SIERRA DE LA PLATA.

Structure of the valley of the Rio Grande—The valley of the Chama—Abiquiu—Copper-mines—Fossil plants—Ruins of Los Cañones—Abiquiu Peak—Plateau country bordering the Upper Chama—Arroyo Seco—Triassic marls—Navajo Spring—Cretaceous sandstones and plateau—Banks of the Nutria—Middle Cretaceous beds—Vada del Chama—Section of valley of the Chama—High mesa of Upper Cretaceous rocks—Laguna de los Cavallos—Divide between the waters of the Rio Grande and San Juan—General view of the structure of the surrounding country—Mountain-chains—Belt of foot-hills—Table-lands—Rio Navajo—Cerro del Navajo—Sierra del Navajo—Rito Blanco—The Pagosa—Sierra San Juan and associated mountain-ranges—Cretaceous rocks and fossils—The Piedra Parada—Rio Piedra—Broken mesa—View from high divide—Rio de Los Pinos—Sierra de Los Pinos—Rio Florido—Valley of the Animas—Ruins on the Animas—Crossing of the Animas—Structure of the mountains drained by the Animas—Rio de La Plata—Delightful camp—Cretaceous rocks and fossils—Sierra de La Plata—Metalliferous veins of the Sierra de La Plata.

CHAPTER V.

GEOLOGY OF THE SAGE PLAIN AND VALLEY OF THE UPPER COLORADO.

General features of the northern portion of the Colorado basin—Aspects and structure of the Sage plain—Mesa Verde—Enormous denudation of the Colorado plateau—Crossing the Sage plain—Rio de Los Mancos—Rio Dolores—Section of Lower Cretaceous rocks—Ruins on the Dolores—Sierra San Miguel—Soronara—Tierra Blanca—Guajolotes—Cañon Pintado—Triassic rocks—Saurian bones—La Seuejal—Eroded buttes—Casa Colorado—Ojo Verde—Sierra La Sal—Excursion to Grand River—Cañon Colorado—Plateau bordering the Colorado River—Eroded monuments—Labyrinth Cañon—Ruined buildings—Summit of the Carboniferous formation—Section of Triassic rocks—Remarkable country about the junction of Grand and Green Rivers—Singular eroded buttes and pinnacles—Net-work of cañons—Cañon of Grand River—Section of Carboniferous strata—Transverse section of the Colorado Valley—Return to Sage plain—Journey southward to the San Juan—Sierra Abajo.

CHAPTER. VI.

GEOLOGY OF THE BANKS OF THE SAN JUAN.

General features of the country bordering the San Juan—Section of Lower Cretaceous strata south of Sierra Abajo—Bird's-eye view of country bordering San Juan—High mesas of the Navajo country—Triassic rocks of Lower San Juan—Lower Cretaceous strata of Camp 37—Middle Cretaceous beds and fossils south of Le Late—The Needles—The Creston—Upper Cretaceous strata at mouth of the Animas—Ruins in the San Juan Valley—Cañon Largo—Sections of Upper Cretaceous strata—Plateau country bordering Cañon Largo—Buttes of marls and sandstones, highest members of the series of sedimentary rocks composing Colorado plateau—General section of Upper Cretaceous strata—Nascimiento Mountain, its structure and relations—Notes on the different formations exposed on its sides—Journey through country bordering western base of Nascimiento Mountain—Divide between San Juan and Rio Grande—Mount Taylor—Cabiezon—Tertiary strata at Jemez—The Valles—Trap plateaus.

DESCRIPTIONS OF CRETACEOUS FOSSILS, BY F. B. MEEK.

DESCRIPTIONS OF CARBONIFEROUS AND TRIASSIC FOSSILS, BY J. S. NEWBERRY, GEOLOGIST OF THE EXPEDITION.

ILLUSTRATIONS.

LANDSCAPE VIEWS.

	Page.
Plate I. Abiquiu Peak, looking westerly	69
Plate II. Near Vado del Chama, upper cretaceous mesa	71
Plate III. La Piedra Parada, looking west	78
Plate IV. The Pagosa and San Juan River, looking easterly	76
Plate V. Rio Dolores and Sierra de la Plata. From near Camp 21	86
Plate VI. Casa Colorado and La Sal Mountains, looking northerly	92
Plate VII. Head of Labyrinth Creek, looking southeasterly	96
Plate VIII. Head of Cañon Colorado. Erosion of Triassic series	98
Plate IX. Lower San Juan, looking west. From near Camp 35	102
Plate X. The Noodles, looking southwesterly	106
Plate XI. The Cabazon, from near Camp 54	112
Trap Dike, Pope's Well, south of Santa Fé, New Mexico	51
The Pagosa, S. W. Colorado	75
Ruins of stone houses on cliffs, Labyrinth Cañon	94

PALEONTOLOGY.

Plates I to VIII, inclusive, at end of Descriptions of Fossils, by F. B. Meek and Dr. J. S. Newberry.

LETTER OF TRANSMITTAL.

UNITED STATES ENGINEER'S OFFICE,
Rock Island, Ill., June 18, 1875.

GENERAL: I have this day forwarded to you the Geological Report of Dr. J. S. Newberry, geologist of the San Juan exploration party, which went from Santa Fé, New Mexico, to the vicinity of the junction of Grand and Green Rivers, in Utah, and back to Santa Fé, in the summer of 1859, and which party was in my charge.

This is the report to which I alluded in my report to you of November 1, 1860, as setting forth whatever the route above mentioned afforded of interest to the public at large or to the man of science. I trust it may be found possible to publish it.

The report is arranged in seven chapters, with a prefatory note, and is accompanied by the following sketches and drawings, viz:

Eleven water-color sketches, showing characteristic scenery of the region in Northwestern New Mexico, Southwestern Colorado, and Southeastern Utah. Also, eleven drawings (eight of fossils and three of scenery), all of which are interesting and important in connection with the report.

My map of the route was engraved on a steel plate, and is on the files of the Engineer Department.

I remain, very respectfully, your most obedient servant,

J. N. MACOMB,
Colonel of Engineers, United States Army.

Brig. Gen. A. A. HUMPHREYS,
   Chief of Engineers, United States Army.

EXPLORING EXPEDITION FROM SANTA FÉ TO JUNCTION OF GRAND AND GREEN RIVERS.

GENERAL REPORT.

REPORT.

WASHINGTON, D. C., No[vember]

SIR: For the information of the War Department, I beg leave to su[bmit the fol]lowing remarks upon the exploration made by me, during the summer o[f 1859, in] New Mexico and Utah.

About the middle of July, 1859, my party set out from Santa Fé, Ne[w Mexico,] and pursued a northwesterly course, crossing the Rio Grande Bravo del No[rte at the] old Indian pueblo of San Juan, and following up the valley of the Rio Ch[ama, pass]ing by the pueblo of Abiquiu, the outpost of settlement in that direction, be[ing about] fifty-two miles from Santa Fé. We continued up the Chama Valley for some [ ] miles more, when we left it and crossed the dividing ridge between the wa[ters of the] Gulf of Mexico and those of the Gulf of California, at a remarkable point, w[here there] is a small lake called Laguna de los Caballos, when we struck upon the h[eadwaters] of the San Juan River, crossing several branches before we came to the m[ain stream.] This we crossed in latitude 37° 14' 48" north and longitude 107° 2' 47" west, [where there] is a hot spring, of temperature about 140° Fahrenheit and of magnificent d[epth.] We looked down through its limpid waters until the power of vision wa[s lost in the] cavernous depths whence the waters flow. From this point our route was w[esterly for] about seventy miles, over a region very much broken and intersected by ra[pid mount]ain streams (branches of the San Juan), which afford an abundant sup[ply of good] water and have the appearance of being permanent. We had fre[quent rains] in this part of our route, and the grazing was thus far excellent. Up to a [point about] forty-five miles westward from the "Pagosa," or great hot spring above m[entioned, we] were accompanied by Mr. Albert H. Pfeiffer, sub-agent for the Utah Ind[ians, and his] interpreter, Neponocino Valdez, to both of whom we are indebted for [much hospi]tality and for facilitating our passage through the country of the Capote[s and other] bands of the Utah Indians, in whose vicinity our route happened to lead u[s.]

In latitude 37° 16' and longitude 108° 4', we passed along the south[ern base of] the mountain group known as "Sierra de la Plata;" hence in a northwesterl[y direction] for about one hundred and twenty miles, over gloomy barrens, covered [with the] *Artemesiæ*, but affording a scanty pasturage in some of the small valleys. [ ] rains favored us, and we had no scarcity of water on our route to the "Ojo [ ] latitude 38° 14' 50", longitude 109° 26' 40", a point about three hundred [ ] miles from Santa Fé. The greater part of our journey from Abiquiu to this [ ] by the old Spanish trail, which has not heretofore been accurately laid down upon any map. This trail is much talked of as having been the route of commerce between California and New Mexico in the days of the old Spanish rule, but it seems to have been superseded by the routes to the north and south of it, which have been opened by modern enterprise.

At the "Ojo Verde" the Spanish trail strikes off more northwardly, to seek a practicable crossing of Grand and Green Rivers. We left the trail here, and, leaving the main body of our party encamped at the spring, with a small party of nine, went to the westward some thirty miles, under the guidance of an Indian, who had joined us many days previously, on our route to look for the junction of the Grand and Green Rivers. This part of our journey was very rough and dangerous, from the precipitous nature of the route, winding down the sides of deep and grand cañons, and it is fortunate that no attempt was made to bring forward our pack-train, as we must have lost many mules by it, and, moreover, there was not sufficient pasture for the few animals that we had with us. I cannot conceive of a more worthless and impracticable region than the one we now found ourselves in. I doubt not there are repetitions and *varieties* of it for hundreds of miles down the cañon of the Great Colorado, for I have heard of but one crossing of that river above the vicinity of the Mojave villages, and I have reason to doubt if that one (El Vado de los Padres) is practicable, except with the utmost care, even for a pack-mule.

On leaving the "Ojo Verde" we traveled south for about seventy miles, passing by the eastern base of the Sierra Abajo, until we struck the San Juan River, in latitude 37° 16' 27" and longitude 109° 24' 43", on the 2d September, 1859. We found bottom-land of the river at this point of a light and loose soil, into which the feet of the mules would frequently sink for some 18 inches. We followed up the river, remaining on its right bank for some one hundred and twenty miles, until we came opposite to the mouth of Cañon Largo, in latitude 36° 43' 28" and longitude 107° 43' 29". In the course of our march we observed many ruins of houses and found quantities of fragments of pottery scattered over the ground, indicating that the valley was once occupied by a race probably of the same origin and character as the Pueblo Indians extant in New Mexico. The fate of those former occupants of that dreary region is involved in mystery. It requires, however, no effort of the imagination to fancy that they may have been starved or frozen to death; for the winters are severe and fuel is very scarce there.

I have no doubt that the warm season is very short there, otherwise more of the valley of the San Juan would be cultivated by the Navajos, who are a corn-growing people, for the river affords abundant water for irrigation, and carries soil enough to enrich and renew the fields.

On the 15th September, 1859, we forded the San Juan, opposite Cañon Largo, with no little danger, the strong current and deep water sweeping down some of the mules, which were recovered with difficulty. We were fortunate in passing through Cañon Largo just after heavy rains, as I learned afterward that the command of Major Simonson, which passed through the cañon in July, had suffered much for the want of water. There is one fine spring in the cañon, about thirty-five miles from San Juan, but no other reliable water until the San José spring is reached, about thirty miles farther to the southeast. From the last-named water we followed down the valley of the Puerco (a branch of the Rio del Norte) for about forty miles, when we crossed the southern spur of the Nacimiento Mountain and came to the old pueblo of Jemez, about fifty-six miles to the west by south from Santa Fé. The route has been passed over by wagons from Santa Fé to a point a short distance to the westward of Jemez, and also from Santa Fé to the upper valley of the Chama, a short distance above Abiquin, but on the remainder of the route passed over by my party there is no evidence of a wagon having ever been seen, and a suitable road for wagons could only be made at a heavy cost for construction, and it would doubtless meet with much opposition on the part of the Navajos and Utahs, whose country it would pass through.

During the expedition my time was taken up with the astronomical observations requisite for laying down the route. In these observations I was assisted by Mr. F. P. Fisher, who noted the time and kept the record for me with accuracy and neatness. Mr. Fisher also carried a barometer throughout the march. All computations required for the astronomical observations were necessarily made by myself.

Mr. C. H. Dimmock made an excellent sketch of the route, which he has drawn in one large map upon a scale of half an inch to the mile. This map I have tested by the results of my astronomical observations and computations with very great satisfaction.

Messrs. Dorsey and Vail carried barometers and thermometers, and kept daily records of the indications of those instruments, chiefly from the readings of Mr. Vail. Mr. Dorsey also assisted the geologist in making some of the collections of natural history specimens.

Dr. J. S. Newberry, the geologist of the expedition, was particularly zealous and energetic in his examinations of the country, and I expect from him a report setting forth whatever there may be of interest in the route either to the public at large or to the man of science.

I am now engaged, under your direction, in preparing for publication, upon a scale suitable for ordinary use, a map of the region visited by my party, which will exhibit with all requisite minuteness and accuracy of detail the features of the country, covering an area of some twelve thousand square miles, which has heretofore been indicated upon the maps under the head of "unexplored."

The expedition was accompanied by a detachment of infantry under the command of Lieut. M. Cogswell, of the Eighth Regiment, to whom we are indebted for our safe escort through a wild and inhospitable tract of country, partly occupied by hostile and treacherous Indians.

I was directed, on my return to Santa Fé, to reduce my party and come in to Washington to prepare my report, and, on my way, to stop at the southwest corner of the Territory of Kansas, to set up a new monument at a point some two and a quarter miles to the east of the one originally placed there. I accordingly diverged from the usual route across the plains from Fort Union and went up the Cimarron to the point indicated, and retraced that part of the thirty-seventh parallel from the old monument to the meridian of 103°, as laid down upon the map accompanying my instructions, and at the intersection of these two geographical lines I erected a rough stone monument. The original monument above alluded to is of earth and sods. This duty was finished about the middle of November, 1859, when the thermometer was ranging from zero to about 16° above.

I was accompanied to this position by a small detachment of troops under the command of Lieut. H. M. Enos, of the regiment of mounted riflemen, to whose vigilance I am indebted for a safe transit to Fort Leavenworth, at a time when the Indians of the great plains had manifested the most decided determination to be troublesome.

I remain, very respectfully, your most obedient servant,

J. N. MACOMB,
Captain Topographical Engineers.

Capt. A. A. HUMPHREYS,
 Top. Engineers, in charge of Office of Explorations and Surveys.

WASHINGTON, D. C., November 27, 1861.

COLONEL: At the time of making my last annual report I was engaged in the preparation of a map of the region visited by the party which I conducted in the summer of 1859. The map was finished, and is now in the hands of an engraver, who promises to give me the finished plate by the month of March next.

The report upon the geology, &c., of the same region has been written by Dr. Newberry, and I hoped to have had it in my possession to send in for publication with the annual report from the Bureau of Topographical Engineers, but, owing to the delay in finishing some of the drawings for illustrating the report, and to the fact that the geologist has for some months been actively employed with the duties of the "sanitary commission" in the West, I am not yet in the receipt of his results. I may add for myself that, as in the case of every available officer of the Government, my time has been so much engrossed by the duties which have pressed upon me, arising out of the existing state of affairs in our country, that I have been prevented from pushing the reports and maps, &c., of the San Juan exploration to a conclusion. I hope, however, that they will all be rendered to me before the close of the session of Congress now about to commence.

All of which is respectfully submitted by your obedient servant,

J. N. MACOMB,
Lieut. Col., Aid-de-camp to Maj. Gen. McClellan, and Major Top'l Engineers.

Lieut. Col. H. BACHE,
 Commanding Corps Topographical Engineers, U. S. A.

GEOLOGICAL REPORT.

BY

J. S. NEWBERRY, M. D., LL. D.,
GEOLOGIST TO THE EXPEDITION.

PREFATORY NOTE.

COLUMBIA COLLEGE,
New York, June 1, 1875.

The following report was prepared for publication at the time indicated by the date of my letter to Captain (now Colonel) Macomb, but the breaking out of the rebellion arrested the publication of all the reports of surveys made by the Government expeditions immediately previous to this event. The reports of the surveys made by Lieutenant (now General) G. K. Warren, United States Engineers, Captain (now General) W. F. Raynolds, the report of the Northwestern Boundary Commission, and some others, were in this category, and much most valuable information in regard to the far West has been lost to the country and the world by the suppression of these important documents.

As attention is now again drawn to the region bordering the San Juan and Upper Colorado, and several parties are occupied in exploring adjacent districts, the results of the explorations made by the San Juan Exploring Expedition have acquired an importance in this connection which has rendered their publication desirable. They are therefore now given to the public. Although much has been learned in regard to the geology of the country drained by the Colorado River during the last ten years, and much that has a bearing on the subject-matter of this report, none of this lately-acquired knowledge is referred to on its pages, but they are printed precisely as written in 1860.

This course has been pursued as the only just and natural one. The observations made fifteen years ago, if accurately made, have equal value now as then; if inaccurate, it is only right that the credit of the correction of errors should belong to those who make such corrections. The geological narrative now given stands, therefore, just as written, and is a fair exponent of the state of our geographical and geological knowledge of the West at the date of its preparation. It is evident that to modify the report so as to conform to all the conclusions more recently reached, would be to falsify the record and greatly impair the independence and value of the statements it includes. The truth or error of these statements will soon be demonstrated by the extension of the explorations of other parties into this field. It is but just that the credit or discredit of the trial to which the report is to be subjected should belong to the writer. Knowing that his work was done honestly, and believing that it was in the main accurately done, he accepts the entire responsibility of it, whether for praise or blame.

J. S. N.

LETTER OF TRANSMITTAL.

WASHINGTON, D. C., *May* 1, 1860.

DEAR SIR: I submit herewith my report on the geology of the country traversed by the San Juan Exploring Expedition, in which I had the honor to serve under your command.

Very respectfully, your obedient servant,

J. S. NEWBERRY.

Capt. J. N. MACOMB,
   Topographical Engineers, United States Army.

CHAPTER I.

GEOLOGY OF THE ROUTE BETWEEN INDEPENDENCE AND SANTA FÉ.

GENERAL GEOLOGICAL SKETCH — INDEPENDENCE TO DRAGOON CREEK — CARBONIFEROUS STRATA — CHARACTER OF COAL AND COAL-MEASURES OF KANSAS — DUE TO WHAT CAUSES—COAL-PLANTS OF KANSAS—MORUSCAS FOSSILS—DRAGOON CREEK TO COTTONWOOD CREEK—PERMO-CARBONIFEROUS AND PERMIAN STRATA — DIFFICULTY OF SEPARATING THESE FORMATIONS—COTTONWOOD CREEK TO WALNUT CREEK—GYPSUM FORMATION—ITS PARALLELISM — WALNUT CREEK TO PAWNEE FORK — LOWER CRETACEOUS ROCKS—SANDSTONES WITH IMPRESSIONS OF CAVES—PAWNEE FORK TO CIMARRON—TERTIARY STRATA—ARKANSAS BASIN—ITS RELATION TO THAT OF WHITE RIVER—CIMARRON TO ENCHANTED SPRING—JURASSIC (?) ROCKS—ENCHANTED SPRING TO COTTONWOOD SPRING—LOWER CRETACEOUS AND TERTIARY BEDS—COTTONWOOD SPRING TO CANADIAN—TRAP BUTTES AND MESAS NEAR RATON MOUNTAINS—CRETACEOUS ROCKS OF THE CANADIAN—TABLE-LANDS SKIRTING THE ROCKY MOUNTAINS — CANADIAN TO LAS VEGAS — TRAP PLATEAU TO BURGEOIN'S SPRING — CRETACEOUS STRATA AT FORT UNION AND LAS VEGAS.

The geology of the country bordering the Santa Fé road is described somewhat in detail in Chapter X of my report to Lieut. J. C. Ives, U. S. A., on the geology of the Colorado country. It will not, therefore, be necessary to devote as much time and space to this portion of our field of explorations as though it were before wholly unknown. In our recent journey from Independence, Mo., to Santa Fé, however, we passed over quite a large area not traversed on the route from Santa Fé to Fort Leavenworth. In repassing also the route formerly traveled, our stopping-places were, in many instances, different; many new exposures of the rocks were examined, and observations were made by which it is now possible to define much more accurately than was formerly done the geographical limits of the different formations met with. I am happy to say that the conclusions arrived at in my former report on the geology of this region, in regard to the relative position of the various strata noticed, were fully confirmed by our later observations; and the value of the facts now reported consists, for the most part, in the more accurate limitation of the surface-boundaries of the formations, and in the paleontological evidence which they furnish of the age of strata before, in a great degree, conjectural. The number of fossils discovered in our late transit of the plains was large in the Carboniferous, Permian, and Cretaceous rocks, but I had constant occasion to regret that our means of transportation were so limited that I was compelled to leave much behind that would have been of great interest if brought in. Among the localities most rich in fossils, to which I would call the attention of future collectors, are the exposures of the Upper Carboniferous series in Eastern Kansas, near Uniontown, at Rockhouse, Walter's Station, and Burlingame; Permo-Carboniferous, at Dragoon Creek and Wilmington; true Permian on the hill-tops east of Council Grove, and on Cottonwood Creek; Lower Cretaceous at the crossing of Pawnee Fork, at Cedar and Cottonwood Springs, and Whetstone Creek; Middle Cretaceous (Upper Cretaceous of former report) in the valley of Red Fork of Canadian, particularly at the "Breaks of Red River."

INDEPENDENCE TO DRAGOON CREEK.

The surface-rocks of all Eastern Kansas and Western Missouri belong to the Coal-Measures. These are exposed in many places along the banks of the Missouri, and include beds of coal which are extensively worked at Lexington. In Kansas I have examined the out-crops of the Coal-Measures at various points on the road from Independence westward, about Leavenworth City, along the valley of the Kansas, on the Stranger, Grasshopper Creeks, &c. Taken as a whole, the Coal-Measures of this region present a marked contrast with those of the northern portion of the Illinois coal-field, and a still greater one with those of the Ohio and Pennsylvania. This difference consists in the much smaller aggregate quantity of carbonaceous matter and in the vast preponderance of organic over mechanical sediments, *i. e.*, of limestones over the sandstones and shales, which make up the great mass of the Carboniferous series in the northern portion of the Allegheny coal-field. As I have formerly remarked, this difference seems to be a consequence of the fact that, during the Carboniferous epoch, the region occupied by the coal-basin of Missouri and Kansas was more remote from the source from which the mechanical sediments were derived, and was much more frequently, or at least for longer periods, submerged beneath the water of the ocean than the region with which I have compared it. Professor Hall has indicated a similar difference of structure between the northern and southern portions of the Illinois coal-field, and has clearly shown how the great calcareous masses of the southern extremity of this coal-basin are the records of the existence of an open sea in the regions where they exist, while the coal, sandstones, and shales were accumulating on the low shores or shallows bordering the continent which lay to the north.

In my former report, I have described the progressive change which was noticed in the structure of the Carboniferous series in going from New Mexico to Ohio, and have shown how the great masses of limestone without beds of coal, and almost without any mechanical admixture, were succeeded in Kansas by a series of thick, but distinctly separated beds of Fusilina limestone, between which were thinner strata of fine argillaceous shale, with a few seams of cannel or cannel-like coal; and that in Ohio the Fusilina limestones, not individually, but as a group, are represented by the thin calcareous bands which separate the greatly-preponderating masses of mechanical sediment. Further examination has fully verified the accuracy of these observations, and has confirmed in all its general bearings the theory by which the phenomena were explained. It should be observed, however, that the change which has been remarked by Professor Hall in the structure of the coal-basins, going from north to south, and by myself from northeast to southwest, is not uniformly progressive throughout their entire extent, but was modified locally by the sinuosities of the shore-line of the northern main-land, and by the presence of islands at a greater or less distance from the shore toward the south and southwest; in illustration of which we may cite the comparative barrenness of the Coal-Measures of Northern and Central Illinois, where, as in Kansas, the calcareous strata vastly predominate, with the greater development of strata and mechanical sediments in Southern Illinois and Kentucky; so also the productive Coal-Measures of the region about Fort Belknap, in Texas, where the quantity of carbonaceous and sandy matter is equal to, if not greater than, that of Kansas directly north. At Sante Fé, also, as will be seen from the description hereafter to be given of the geology of that vicinity, the Carboniferous series includes a great thickness of coarse sandstone filled with the impressions of land-plants, evidently transported no very great distance from their place of origin. As we progress southward, however, we ultimately reach the limit of traces of the existence of terrestrial surfaces during the coal period, as in Southern and Southwestern New Mexico, where the entire Carboniferous series is represented by a calcareous mass, all an organic or chemical precipitate from the waters of the ocean, and the proof of the uninterrupted existence of an open sea in that region throughout the entire carboniferous epoch.

Coal.—The coals of Missouri and Kansas have all, to a certain extent, a common character, as compared with those of the Alleghany coal-fields; they are softer, and contain a larger amount of volatile matter, of water, and of sulphur. Some of them are cannel, frequently handsome and of good quality, and those which are not strictly cannel are more or less like it in chemical composition and physical structure, and they frequently have layers of cannel running through them. They are generally quite tender, and when exposed to the action of the weather, like the Cretaceous and Tertiary coals of the western part of the continent, which they so much resemble, they are prone to "slack," or to break up into innumerable rhomboidal or cubical fragments.

The causes of the peculiar character of the coals of Kansas are to be sought, I think, in the physical conditions attending their formation, rather than in any peculiarity of the vegetation from which they were derived. In a paper, published in the American Journal of Science, of March, 1857, I have attempted to show that the characters which distinguish cannels from other bituminous coals are for the most part due to the excess of water in which they were submerged during the process of their formation. I have also been led to suppose that this cause has, to a considerable degree, given to the western coals the characters they exhibit; that the carbonaceous matter composing them was, during its accumulation, more thoroughly saturated or more completely submerged than that composing the coal-strata of the Alleghany basin; and that when the coal-seams had attained their entire thickness they were not immediately buried beneath heavy masses of mechanical sediment, by the weight of which all the effects of great pressure would be obtained, but, instead, were submerged perhaps deeply beneath water, the pressure of which would be expended in all directions, and would, therefore, not act as a distinct compress on the saturated mass. That the chemical characters of these coals have been in any great degree modified by this cause

I will not insist, but by submerging a porous body, such as a sponge, it will be seen that the pressure of the superincumbent water has no tendency to bring its particles in contact or consolidate it. The excess of sulphur is doubtless due to the decomposition of the numerous marine organisms which inhabited the water by which the coal was saturated or submerged.

Fossils.—The conditions under which the coal-strata of Kansas have been formed were not favorable to the preservation of a large number of plants; less than a dozen species having been discovered there up to the present time. These are *Cordaites borassifolia, Annularia sphenophylloides, Sphenophyllum dentatum, Alethopteris Serlii, Pecopteris arborescens, Neuropteris flexuosa, N. hirsuta,* and *Sigillaria Menardi.* These plants are all found in the coal-formation east of the Mississippi.

The molluscous fossils of this region have been pretty thoroughly worked up by Messrs. Shumard, Swallow, and Meek. They are enumerated in the papers of these gentlemen in the proceedings of the Saint Louis and Philadelphia academies; and in Chapter X of my report on the Geology of the Colorado Country.

In some portions of Eastern Kansas the Upper Carboniferous limestones contain the remains of echinoderms, of which the spines and plates sometimes almost completely cover the weathered surfaces of the rocks. They all belong to the genus *Archæocidaris,* and constitute several species described by Messrs. Shumard and Hall. These fossils present a new feature in the Carboniferous fauna to one who has studied that formation only east of the Mississippi, where they are exceedingly rare. They are, however, equally common in the Carboniferous rocks of New Mexico; one of the Kansas species recurring in great numbers at Pecos Village, near Santa Fé, and several others of large size, described in my report to Lieutenant Ives, are conspicuous features in the limestones, equivalents of the Coal-Measures, on the banks of the Colorado.

The Fusilinas, which give character to the Fusilina limestones of Missouri and Kansas, have attracted the attention and excited the surprise of every geologist who has visited that region. The Coal-Measure limestones are almost everywhere crowded with them, and in many instances they compose by far the greater portion of their mass. It is not easy to say what influences could have fostered this enormous development of Foraminiferous life in the sea from which the Kansas limestones were deposited; for these fossils, like the echinoderms of which I have spoken, are almost unknown east of the Mississippi; but, unlike them, are comparatively rare in the limestones of New Mexico.

DRAGOON CREEK TO COTTONWOOD CREEK.

The Carboniferous rocks which I have described as so characteristic of Eastern Kansas, prevail without interruption over all the interval between Independence, Mo., and Dragoon Creek. Although the exposures of the underlying rocks are frequent along the Santa Fé road, the surface is merely undulated, nowhere broken, and there are no deep excavations formed by the draining streams. As a consequence the order of succession of strata could not be fully made out, and it is probable that not every number of the series is anywhere visible along our line of examination. It is not certain, therefore, that there are not beds of coal or other valuable minerals still lying concealed by the prairie-grass or beneath the widely-spread Drift deposits over which passes the great thoroughfare of the Santa Fé road. As far as I could see or learn, however, the Coal-Measures are there generally barren of useful minerals. The iron-ores and the fire-clays, so abundantly associated with the coal-beds in Ohio and Pennsylvania, are almost entirely wanting, and but a single outcrop of a coal-seam of workable thickness—that of Burlingame, described in my former report—is known in the vicinity of our route. The coal-strata of this region are, however, not only less numerous, but less continuous than are those east of the Mississippi, and it is highly probable that local but valuable deposits of mineral-fuel will hereafter be discovered where their existence is not now suspected.

At Dragoon Creek we reach the extreme summit of the Carboniferous formation, and first meet with those which may be regarded as distinctly Permian. As has been remarked, in the discussion of this question on a former occasion, it is exceedingly difficult, if not impossible, to separate these two formations in this region by any well-defined line. This is clearly shown also by the able analysis of the geological structure of Eastern Kansas by Messrs. Meek and Hayden, and Swallow and Hawn, and especially by the difference of opinion which still exists among these gentlemen as to where the line of demarcation should be drawn. The rocks of that country are conformable throughout, and the materials composing them are so similar as to indicate great uniformity in the physical conditions which attended their deposition. The fossils which they contain must therefore be our only guide in their classification; and these, though numerous and well marked, are so distributed as to give fair ground for considerable difference of honest opinion

Beneath the variegated non-fossiliferous series of the Trias, are certain beds of magnesian limestone which contain a large number of fossils, for the most part generically identical with, and specifically closely allied to, the most characteristic forms of the Permian of Europe. These consist of species of *Bakevellia, Leda, Axinus, Monotis, Pseudomonotis, Myalina, Pleurophorous, Productus, Athyris, Chonetes, Nautilus, Bellerophon, Murchisonia,* &c. Of these one species of *Monotis,* and another of *Myalina,* are scarcely distinguishable from those which occur in the Coal-Measures below, though very possibly distinct. The *Athyris,* however—a variety of *A. subtilita,* but broader and more gibbous than the common form—recurs in the underlying strata with a fauna decidedly Carboniferous. The same is probably true of a species of *Bellerophon* common in these magnesian limestones. The *Productus* mentioned (*P. Calhounianus*) is scarcely different from *P. semireticulatus.* With the possible exceptions I have enumerated the fauna of this group is decidedly Permian in character; and if the Permian formation is to be regarded as distinct from the Carboniferous, which is scarcely to be doubted, although the separation would not have been made if our American strata had been the basis of geological classification, this upper group of magnesian limestones should undoubtedly be called Permian. Below the magnesian rocks to which I have referred, occur numerous alternations of magnesian limestones and variously-colored clays which contain a mingling of Carboniferous and Permian fossils, or perhaps more properly a mingling of the species contained in the upper group of magnesian limestones with others common in the Carboniferous strata below, added to which are a few species that seem to be restricted to this geological horizon. In the upper part of this intermediate group of strata, we have the *Bakevellia, Pleurophorous, Axinus, &c.,* of the beds above, and a fauna perhaps more Permian than Carboniferous, but below we soon reach a level where the Carboniferous types predominate. This group of strata has been regarded by Professor Swallow as all of Permian age, while Mr. Meek terms it Permo-Carboniferous, drawing the line which marks the base of the Permian at the base of the first group of magnesian limestones, and restricting this term to those members of the series in which the Permian fauna predominates over the Carboniferous.

From this interlocking of the Carboniferous and Permian faunae, it is evident that the line of separation between the two formations must continue to be debatable ground; and as there is, in fact, a group which contains a mingled fauna—in truth, a Permo-Carboniferous group—we must introduce this new member into the geological series, or fix upon some conventional line which shall form the boundary between the summit of the Carboniferous and the base of the Permian formations. To avoid complicating the geological scale, the latter course would undoubtedly be the wiser one; and since there is neither physical nor vital break in the series, it is perhaps not a matter of great consequence whether the line be drawn at the horizon where the first Permian type makes its appearance, or at the horizon beyond which the last Carboniferous species ceases to exist, or even at the point, if indeed it were determinable, where the species of the two formations are represented in equal numbers; in other words, whether at the top, bottom, or middle of the Permo-Carboniferous group. It will be seen by reference to the papers which have been before cited, that, while containing several Permian types, the fauna of the "Lower Permian" group of Swallow and Hawn has considerably more of the Carboniferous than Permian character; and as great bodies attract more strongly than small ones, it seems more natural that the debatable ground should be ceded to the great and well-defined Carboniferous series, of which the symmetry would suffer without it, rather than to the comparatively insignificant and ill-defined Permian formation. It seems probable, therefore, that the "Lower Permian" group of Swallow and Hawn will be regarded as an integral portion of the Carboniferous system, while the term Permian will be restricted to the Permian of Meek and Hayden, to the "Upper Permian" of Swallow and Hawn. It is evident that only those strata should be regarded as Permian in which the Permian fauna predominates.

In the hills bordering Dragoon Creek I first found limestones containing the group of fossils—*Pleurophorous, Bakevellia, Axinus, Bellerophon,* &c.—to which I have referred above. Farther west, toward Council Grove, the hills are capped with yellow magnesian limestone, in many places crowded with the valves of *Bakevellia parva.* Over a considerable area in this vicinity the highlands are occupied by what may be considered true Permian strata, while the valleys of all the water-courses are excavated to and into the Permo-Carboniferous, or, as I have called them, Upper Carboniferous strata.

At Council Grove, Diamond Spring, Lost Spring, and Cottonwood Creek, observations were made and fossils collected by Major Hawn, Messrs. Meek and Hayden, and myself last year. The geology of all these points is nearly the same. At each the

Permian magnesian limestones occupy the general surface, but are cut through by the valleys of the draining streams. Below them are exposed strata containing *Orthisina umbraculum Productus Calhounianus*; spines of a species of *Archæocidaris*, regarded by Professor Swallow as identical with *A. Verneuiliana*, King; a small *Athyris*, and a *Rhynchonella*; all of which belong rather to the Carboniferous than to the Permian fauna. Near Cottonwood Creek the Upper Magnesian limestone, or true Permian, is highly fossiliferous; containing great numbers of *Myalina perattenuata, Monotis (Pseudomonotis), Hawni, Bakerellia parva*, and many other species described by Meek and Hayden, who collected largely at this locality.

COTTONWOOD CREEK TO WALNUT CREEK.

THE GYPSUM FORMATION.

On the west side of Cottonwood Creek, the Permian limestones pass beneath the surface, and are not distinctly recognizable at any western point upon the Santa Fé road. They are succeeded by a series of reddish-yellow and white indurated marls, forming a part of the great "Gypsum formation," which is so conspicuous a feature in the geology of the Indian Territory, New Mexico, and Western Texas. This group fills the interval between the Permian strata, which I have described, and the base of the Cretaceous system; including representatives of perhaps portions of the Permian, the Triassic, and Jurassic formations of the Old World. The magnificent exposures of this series which abound in New Mexico, have been noticed by every geologist and almost every traveler who has entered that country. It will be seen by reference to the reports upon the geology of the Southwest made to the Government by the writer or others, that this formation is everywhere characterized by great poverty of fossils, and for this reason, as well as from the general similarity of its lithological characters from base to summit, and in different localities, it has been hitherto impossible to separate it by satisfactory dividing lines, or to determine with accuracy the equivalence of any of its parts with the different formations which it may be supposed to represent. The study devoted to this group of strata by the writer, while connected with the party under the command of Lieutenant Ives, was not wholly fruitless, but it must be confessed that, as far as regards the determination of the parallelism of its subdivisions with the strata to which they have been referred, it enables him rather to say what they are not, than what they are. The observations made upon this formation in our recent explorations of the country bordering the San Juan and Upper Colorado Rivers—where it is very largely developed—will be detailed in the subsequent chapters of this report, and it is hoped that they will serve to throw some additional light on this difficult and perplexing subject.

The materials composing the Gypsum formation are usually so soft that in a country well supplied with rain and covered with vegetation they present few satisfactory exposures, and are even usually wholly concealed from view. This is the character of the district now under consideration, and it is only here and there that the traveler can obtain even a glimpse of its geological substructure. It is evident, however, from the limited space occupied by the outcrop of this group, taken in connection with the nearly horizontal position of the strata, that the interval which here separates the Carboniferous and Cretaceous series is far less than at any point where it has been examined farther to the south and west. This is also proved from the sections given by Messrs. Meek and Hayden in the report of their explorations in Kansas, where it is shown that the rocks filling this gap have not more than one-third or one-fourth the thickness of those which occupy the same relative position in New Mexico.

The interesting discovery by Dr. Hayden of a group of strata in the Black Hills, which represent a portion of the Gypsum formation and yet contain numerous well-marked Jurassic fossils, shows that this series exhibits in different localities considerable diversity of character and development, and encourages us to hope that hereafter similar industry and energy, by bringing to light other localities where these strata are fossiliferous, will permit an accurate classification to be made of them on paleontological grounds. It may then be possible to establish a parallelism between subdivisions of this group and the Jura and Trias of Europe, but it is evident that until unmistakable Triassic fossils are discovered in the Southwest, even this general parallelism can hardly be said to be established. That it will ever be possible to identify in the members of the Gypsum formation the Oolite, Lias, the *Marnes-Irisées*, the *Muschelkalk*, and *Gres-bigarré*, is more than doubtful.

On the banks of the Little Arkansas there is an exposure of laminated, yellowish-white, fine-grained, rippled-marked sandstone, and a singular cellular amygdaloid-like magnesian (?) limestone, which apparently belong to the Gypsum formation, yet which exhibit lithological characters such as I have not elsewhere seen in any member of that group. As far as observed they contain no fossils whatever, and without further evidence it is impossible to say what are their precise equivalents in other localities.

I shall soon have occasion, in speaking of the geology of the region bordering the Upper Cimarron, to refer to another group of strata which underlie the Lower Cretaceous rocks and hold a place usually occupied by a portion of the Gypsum series. These strata present characters somewhat at variance with those usually exhibited by the Gypsiferous group, and such as have led me to suspect that they form part of a somewhat local deposit, which may be the representative of the Jurassic strata, discovered by Dr. Hayden in Nebraska. I have been able to discover no evidence of the existence of similar rocks, beneath the Cretaceous and above the Permian, east of Walnut Creek.

WALNUT CREEK TO PAWNEE FORK.

LOWER CRETACEOUS ROCKS.

Before reaching Walnut Creek, the Santa Fé road enters the valley of the Arkansas, which is several miles in width, and is bounded on the north and west by the abrupt edges of the "high prairie," a nearly level plateau, which occupies an immense area west of this point. In this plateau the tributaries of the Arkansas have excavated valleys of greater or less breadth, but they are generally narrow and are separated by "divides" of the high prairie, which to the eye are as level as the surface of still water, and are everywhere covered with a velvety carpet of buffalo-grass. Smoky Hill Fork of the Kansas, Cottonwood Creek, the Little Arkansas, Cow Creek, Walnut Creek, &c., all traverse, at least through a part of their courses, channels, which they have excavated in the "high prairie."

Throughout the greater part of the area drained by these streams the geological substratum of the plateau I have described is the Lower Cretaceous sandstone, or, more properly, a *group* of strata, though sometimes consisting of but a single bed, which forms the base of the Cretaceous system; No. 1 of Meek and Hayden's Nebraska section of the Cretaceous series. This group is composed principally and sometimes exclusively of thick-bedded, coarse-grained, ferruginous sandstone, containing as characteristic fossils a large number of species of angiospermous leaves. Around the edge of the high prairie this sandstone caps or composes many isolated buttes which have been severed from their connection with the plateau by aqueous erosion. Such, we learn from Messrs. Meek and Hayden, is the structure of the Smoky Hills, from which they obtained a large part of the impressions of leaves described by the writer, and such also is the structure of Pawnee Rock, which stands near the road between Walnut Creek and Pawnee Fork. At Allison's ranch, on Walnut Creek, this sandstone has precisely the lithological characters of that from the Smoky Hills, but I was not able to detect in it any traces of fossils. At Walnut Creek, however, twenty-five miles distant, vegetable impressions are abundant, including, apparently, some of the same species obtained from Smoky Hill, Blackbird Hill, &c.

The geological horizon marked by this Lower Cretaceous sandstone group is perhaps the best defined of all in the entire geological series in the Southwest, and more generally useful as a plane of reference than any other. From the resistant character of the materials composing this group, it has held its place over an immense extent of country from which the softer superior strata have been removed. When the upper members of the Cretaceous formation are present, as is the case in much of the country hereafter to be described, the Lower Cretaceous sandstones are covered with more than a thousand feet of limestones, or calcareous shales filled with the remains of marine organisms, and evidently a deposit from the waters of the ocean. In an analysis of the Cretaceous formation, to be given in a succeeding chapter of this report, I shall attempt to deduce, from the composition and fossil contents of the different members of this series, something of the history of the changing phases of the physical geography of the central portion of the continent during their deposition. I may say, however, in passing, that these coarse Cretaceous sandstones are exclusively mechanical deposits, and such as have not been transported any very great distance from their place of origin; that, extending as they do from the vicinity of the Mississippi all the way to the base of the Rocky Mountains, they mark a period of general subsidence in all this portion of the continent—a period through which the sea was gradually encroaching upon the land. The shore-line was then constantly marching inland, leaving behind it proofs of the power of its littoral waves; which comminuted and sifted the barriers opposing their progress, and formed of their ruins these beds of stratified sands and pebbles, which may be regarded as only an unbroken series of ancient sea-beaches. The finer materials, washed by the shore-waves, were taken into suspension or solution by the sea-water, and, mingled with or composing the remains of marine animals, were spread over the ocean bottom as the shales and limestones of which I have before spoken. This encroachment of the sea took place from east to west, and the invading flood is now represented by the Gulf of Mexico. This is indicated by the facts that the Lower Cretaceous sandstones thin out and disappear toward the south and east, where nearly the entire Cretaceous series is represented by marine and organic sediments; while, as we go toward the west and northwest, on the contrary, the sandstones increase in thickness, the superincumbent strata become less and less calcareous, until ultimately, as we approach the shores of the continent not submerged by the Cretaceous ocean, the mechanical sediments greatly preponderate over the organic, and beds of sandstone and shale of enormous thickness, the direct *débris* of the land, represent all the subdivisions of the chalk formation.

I have spoken in my former report of the parallelism between the Lower Cretaceous strata of New Mexico and those of Nebraska, as described by Meek and Hayden, and those of New Jersey, by Professor Cook. How accurately the Lower Cretaceous rocks of the district now under consideration represent those of the regions just mentioned will be seen in the following section:

Section of Lower Cretaceous rocks at the crossing of Pawnee Fork.

No. 1. Soft, coarse sandstone, dark reddish-brown, yellow, or nearly white; lower part finer, and containing impressions of dicotyledonous leaves (*Salix*, &c.) to summit of cliff, about 50 feet.

2. Light dove-colored clay, with lignite and broken leaves, 10 feet.

3. Yellow sandy clay with vegetable impressions to bed of stream; about 15 feet exposed.

I had not time fully to explore this locality, but the fossils are quite numerous and very accessible. The species of *Salix* referred to is apparently identical with *S. Meekii*, obtained at Smoky Hill by Meek and Hayden. The dove-colored clay which underlies the sandstone is scarcely distinguishable from that which holds a similar position in New Jersey, and which, like this, is filled with vegetable matter.

By reference to the section of the rocks of Kansas given by Messrs. Meek and Hayden, in the Proceedings of the Philadelphia Academy, January, 1859, it will be noticed that the "red, brown, and yellowish coarse-grained sandstone, containing leaves of dicotyledonous trees, forming the summits of the Smoky Hills," is underlaid by "whitish, very fine-grained, argillaceous sandstone, with bluish, purple, and ash-colored clays." Though containing at that locality no vegetable impressions, it is evident that these latter beds are the equivalents of those exposed beneath the sandstone on Pawnee Fork.

PAWNEE FORK TO CROSSING OF CIMARRON.

TERTIARY STRATA.

After leaving Pawnee Fork the Santa Fé road crosses the margin of an immense Tertiary basin, to which I first called attention in my report on the geology of the Colorado country, and designated by the name of the "Tertiary basin of the Arkansas."

During my former transit of the plains I formed the opinion that the western boundary of this Tertiary belt was passed near the crossing of the Cimarron; and it is still possible that Tertiary strata will not be found west of that point which are continuous with those forming the table-lands bordering the Arkansas, but during the past season I noticed similar beds recurring at various points quite up to the bases of the Rocky Mountains, and I think we have evidence that at one time Tertiary rocks occupied the surface of a large territory in this region, from which they have been entirely removed, or so nearly so as to be represented by isolated and often widely separated patches.

As will be seen by reference to the sections exposed at various points along the western portion of the Santa Fé road, these Tertiary rocks are entirely unconformable to those upon which they rest; are of very much later date, and were deposited, not only subsequent to the period when the entire series of Cretaceous strata had been laid down, but after they had been much disturbed, and elevated to such a point that valleys, eroded by surface action, had been cut down to and through the base of that series. In different localities the Tertiary strata rest up on the Middle or Lower Cretaceous rocks, or even on the underlying Triassic formation.

The vicinity of the Raton Mountains has, in former times, been the theater of violent and wide-spread volcanic action. At that time numerous mountain masses and subordinate buttes of trap were thrown up, and floods of lava poured out, covering an extensive area in their vicinity. During this period of violence the Cretaceous rocks were locally much disturbed and metamorphosed, and the lowest members of that series elevated to, and perhaps far above, the surface of the ocean. At some time subsequent to the period of greatest volcanic activity, and yet apparently before the fires in this great furnace were entirely extinguished, the Tertiary strata began to be deposited in the depressions, and over the irregularities which then existed on the surface. Unfortunately, in all the localities where I examined these strata, they seemed to be destitute of fossils. We are, therefore, as yet without the light which they would throw upon the conditions of their deposition, and the conclusions to which I have arrived in reference to the precise age of these beds are to a certain extent conjectural, and liable to be modified by future discoveries, yet there seems to be good reason for supposing that they are what I have called them, Tertiary, and that they are continuous with the Tertiary basins of Northwestern Kansas and Nebraska. The reasons for this conclusion are, first, that these deposits are considerably more recent than any portion of the Cretaceous series represented in the region in which they exist; second, that in their lithological characters and the circumstances of their deposition they are the exact counterparts of the fresh-water Tertiary strata of the basins to which I have referred, and which are also only locally and rarely fossiliferous; third, that the Tertiary strata of the Upper Platte extend southward toward the Arkansas, where their only possible representatives are those under consideration; fourth, Tertiary fossils are said to have been found in these beds on the banks of the Arkansas, above the crossing.

In lithological characters the Tertiary rocks of the Arkansas basin are considerably unlike any marine deposit with which I am familiar, but the greater portion of them strikingly resemble the fresh-water Tertiary limestones of the Paris basin; and, as I have said, are undistinguishable from those of the "bad-lands" of the Upper Missouri, shown by their fossils to be all of fresh-water or estuary origin. The great mass of the Arkansas beds is made up of white or cream-colored limestone, closely resembling much of the calcareous tufa deposited from springs, and frequently containing masses of black or red, very light and porous scoria; with this tufaceous limestone are associated strata of more compact laminated cream-colored limestone; a bed of coarse, friable light-colored sandstone, frequently a conglomerate; and at a higher level a stratum of exceedingly coarse conglomerate, of which the pebbles, if such they can be called, are often 6 or 8 inches in diameter. These pebbles are principally composed of quartz or the harder erupted rocks, basalt, porphyry, &c., with occasionally a fragment of Carboniferous limestone. I noticed that in going toward the west the materials composing these sandstones and conglomerates became much coarser, showing that they had been derived from the direction of the Rocky Mountains. Although the Tertiary basins of the West have been studied in but a small portion of their extent, and we are as yet very far from being in possession of all the facts in reference to their areas, their structure, or their fossils, which will permit us to write in full the history of their deposition, the observations already made all seem to point to the conclusion that the Tertiary epoch was an era of progressive elevation over all the central portions of our continent; and that during the greater part of this epoch, the continent had nearly the form and area which it has at present. The purely marine Tertiaries appear to be restricted to the immediate vicinity of the present ocean; and to a narrow belt along the valley of the Mississippi, which continued to be occupied till a comparatively recent period by an arm of the Gulf of Mexico. So far as at present known, all the Tertiary strata which are found between the Mississippi and the Sierra Nevada are of fresh-water or estuary origin. The gradual retrocession of the ocean is also indicated by the fact reported by Dr. Hayden that where estuary shells are found in the Tertiary strata of Nebraska they are generally restricted to the lower beds of the series; the overlying strata containing fresh-water species. We are led to infer, therefore, that the Tertiary basins which skirt the bases of the Rocky Mountains, were once the beds of rivers and lakes of the Tertiary continent; and, except in the immediate vicinity of the coast-line, were wholly occupied by fresh water. It is also probable that some of these basins occupy former lines of drainage from the Rocky Mountains; and that the beds of coarse sand and gravel made up of fragments of crystalline rocks, wholly foreign to the localities where they are found, but abundant in and peculiar to the Rocky Mountains, were transported from their distant places of origin by the rapid currents of these ancient rivers. The further consideration of these facts, as well as others bearing on the subject of the physical geography of the central portions of the continent during the Tertiary epoch, must be deferred to a subsequent portion of this report, where it will more properly find place.

The details of structure of the Tertiary basin of the Arkansas will be, perhaps, most readily understood by a few extracts from my notes, made at various points along our route where the Tertiary strata are exposed. "After leaving Pawnee Fork, the road passes over level bottom-lands for several miles, where it divides; the left-hand branch following the windings of the Arkansas; the other, called the 'dry road,' rising on to and crossing the table-land which separates the valleys of Pawnee Fork and the Upper Arkansas. This table-land is underlain by a white tufaceous limestone, exposed in the bed of the Coon Creeks, and still better at the point where the dry road comes down again to the Arkansas. It is also thrown out in many different places from the burrows of the prairie-dogs. In lithological characters, this rock is precisely like a portion of the strata of the 'bad-lands' of Nebraska; contains no fossils, but a few pebbles of crystalline rock. At the Caches, sixteen miles below the crossing of the Arkansas, the same stratum is seen overlaid by some thirty feet of coarse, soft, light-brown conglomerate, much cross-stratified. The cement is coarse silicious sand; the pebbles, from the size of an egg downward, of granite, trap, quartz, porphyry, trachyte, jasper, quartzite, chert, &c., with a few of Carboniferous limestone."

"At the crossing of the Arkansas, the following section is exposed:

"1. Spongy tufaceous limestone like that on Dry road.
"2. Coarse, soft conglomerate, same as at Caches, 35 feet.
"3. Tufaceous limestone, like No. 1, to base."

"The sand-hills, which border the Arkansas on the south side, seem to have been derived from the decomposition of the Tertiary conglomerate."

"The same stratum forms the banks of the Cimarron, and has apparently given character to its sandy and sterile valley. The 'Jornada,' the divide between the Arkansas and Cimarron, is another portion of the high prairie, precisely like, in physical and geological structure, that crossed by the 'dry road.'"

"At Eighteen-mile ridge, on the Cimarron, the coarse conglomerate and chalky tufa are exposed, as at many points below. The conglomerate is composed of a coarse sandy cement, with pebbles from the size of shot to eight inches in diameter. The larger ones are compact, fine-grained, reddish-yellow sandstone, doubtless of Lower Cretaceous age, and such as comes to the surface farther westward. Others are composed of granite, amygdaloid, clay-slate, quartz, jasper, &c. The greater size of the pebbles in this conglomerate perhaps indicates that, in going westward, we are approaching the source from which they were derived. The conglomerate would seem to be a drift from the Rocky Mountains, where, and where only, as far as I am aware, such materials occur in place. If this is true, when on the Cimarron, we were doubtless standing in the channel of a great line of drainage of the Tertiary epoch."

At the middle spring of the Cimarron a very instructive and interesting section is exposed, in which we again see the base of the Tertiary series. On Pawnee Fork, the tufaceous limestones and conglomerate which I have described rest upon the coarse ferruginous Lower Cretaceous sandstone. Here we find them underlain by soft yellow or red sandstone, of which the place is considerably lower than that last mentioned. In other localities further west we shall see that these Tertiary beds rest first on Lower Cretaceous sandstone, then on trap, again upon the Middle Cretaceous limestones and shales, and, finally, upon the red calcareous sandstones of the Trias. The elements composing the section of the middle spring of the Cimarron are indicated in the following table:

Section of strata at Middle Spring of Cimarron.

	Feet.
1. Coarse gravel from disintegrated conglomerate	6
2. Spongy, tufaceous limestone, cream-colored	3
3. Soft, chalky tufa, cream-colored	2
4. Laminated, tufaceous limestone, cream-colored	6
5. Massive, tufaceous limestone, upper part hardest, containing balls of red and black scoria	50
6. Cream-colored tufa, similar to No. 5, but softer	19
7. Hard, foliated tufaceous limestone	5
8. Yellow or reddish, soft, massive sandstone	40

The cream-colored tufaceous limestones of the above section are the equivalents of the lower tufaceous limestone of the Arkansas, and, though containing no fossils, are doubtless Tertiary. The balls of scoria which they include, though not positive evidence of the fact, may be regarded as an indication that volcanic action was going on somewhere in this vicinity during their deposition. If this was the case, the scoria must have been derived from the vicinity of the Raton Mountains, where volcanic eruptions were taking place, geologically speaking, about that time.

Scoria is very frequently contained in the Tertiary strata near the Rocky Mountains; a fact which has suggested the thought that the water from which these tufaceous limestones were deposited may, in some instances, have been heated, and that this is one reason why they contain so few fossils.

The sandstone which forms the base of the section, at the Middle Spring of the Cimarron, will be soon noticed, in connection with the group to which it belongs; but its place in the series, as has been stated, is below the Lower Cretaceous sandstone.

We have here abundant evidence of the entire unconformability of the Tertiary beds with those on which they rest, and that they were deposited in basins scooped out of the underlying rocks, doubtless by subaerial action, precisely as similar valleys or basins are forming at the present day.

A few miles further westward the Lower Cretaceous, and even some portions of the Middle Cretaceous strata, are found in place, and there is no question but that they once stretched over all the adjacent country, and occupied the place since held by the Tertiary beds, but, by the long action of eroding agents, they had been entirely removed or deeply excavated before the Tertiary limestones began to be deposited; and that subsequently this latter series filled up and obliterated all traces of that ancient denudation. During the present epoch the process of erosion has again begun, and the valleys of the Cimarron and Arkansas are being for the second time excavated.

CROSSING OF CIMARRON TO ENCHANTED SPRING.

JURASSIC ? ROCKS.

At the crossing of the Cimarron, and for some miles west of that point, the Tertiary strata have been entirely removed; the bottom of the basin exposed and deeply eroded. It is here composed of a series of strata of which the sandstone, lying at the base of the cliff at the Middle Spring, forms a part. This series consists of a number of alternations of strata which are quite different in color, texture, and composition. They are, as far as my observation extended, destitute of fossils, and it is therefore impossible to fix accurately their place in the geological scale. It will be seen from the section given below that they underlie the coarse red and yellow sandstones of Lower Cretaceous age, which have been so frequently referred to in the preceding pages. They are, however, in lithological characters quite unlike the strata which are generally found immediately beneath the Lower Cretaceous sandstones of New Mexico. The position they hold is apparently the same with that of the Jurassic rocks discovered by Dr. Hayden in the Black Hills. It is possible, therefore, and perhaps probable, that they are of the same age. It will, however, be necessary to wait the detection of fossils in the group before its place in the series can be more than conjectured. The section taken from the summits of the hills at Enchanted Spring, down the side of the valley toward the Cimarron, as far as the rocks were exposed, is as follows:

1. Gray, yellow, or brown coarse sand-rock, the equivalent of that of the Smoky Hills, here containing obscure impressions of large dicotyledonous leaves, 70 feet.
2. Thin layers of laminated brown sandstones, with very smooth surfaces, 20 feet.
3. *Hard light-blue or dove-colored limestone in thin layers, Jurassic?* 50 feet.
4. Slope covered, about 30 feet.
5. Yellow or reddish quartzose sandstone, 2 feet.
6. Red shale, 5 feet.
7. Yellow calcareous sandstone or silicious limestone, with ferruginous concretions, 20 feet.
8. Brecciated conglomerate, 5 feet.
9. Blood-red shale, 25 feet.
10. Yellow calcareous sandstone, similar to No. 7, 8 feet.
11. Blood-red shale, with one or two narrow bands of green, 10 feet.
12. Red and yellow argillaceous limestone, somewhat concretionary, often laminated, sun-cracked and ripple-marked, pierced by vertical cavities from one to two inches in diameter, to base, 8 feet.

Much of the coarse sand-rock, No. 1 of the section, is precisely like that containing the fossil plants of Blackbird Hill, Nebraska; being partly dark-brown and ferruginous, and partly gray, quartz-like, and intensely hard. Other portions of the mass are yellow and softer, in this respect resembling the general aspect of this rock in New Mexico. The limestone, No. 3 of the section, is the most interesting feature of the group, and the one to which we must look for fossils that shall determine its age. It is a fine-grained, homogeneous rock, such as I have nowhere seen near the same geological horizon in the Southwest. With the exception of the limestone, I should have no great difficulty in supposing that this group represented the strata which in New Mexico immediately underlie the Lower Cretaceous sandstones; but the limestone is entirely foreign to the geology of those portions of New Mexico which I have examined. I am strongly inclined to believe that it is a member of the series not represented further to the south and west, and I shall be surprised if it does not yield to future explorers well-marked Jurassic fossils.

ENCHANTED SPRING TO COTTONWOOD SPRING.

TERTIARY AND LOWER CRETACEOUS STRATA.

At Enchanted Spring the Lower Cretaceous sandstones form a line of bold bluffs, which border the excavated valley of the Cimarron. From this point up to the base of the mountains the surface has nothing of the monotony of the plains below, but is greatly varied, and the scenery is frequently impressive, occasionally grand. With the exception, however, of the volcanic outlayers of the Raton Mountains, there are few evidences of the action of violent disturbing causes, and the variety which the scenery presents is due almost entirely to the erosion of nearly horizontal strata by the drainage from the Rocky Mountains. Here the traveler, journeying to New Mexico, obtains his first view of the peculiar and impressive scenery so characteristic of nearly all portions of the great central plateau of the continent. Here he first hears the word *mesa*, and sees it embodied in the long lines of table-lands which fill the horizon and stretch away in perspective, like the walls of Cyclopean cities. I have, in a former report, described somewhat in detail the phenomena of erosion which are presented by the high table-land bordering the Rocky Mountains. It is, therefore, only necessary for me to say in this connection that the views then advanced in reference to the origin of the great natural features of that region, its *mesas* and *cañons*, have been fully confirmed by subsequent observation, and that there can be no question that they are to be regarded simply as phenomena of surface erosion, of which they are the grandest examples known.

The geology of the region lying between Enchanted Spring and Cottonwood Spring is similar throughout. The rocky basis of the country is formed by the Lower Cretaceous sandstone, covered here and there with patches of white tufaceous Tertiary limestone. These Tertiary beds were, perhaps, once continuous, but now form only a relatively thin covering over the divides between the streams, being wholly removed from the valleys and low lands. As on the Arkansas, they are without fossils as far as observed, and were deposited nearly horizontally over the irregular surface of the underlying sandstone.

A section of the strata at Cedar Spring is as follows:

(a.) *Tertiary.*

1. White, chalky, tufaceous limestone, with hard, gray, compact bands ..... 15 feet.
2. Cream-colored, spongy, tufaceous limestone, (similar to that on the Arkansas and Cimarron) ..... 40 feet.

(b.) *Cretaceous.*

1. Yellow fine-grained sandstone, with obscure impressions of fucoids ..... 6 feet.
2. Light blue or white shale, with many obscure vegetable impressions, about ..... 4 feet.
3. Yellow sandstone, soft and rather coarse, in thin (often rippled-marked) layers, containing impressions of dicotyledonous leaves, resembling those of *Salix* and *Quercus* ..... 5 feet.

4. Bluish shale, containing impressions of leaves, and a thin bed of lignite.... 4 feet.
5. Yellow soft sandstone, with impressions of dicotyledonous leaves, apparently identical with some of those from Smoky Hill, to base of section....... 50 feet.

From Cedar Spring to McNee's Creek the road passes over a high prairie underlain by Tertiary limestones. At McNee's Creek the Tertiary rocks are cut through and the Cretaceous series freely opened. No fossils were found here, but the rock is generally similar to that at Cedar Spring. At Cottonwood Spring the surface rock is Tertiary tufaceous limestone, which is cut through by the stream, and its line of junction with the underlying Cretaceous rocks exposed. The sandstone is here considerably disturbed and metamorphosed apparently by the upheaval of the erupted mass of the "Rabbit-ear Buttes," which are near by. Upon the uneven surface of the sandstone the Tertiary strata are laid down nearly or quite horizontally, and have evidently been but little disturbed since their deposition. In the upper part of the Cretaceous sandstone near the spring I found many vegetable impressions, generally trunks of trees and fragments of wood, and also some leaves. One of these is apparently a *Salix*, and perhaps identical with *S. Meekii*. There are also others, which are similar to the leaves found at Smoky Hill. The metamorphosis of the Cretaceous strata is shown not only in the peroxidation of the iron which they contain, but an associated clay-shale is rendered nearly as white and as hard as porcelain; the contained iron being segregated in thin vein-like bands.

COTTONWOOD SPRING TO RED FORK OF CANADIAN.

TRAP, TERTIARY, AND CRETACEOUS ROCKS.

The interval indicated by the above heading includes a portion of the volcanic district adjacent to the Raton Mountains, to which I have before alluded. Rabbit-ear, Round Mound, Wagon Mound, &c., form part of a group of trap buttes, which are scattered over the prairie for a long distance east of the mountains. They are in some cases entirely isolated, and seem to mark minor vents, where a portion of the molten matter contained in some vast subterranean reservoir found exit. Others are connected by sheets of trap, and in some instances are but portions of a volcanic flood, separated from their connections by subsequent erosions. Toward the mountains the erupted material more completely covers the country, and forms extensive mesas, or high table-lands, which have been deeply cut by the cañons of the streams once flowing over but now through them. They have also been left in strong relief by the cutting down of the country bordering them on the east.

In many places the sheets of trap are covered by Tertiary tufa, which has been deposited quietly and uniformly over their surfaces, and is evidently much more recent than they. This Tertiary bed is here not of great thickness, and perhaps represents only the extreme upper portion of the series described in the preceding pages.

Wherever the trap is cut through in the stream-beds it is found resting on the Lower Cretaceous sandstones, which are in such cases somewhat metamorphosed; being vitrified, or at least hardened; the iron being peroxidized, and more or less segregated in bands or veins. In other localities the Lower Cretaceous sandstone is covered by the Tertiary tufa; but, over large areas, it is itself the surface rock. At Whetstone Creek this group is exposed in the banks of the stream, and shows a great number of alternations of very fine-grained, laminated sandstone, with more argillaceous bands. These strata contain fossil plants in large numbers, which would undoubtedly well reward collectors who could have more time to devote to the locality than was at my command. Several of the species noticed there are apparently different from those obtained from outcrops of this formation from other localities, but a narrow leaf, perhaps a *Salix*, seems to be identical with one obtained at Smoky Hill, Pawnee Fork, &c.

A remarkable fissure has been opened by volcanic force in the rocks containing these plants. It is about four and a half feet wide following the main jointings of the sandstones, which here run nearly east and west. No trap fills the fissure, but it is evident that it was once a kind of flue through which a vast amount of heat escaped from below. Its sides are blackened, glazed, and blistered, and the sandstone which forms its immediate walls is considerably metamorphosed; to the depth of an inch it is vitrified; back of this it is converted into a hard, blue, sonorous rock, resembling a compact basalt. The effect of heat is noticeable in the changed condition of the sandstone several feet from the sides of the fissure, but at a distance of twenty feet the rock again exhibits its normal appearance.

VALLEY OF THE CANADIAN.

MIDDLE CRETACEOUS STRATA.

The valley of the Red Fork of the Canadian is a broad eroded trough, excavated almost entirely in the great group of limestones and calcareous shales which rest upon the sandstone group I have so frequently referred to as the Lower Cretaceous sandstones. The overlying calcareous mass, which contains immense numbers of Cretaceous fossils, is apparently the equivalent of Nos. 2, 3, and 4 of Meek and Hayden's Nebraska section.

In my former notes on the geology of this region, I designated this series as Upper Cretaceous, to distinguish it from the Lower Cretaceous sandstone group. At that time I had seen no evidence of the existence in New Mexico of higher members of the Cretaceous formation. In our recent explorations of the San Juan country, where this series is very largely developed, I found the equivalents of the strata under consideration covered by soft sandstones and marls, which I regarded as also members of the great Cretaceous formation. This latter group is, therefore, more properly Upper Cretaceous, and the calcareous strata of the Canadian and their equivalents will be designated in the subsequent portions of this report as Middle Cretaceous.

In describing the Cretaceous strata of the country bordering the San Juan, I shall have occasion to return to the subject of the classification of the rocks belonging to this series, as developed in New Mexico, and, as far as practicable, establish a parallelism between them and those of the Upper Missouri, as described in the Nebraska section of Messrs. Meek and Hayden. I may here say, however, that the division of the Cretaceous rocks of New Mexico into three great groups—Upper, Middle, and Lower—will be found to be the most convenient, if not the only one practicable

Wherever I have observed them these different divisions are marked by obvious and distinctive lithological characters, and the fossils contained by each group are usually recognizable at a glance. Those of the Lower sandstone group being generally angiospermous leaves; those of the Middle group, marine shells and the remains of fishes; those of the Upper division, as far as yet observed, being leaves and trunks of trees different from those found below. It is true, that in Southeastern New Mexico and Texas there is very little sandy matter in any of the Cretaceous rocks, while in the Rocky Mountains the upper and lower arenaceous divisions are greatly developed, and the limestones have nearly disappeared from the middle division. This latter group is, however, distinctly marked even there; consisting of calcareous shales, with thin bands of limestone and beds of lignite, interstratified with layers, of greater or less thickness, of fine-grained sandstones, usually containing considerable lime.

On the banks of the Canadian, from 800 to 1,000 feet of the Middle Cretaceous strata all exposed.

The section from the summit of the hills at the "Breaks of Red River," down to the bed of the stream, is as follows:

1. Rolled gravel, composed of fragments of porphyry, trap, Paleozoic limestone, &c., drift from the Rocky Mountains.

2. Light-blue compact limestone, on exposure cracking into flattish chips or "spalls," containing *Inoceramus problematicus*, *Gryphæa Pitcheri*, &c.

3. Ferruginous, laminated, sandy limestone, with rounded concretions, one to five feet in diameter, of compact blue limestone, much cracked, and fissures filled with crystallized carbonate of lime. This rock is a great store-house of fossils, of which, perhaps, the most abundant is a remarkably neat little *Ostrea*, hitherto undescribed, which I have called *Ostrea elegantula;* one of the most common and widely distributed Middle Cretaceous fossils of New Mexico. With this are *Inoceramus fragilis*, H. & M., *I. Crispii?*, *Ammonites percarinatus*, Shark's teeth (*Lamna* and *Oxyrhina*), &c. The surfaces of the layers of this stratum are covered with small *Ostreas* (*O. congeata*), and fragments of *Inoceramus*, which resemble fish-scales; thickness 80 feet.

4. Light-blue compact limestone in thin beds, weathering white, similar to No. 2; about 30 feet exposed. From this point to the bed of the river, some 700 to 800 feet, the cliffs are composed of blue compact limestone in thin beds, alternating with dark-blue and brownish bituminous calcareous shales, which underlie the preceding members of the section, and rest upon the Lower Cretaceous sandstones. In every part of these lower limestones *Inoceramus problematicus* is exceedingly abundant. They also contain large numbers of *Gryphæa Pitcheri*, of which remarkably large and fine specimens were collected a short distance east of the crossing.

All the foregoing calcareous beds rest upon the sandstones of Lower Cretaceous age to which I have so frequently referred. These sandstones form the bed of the Canadian at the crossing and the walls of the cañon below, and here exhibit nearly the same lithological characters as at many localities where they are exposed farther eastward. They seem to be somewhat disturbed and hardened, and it is possible that a slight unconformability may be discovered between them and the overlying rocks. This is a mere suspicion, however, which I could not verify or disprove in the time at my command. The divide between the valleys of the Red Fork and its tributary, the Ocaté, as well as the western bank of the Ocaté, is formed of the Middle Cretaceous limestones and marl, enumerated in the preceding section.

The structure of the picturesque table-lands from which these streams issue I had no opportunity of determining, as they lie several miles north of the road, but I could see that they are in part covered by a thick layer of trap, to which their nearly horizontal surfaces and precipitous sides are doubtless due.

VALLEY OF THE CANADIAN TO LAS VEGAS.

As far westward as Burgwin's Spring, patches of Tertiary tufa appear in numerous localities, usually resting upon trap, which is the prevailing surface-rock, and which caps the picturesque mesas bordering the road on either side. Here, as farther east, numerous trap buttes stud the prairies, and there are several lines of trap hills which run off toward the south as diverging spurs from the Raton Mountains. Near Dragoon Spring, by a long and painful ascent we reached the summit of a trap mesa, apparently the continuation of the table-lands bordering the Upper Canadian. The underlying sedimentary rocks are here concealed by the *débris* of their trappean covering. A few miles farther westward, however, the Lower Cretaceous sandstones again come into view, and it is probable that they here form the surface over which the volcanic flood was poured. The trap of all this region exhibits great similarity of character; its weathered surfaces are black, while within it is dark brown or gray. It is generally more or less vesicular, sometimes quite scoriaceous.

About Fort Union the only rocks visible are a mass of vesicular trap similar to that just described, apparently only a narrow and local lava-stream, and the Lower Cretaceous sandstones, which are very fully exposed. This latter group has here a thickness of at least 300 feet, perhaps considerably more, as its line of junction with the underlying rocks is nowhere reached. It forms the hills at the base of which the fort is located, and a large part of Gallinas Mountain. Probably still older strata are thrown up at the latter locality, but I had no opportunity to look for them. Just below Fort Union the Cretaceous sandstones, dipping to the south and east, away from the mountains, pass beneath the surface, and are succeeded by the Middle Cretaceous limestones so fully exposed on the banks of the Canadian. These rocks occupy all the interval between this point and Las Vegas. On my former visit to Las Vegas I was unable to discover any fossils in the blue limestone which crops out there, though I regarded it as equivalent to the Middle Cretaceous beds elsewhere examined. This conjecture I was able more recently fully to confirm by finding in it *Inoceramus problematicus* and other fossils of that horizon.

At Las Vegas the road leaves the prairies, and thence to Santa Fé is constantly involved in the foot-hills of the Rocky Mountains. As the geology of this portion of our route is somewhat complicated, and was studied principally on excursions made at different times from Santa Fé, it will perhaps more properly form part of a distinct chapter, where the structure of a limited geographical district is considered by itself, and where the light derived from this one of its parts may serve to illuminate the others. This division is the more natural, as in this vicinity we passed out of the great basin in which we had so long been journeying—the valley of the Mississippi—and entered that of the Rio Grande. At Las Vegas, too, the granite of the Rocky Mountains is first seen in place, forming the axis of a subordinate anticlinal, on the eastern flanks of which the Triassic and the Carboniferous formations re-appear in succession, thus bringing us to the base of the section which has occupied our attention in the preceding pages. The exposures of these strata are much less full and satisfactory here than nearer Santa Fé, where they are also less metamorphosed and more fossiliferous, and where the contrast and coincidences which their exposures present with their eastern outcrops may be more accurately determined.

CHAPTER II.

GEOLOGY OF THE VICINITY OF SANTA FÉ.

GENERAL GEOLOGICAL FEATURES—SANTA FÉ MOUNTAINS—GRANITE—ITS CHARACTER AND CONTAINED MINERALS—RELATIONS OF THE SANTA FÉ MOUNTAINS—PLACER MOUNTAINS—CRETACEOUS AND TRIASSIC ROCKS—CRETACEOUS LIGNITE CONVERTED INTO ANTHRACITE BY AN OUTBURST OF TRAP—GOLD OF THE PLACER MOUNTAINS—COPPER—IRON—THE CERRILLOS—GOLD—SILVER—LEAD—COPPER—IRON—TURQUOISE—ANCIENT CHALCHUITL MINES—THE SANDIA MOUNTAIN—THE VALLES—STRATIFIED ROCKS—CARBONIFEROUS FORMATION—SANTA FÉ SECTION—SECTION AT PECOS VILLAGE—PERMO-CARBONIFEROUS BEDS—GYPSUM FORMATION—SECTION AT SAN JOSÉ—FOSSIL PLANTS—CRETACEOUS FORMATION—SUBDIVISION OF THE SYSTEM—YELLOW SANDSTONES OF CAÑON BLANCO CRETACEOUS—SECTIONS AT GALLISTEO AND POPE'S WELL—TERTIARY BEDS OF FRESH-WATER ORIGIN.

The region about Santa Fé has occupied the attention of several geologists who have visited New Mexico, among whom Messrs. Wislizenus, Marcou, and Blake have given full reports of their observations upon it. I also was able to devote a short time to its study while connected with the party of Lieutenant Ives in 1858, a *résumé* of the observations then made being given in my report to that officer. It might, therefore, be supposed that this subject was by this time freed from all obscurity, and, perhaps, exhausted of all interest. This is, however, far from being true, as may be shown in few words. The geological structure of that region is complicated by several distinct lines of upheaval, which have been classed together in the so-called Rocky Mountain system; and yet the relations of these groups and chains of mountains are far from being fully understood, or at least demonstrated. They have been regarded, perhaps justly, as of the same age, but, as will be seen, when we come to speak of them more in detail, evidence of complete synchronism is yet wanting, while there are some facts which seem to point to a contrary conclusion.

Aside from the obscurity which hangs over the erupted rocks, an obscurity that cannot be dissipated without much careful study in the field as well as in the laboratory, the splendid exposures of the three great groups of sedimentary strata, the Carboniferous, the Triassic, and the Cretaceous—to say nothing of the Tertiary beds largely developed, but without fossils—deserve and demand for their full analysis more time than has yet been devoted to them. The three months spent in the vicinity of Santa Fé during the past season by our party have, I trust, not been entirely without value, as regards the determination of doubtful points in the geology of this region. It must be confessed, however, that many questions are left unsettled which we had hoped to solve, and I am convinced that there are few localities within the field of the American geologist where patient and accurate investigation would be so likely to result in the discovery of facts of high scientific value as in that under consideration.

SANTA FÉ MOUNTAINS.

As I have mentioned in my former report, the great mass of the Santa Fé Mountains is composed of coarse, red, feldspathic granite, which ,if not peculiar to, is at least highly characteristic of, many of the mountain ranges of the central portion of the continent included in what is known as the Rocky Mountain system. As we shall see further on, a granite to the eye identical with this forms the core or axis of the Nascimiento Mountain, the Sierra de la Plata, and other of the more westerly ranges of this system. In the Coast Mountains of California or Oregon, in the Cascade Mountains, or in the Sierra Nevada, though I have examined outcrops of granite in many thousand different localities, I have never seen even a hand specimen similar in character to the red granite of the Rocky Mountains. It will be seen, by reference to the description formerly given of the country bordering the Lower Colorado, that the granites of all the mountain ranges which cross that stream in the lower 500 miles of its course are like those of the Pacific coast, white or grey, and contain a large quantity of albite. In the bottom of the cañon of the Great Colorado, north of the San Francisco Mountain, where the river flows in a granitic trough, this rock, which is covered by several thousand feet of Paleozoic strata, is generally grey and fine-grained. It is, however, in many places penetrated by veins, or replaced by masses of a bright-red granite very similar to that of the Santa Fé Mountains. This was the first locality in which, coming eastward from the Pacific, I met with a rock of this character. In the Alleghanies, or the mountains of New England, I have never seen any granite like that of the Rocky Mountains, but, in the bowlder-drift of the Mississippi, and in places north of the great lakes, a rock is found much more closely resembling it. In this, however, the crystals of feldspar are of a less decided red than those of the Canadian rock, being pale rose-red, those of Santa Fé a bright brick-red. To the erosion of the red granites of the Rocky Mountains, during the Paleozoic and Secondary ages, I have been inclined to attribute the prevailing red color of so large a part of the sedimentary rocks. On the banks of the Colorado, several hundred feet of the Carboniferous strata consist of blood-red sandstones and shales, with large quantities of gypsum; nearly the entire interval between the summit of the Carboniferous system and the base of the Cretaceous is filled with similar materials, and some portions of the Upper Cretaceous strata have the same decided tint.

The granite of the Santa Fé Mountains is not universally of the character I have described; occasionally it is seen to be light-colored, grey or white, as it is near Rock Corral, a few miles east of Santa Fé, on the Independence road. Veins of quartz and epidote are very common in the granite of the Santa Fé Mountains; the former being numerous and large. I was never able, however, to discover in them any traces of metallic minerals. They are certainly not the repositories of the copper, lead, silver, and gold which are found in the region immediately about Santa Fé.

The relations which the Santa Fé Mountains sustain to the geology of the surrounding region may be given in a few words. Like most of the ranges which go to make up the complex group of the Rocky Mountains, though attaining a great altitude, this is comparatively short. How far it may be traced to the north, we are at present not able to say; probably not more than fifty or sixty miles. It is then succeeded by other ranges, which, with more or less interruption, extend to and beyond the parks, forming the broad mountain belt which gives character to the topography of the central portions of the continent. On the south it falls off abruptly near Santa Fé, and either wholly disappears or is represented at a distant point by some of the mountain chains which lie east of the Rio Grande. The trend of this chain—a few degrees west of north and east of south—would, if prolonged, strike altogether to the eastward of its nearest neighbors on the south, Placer and Sandia Mountains. The altitude of its highest peak is supposed to be between twelve and thirteen thousand feet.

Upon the flanks of the Santa Fé Mountains, where not removed, the sedimentary rocks rest in regular order, and are, with the exception of the Tertiary, nearly or quite conformable.

THE PLACER MOUNTAINS.

From the southern base of the Santa Fé Mountains the surface descends toward the south, to the valley of Galisteo Creek, some twenty miles distant; thence it rises again, three or four miles, to the base of the Placer Mountains; the course of Galisteo Creek being nearly east and west, following the line of greatest depression between the adjacent mountain groups. This depression forms a natural pass from the plains to the valley of the Rio Grande, affording a practicable and convenient railroad route. Viewed as a whole, the interval between the Santa Fé and Placer Mountains may be regarded as a plain, the inequalities of the surface being slight compared with those of the surrounding country. It is cut, however, by numerous eroded valleys and ravines, and a limited portion of it is occupied by a group of erupted hills—Los Cerrillos—some of which have an altitude of several hundred feet.

The rocks exposed in the valley of Galisteo Creek are mostly of a sedimentary character, representing portions of the Triassic, Cretaceous, and Tertiary formations. East of the Cerrillos, though much disturbed, these are but little changed in structure; the Cretaceous strata abounding in fossils characteristic of the middle and lower beds —the first, mollusks; the second, angiospermous leaves—the Triassic rocks containing great numbers of silicified trunks of coniferous trees similar to those so frequently met with in the same formation farther westward. The stratified rocks are, however, in several localities, cut by trap dikes, which, offering greater resistance to erosion, have been left in strong relief above the surface. Two of these, one north, the other south of the village of Galisteo, are particularly conspicuous, running with a nearly parallel course in an east and west direction for several miles across the country. Of these the southern is the most remarkable, standing like a huge, nearly-continuous wall, its crest being in many places a hundred and fifty feet above the plain bordering it on either side. West of the Cerrillos similar but smaller dikes are common, and a large area on both sides of the Rio Grande is nothing less than a lava-plain, the flood which formed it having apparently flowed from one or several volcanic vents near the eastern base of the Valles, the mountain-chain forming the western boundary of this portion of the valley of the Rio Grande. In this lava-plain the Rio Grande has excavated the cañon through which it flows above Santo Domingo, and its cut edge forms the high mesa-wall which borders Galisteo Creek on the north, from the Cerrillos to its mouth.

It is only near the Rio Grande that the Tertiary beds to which I have referred make their appearance. Here they are altogether similar to those I have described as occurring on the Arkansas and other localities east of the mountains, viz, white tufaceous limestones and beds of conglomerate, the pebbles mainly of pumice or trap, and all without fossils.

On both sides of Galisteo Creek the Cretaceous strata contain beds of lignite. On the south side, in the foot-hills of the Placer Mountains, an outburst and overflow of trap has, over a limited area, changed the lignite into bright, hard anthracite coal. This will doubtless have considerable economical value. The bed is four to five feet thick, included between strata of bluish argillaceous shale, with bands of nodular iron-ore, the whole forming an accurate copy of the most characteristic sections afforded by the Coal-Measures of the Mississippi Valley.

The Placer Mountains form a group rather than a chain, their extent east and west being nearly or quite equal to that north and south. They are made up, however, of a series of short lines of upheaval, having a trend somewhat north of west and south of east. Like most isolated mountains and mountain *groups*, as distinguished from the *chains* which have come under my observation in Central and Western North America, they are composed, for the most part, of rocks decidedly eruptive in character, and to a much less degree than their neighbors the Sandia and Santa Fé Mountains, consist of granite or stratified materials.

The principal constituents of the Placer Mountains are porphyry, trachyte, tufa, and trap, with masses of granite and mica-slate. About their bases, and in some cases upon their flanks, the stratified rocks of the country may all be found, but are less fully exposed than in the more important mountain ranges of this region. The Placer Mountains have received their name from the gold which they furnish; considerable quantities having been taken during a long period of years from the placers of their bases and slopes. More recently, systematic mining operations have been commenced in the auriferous rocks, and a limited amount of gold has been extracted from them. The gold of the Placer Mountains is of remarkable purity, and there is no question but that a great deal of it exists there, yet it is quite doubtful whether these gold-diggings will ever become very productive, from the fact that it will be difficult, if not impossible, ever to bring to the placers an adequate supply of water, and the gold is so sparsely and widely distributed through the metalliferous rock that mining and crushing it will be but moderately compensated by the quantity obtained.

The "Old Placer" has been worked by the Mexican population since the first occupation of the country by the Spaniards, and probably was a place of resort by their predecessors the Pueblo Indians. The gold is obtained in the bed of an intermittent stream flowing through a ravine which separates two of the principal peaks, and in and beneath the *débris* which has accumulated where this gorge opens into the valley of

Galisteo Creek. It generally occurs in fine scales, and but few nuggets of any considerable size have been found. The supply of water for washing out the metal is so small and irregular that gold-digging here is too uncertain a business to be depended upon as a means of subsistence by any considerable number of miners. Only a few Mexican families reside in the vicinity, and these employ but part of their time in gold-washing. When the quantity of water is sufficient to enable them to wash out the gold, the average gain of each man provided with shovel and shallow wooden wash-pan, *batea*, may perhaps be estimated at a dollar per day.

Some Frenchmen formerly resided here, who, for a long time, carried on mining operations in a somewhat systematic manner. They excavated the gold-bearing rock; crushed it between blocks of porphyry, made to revolve by mule-power; the gold being extracted by quicksilver. The auriferous rock is said to have yielded about thirty dollars of gold to the ton. With their rude processes of obtaining the gold it is probable that the operations of those parties were not very remunerative, as they have been now for some years discontinued. An American company has recently purchased a proprietorship at the Old Placer; but, as they represent, from the want of proper machinery and the difficulty of obtaining laborers skilled in the business, the experiment has so far been unsuccessful. The quantity of gold which exists here is, however, evidently large, and it is quite possible that, with more ample means, with more skillful operators, and better machinery, these mines might be worked with profit to the proprietors. It is possible, too, that something might be done by building reservoirs to increase, or at least to regulate, the supply of water for the placer, and thus render it more productive. It is true, however, that the fall of rain in all this region is both small and exceedingly irregular, and the structure of this mountain group, so limited in extent and so simple, would render it difficult, if not impossible, to utilize fully the few and fitful rains by which it is visited.

The rock containing the gold at the Old Placer has been regarded by some who have visited the locality as an altered sandstone, but there can be, I think, little doubt that it is the gossan of an auriferous quartz vein. The material now excavated is a cellular silicious rock, of which some portions are soft and ochrey, others hard and quartz-like. In some localities it is associated with a soft yellow tufa, in others with a hard trachyte or porphyry. The same rock recurs in the Cerrillos; and I have received from the gold diggings of Pike's Peak specimens of auriferous vein-stone presenting precisely the same characters.

Copper.—Considerable copper is found at the Old Placer, though as yet no effort has been made to turn it to account, and it is doubtful whether the quantity is sufficient to make it a proper object of attention in an economical point of view. I obtained from there, however, very beautiful specimens of the sulphides of copper and iron, both yellow and variegated (chalcopyrite and bornite).

Iron.—Many large masses of magnetic iron ore were noticed about the Old Placer, and it is said to occur in abundance there in place. This ore is very pure, of a nearly uniform dull black color, less crystalline in appearance, and containing less silica than the Champlain and Canada ores. That which is freshly mined is highly magnetic in character, and often exhibits the properties of the loadstone.

LOS CERRILLOS.

These are a group of hills or small mountains between Santa Fé and the Placer Mountains, on the north side of Galisteo Creek. The highest has an altitude of perhaps a thousand feet; they are somewhat conical in form, and have no distinct linear arrangement. West of them are several smaller hills, extending off toward the Rio Grande, of which one, from its perfect symmetry called the Potato Hill, will probably attract the attention of all who visit that region. The Cerrillos are wholly eruptive in character, mainly trap and trachyte, and by their upheaval seem to have little disturbed the sedimentary plateau on which they rest. They are principally interesting from their minerals, and contain many old mines worked by the Spaniards or Indians. There are found there gold, silver, lead, copper, iron, and turquoise or "chalchuitl." The gold apparently exists in but small quantity; a single locality only, so far as known, having furnished it. It there occurs in a quartz vein, running through a yellow silicious trachyte similar to that of the Placer Mountains. The silver is found, in combination with lead and copper, in veins in trachyte. These veins have a direction a little west of north and east of south. By many it is believed that the silver mines of the Cerrillos are very rich, and that they will at some time be a source of great wealth to their possessors. The veins which I examined, however, are not promising; where exposed they are not rich, and the evidence is wholly wanting that they will prove more so upon further exploration. The most interesting mines of the Cerrillos are those from which the *chalchuitl* was taken by the ancient inhabitants of the country. Of these there are several, but one much more extensive than the others—that so fully described by Mr. W. P. Blake, Amer. Jour. Science, Vol. xxv, p. 227. The *chalchuitl* occurs in a yellow, porous, trychytic porphyry, in numerous thin and interrupted veins. The mineral is rather abundant, but most of it is of an inferior quality, being of an apple-green color. Pieces of the requisite blue tint, and of sufficient size to form the ear-drops or nose-jewels worn by the Indians, could probably only be obtained by long and laborious excavation; the value which they have always borne attesting their rarity. We found but a single specimen of the requisite purity after some hours' search, and that less than a fourth of an inch in diameter. These mines have undoubtedly been worked for ages; the conical cavity which marks the site of the most extensive one being still a hundred feet in depth by nearly two hundred feet in diameter. Probably no excavation has been made here since the occupation of the country by the Spaniards, but the Pueblo Indians and the Navajoes are still in the habit of visiting the spot and digging in the loose rock thrown out by the ancient miners for fragments which they have overlooked. The *chalchuitl* is not unfrequently found about the ruins which are scattered over New Mexico, and the value set upon it by the ancient inhabitants is still retained by the modern Indians. I have seen ornaments of it worn by the Apaches, Mohaves, the Navajoes and Pueblos, and so highly prized that a fragment of fine quality no larger than the nail of one's little finger and one-eighth of an inch in thickness was regarded as worth a mule or a good horse. The Indians are excellent judges, too, of the quality of the article, discriminating accurately between the different shades of color, and not to be deceived by any base imitation.

6 s p

Of the two great mountain chains visible from Santa Fé, referred to in the preceding pages, the Sandia and the Valles, the former is so fully described in the reports of other geologists (Messrs. Marcou and Blake), and in my report upon the geology of the country bordering the Colorado, that it is scarcely necessary that anything more should now be said in reference to it. The Valles, lying west of the Rio Grande, will be more appropriately noticed hereafter in the description to be given of the geology of the country between the Rio Grande and the Colorado along the route of our expedition. This region includes numerous important mountain ranges, which will be best examined from a point of view where their relations can be most clearly seen.

The stratified rocks of the neighborhood of Santa Fé now claim our attention, and the features which they present will perhaps be most readily appreciated from a *résumé* of each formation considered by itself.

CARBONIFEROUS STRATA.

The rocks of this age are exposed in numerous localities in the vicinity of Santa Fé, and are apparently the oldest sedimentary strata represented in that region. It is possible that Devonian and Silurian rocks exist in this part of New Mexico; but if so, they have hitherto escaped detection, and are probably concealed by a covering of more recent materials. It is certain that at Santa Fé, in several localities where I had an opportunity of seeing the line of junction of the sedimentary and crystalline rocks, the Carboniferous limestones, the equivalents of the Coal-Measures, rest directly upon the granite, or a layer of coarse sandstone two or three feet thick intervenes, the only possible representative of the older rocks. It will be remembered by those who have read the description given in the report of Lieutenant Ives of the section presented in the cañon of the Great Colorado, that in the table-lands west of the Rocky Mountains an interval of over three thousand feet occurs between the base of the Coal-Measure limestones and the surface of the granite. This interval is filled by a series of limestones, shales, and sandstones, which I have supposed to represent the Lower Carboniferous, Devonian, and Silurian formations. All that great mass of sediment is wanting at Santa Fé. It is wanting, too, on the more westerly ranges of the Rocky Mountains, and also from those which border the table-lands at their western verge. The absence of this group of rocks in all these localities seems to me to be accounted for only by supposing that they were deposited after some of the great lines of upheaval which traverse the central portion of the continent had already attained considerable elevation above the surfaces which bordered them. The facts revealed in the cañon of the Colorado show plainly that the granitic basis of this country was consolidated previous to the deposition of the Paleozoic strata, and that over many of the minor irregularities of the sea-bottom the older sedimentary rocks were quietly and horizontally laid down, surrounding and abutting against granitic pinnacles, which rose above the shallow waters in which they were deposited. These inferences, if confirmed by future observations, will considerably modify the hitherto accepted ideas in regard to the age of the ranges of the Rocky Mountains. We are at least warranted in the conclusion that these great lines of fracture in the earth's crust are few of them wholly of modern date, and it even seems probable that through all the geological ages they have served as hinges upon which the great plates of the earth's crust turned, as, in repeated elevations and depressions, the angles which they inclose have been ever varying.

The following detailed sections of the Carboniferous strata, exposed in the hills immediately back of Santa Fé, will be read with interest by all those who are familiar with the Carboniferous rocks of the valley of the Mississippi.

Section of strata at Santa Fé.

No. 1.

Feet.
1. Soft reddish-yellow conglomerate..........
2. Red shale and sandstone, without fossils.......... 45
3. Yellow magnesian, shaly limestone, containing large numbers of *Orthisina umbraculum* and *Productus semireticulatus*.......... 8
4. Red and yellow shale without fossils.......... 25
5. Red and yellow argillaceous shale, with thin bands of ferruginous sandy limestone.......... 20
6. Yellow and pink shale, with bands of calcareous nodules.......... 8
7. Yellowish-pink (flesh-colored) limestone, containing *Productus nodosus*, *Spirifer cameratus*, *Retzia mormoni*, &c.......... 7
8. Red and yellow shale, with layers of limestone nodules.......... 15
9. Yellow limestone, with partings of shale.......... 6
10. Soft red shales, with two bands of intensely hard, grey, quartzose, fine conglomerate, with numerous but obscure impressions of stems of plants.... 45
11. Yellowish-blue compact limestone, with *Productus semireticulatus*, *Spirifer cameratus*, etc., in great numbers.......... 8
12. Purple, pink, and yellow shales, with thin bands of ferruginous limestone, containing the same fossils as the bed above.......... 50
13. Coarse, brown, sandy limestone, full of crinoidal columns.......... 16
14. Coarse, gray sandstone.......... 5
15. Gray clay.......... 3
16. Coarse, reddish sandstone.......... 7
17. Coarse, massive, silicious sandstone, with large grains of quartz, containing *Spirifer cameratus*.......... 10
18. Gray clay.......... 3
19. Gray limestone, with *Productus semireticulatus*, *P. nodosus*, &c.......... 8
20. Pinkish and variegated sandstone.......... 12
21. Gray limestone.......... 4
22. Ferruginous and micaceous sandstone.......... 6
23. Ferruginous foliated limestone, with *Orthisina umbraculum*, *Spirifer cameratus*, *Athyris Roysii*.......... 7
24. Reddish-gray, compact limestone, with *Spirifer cameratus*, *S. lineatus*, *Productus nodosus*, *P. Rogersi*, *P. scabriculus*, *P. semireticulatus*, *Athyris subtilita*, &c.......... 5

		Feet.
25.	Gray shale...	2
26.	Ferruginous sandstone...	3
27.	Gray shale..	7
28.	Dark-red or coarse gray sandstone, with obscure impressions of *Lepidodendra* and *Sigillaria*..	8
29.	Gray and red shales, or indurated clays..............................	5
30.	Dark-red ferruginous limestones, with nodules of red chert...............	15
31.	Grayish-blue or reddish silicious limestone, rather massive, without fossils..	30
32.	Compact crinoidal limestone, reddish or gray in places, made up of bodies and stems of crinoids, the latter often large; also containing fish-teeth, spines of *Archæocidaris* and great numbers of *Productus nodosus*, *P. Rogersi*, *Athyris subtilita*, *Spirifer cameratus*, &c...........................	25
33.	Dark-red ferruginous sandstone, sometimes a conglomerate and quartzose, in other localities soft and coarse.................................	10
34.	Red, blue, green, and yellow, and mottled indurated clay, with nodules of jaspery chert at bottom......................................	18
35.	Cherty concretionary limestone, gray, yellow, blue, red, and contains a few Spirifers of an undescribed species..................................	35
36.	Foliated silicious limestone, gray, yellow, or mottled, with dendritic manganese in the joints; no fossils; like the last, frequently a handsome marble..	20
37.	Red massive granite to base.	

In the preceding section bed No. 1 is certainly not a member of the Carboniferous series, but is probably the base of the Triassic formation. It is, however, less coherent and of lighter color than any of the lower members of this group as they appear when exposed near Santa Fé. It is conformable to the rocks below, while the Tertiaries of that vicinity are, I believe, always unconformable. It will be seen that in this section well-known Carboniferous fossils are found within less than 50 feet of the granite. If, therefore, the older rocks are represented here, they are restricted to a portion of that limited space. Without positive evidence to the contrary, I must regard all the rocks of the section, except bed No. 1, as Carboniferous, and as the equivalents of the upper division of that great formation; that is, the Coal-Measures. As before remarked, in the walls of the cañon of the Great Colorado is a limestone mass, lying beneath the Coal-Measure limestones, which I have supposed might be the Mountain limestone; but of whatever age, that rock and the strata which underlie it are here wholly wanting. There are doubtless some geologists who will regard the granitic base of the preceding section as a metamorphosed condition of the sedimentary rocks which are here due beneath the Carboniferous strata; but this view of the case seems to me wholly untenable. The massive, unstratified, red granite of the Santa Fé Mountains presents characters, both in its physical structure and chemical composition, which could never be assumed in any possible phase of metamorphism by the older Paleozoic rocks of the Colorado Cañon. Much the greater part of their mass is calcareous, and only the extreme upper and lower portions are red. Again, the lower members of the series of sedimentary strata at Santa Fé are but slightly, if at all, metamorphosed. Even if those which rest on the granite in the preceding section be supposed to be changed from their original condition, in the succeeding section, taken in a locality less than two miles distant, the lowest sedimentary rock is not in the least affected by the proximity of the granite. These facts conclusively show, as it seems to me, that the granite was already consolidated before the sedimentary rocks were deposited upon it, and that the reason why the strata underlying the Carboniferous rocks in the Colorado basin are here wanting is simply this: that the surface of the granite upon which they should have been deposited was here too high to receive them. It will be noticed that in the foregoing section of the Coal-Measure strata there are no beds of coal, and yet the preponderance of mechanical over organic sediments, that is, of shales and sandstones over limestones, and especially the presence of coarse sandstones and conglomerates, give to this section a character strongly contrasting with that of the strata of the same age in Kansas—a character unquestionably due to the closer and more constant proximity to high land.

Section of the Carboniferous rocks in the gorge of Santa Fé River.

No. 2.

	Feet.	Inches.
1. Compact blue limestone	10	
2. Gray, brown, and black shales	12	
3. Pinkish shelly limestone, a mass of fossils, containing *Athyris Roysii*, *A. bovidens*, *A. subtilita*, *Spirifer cameratus*, *S. lineatus*, *Productus nodosus*, *P. semireticulatus*, *P. scabriculus*, *P. Rogersi*, *Orthisina umbraculum*, *Orthis Michilini* (?), *Rhynchonella uta*, *Platyceras*, sp., *Nautilus*, sp., &c.	5	
4. Brown, black, and greenish shale	4	
5. Gray limestone	6	
6. Coal		4
7. Green and blue shale	10	
8. Crinoidal limestone, equivalent of No. 32 of preceding section; very fossiliferous	4	
9. Bituminous and argillaceous shale	1½	
10. Crinoidal limestone, equivalent of No. 32 of preceding section	6	
11. Gray and blue shale, with bands of bituminous shale and coaly matter, with *Calamites* and leaves of *Cordaites*	5	
12. Ferruginous sandstone	4	
13. Gray and blue shale	8	
14. Massive concretionary and brecciated gray limestone, containing crinoidal columns, *Athyris subtilita*, *Productus semireticulatus*, &c.	6	
15. Foliated limestone, gray and mottled, with dendritic manganese	15	
16. Coarse, soft, white sandstone	3	
17. Red granite, passing into mica slate, to base.		

In this section the Carboniferous fossils approach nearer the granite than in the preceding one, and the sandstone No. 16 is very soft, and exhibits no trace of metamorphism. Another section, (No. 3), taken at the south base of *Cerro Gordo*, will, with the preceding one, suffice to give a clear idea of the character of the Carboniferous strata near Santa Fé.

Section No. 3.

	Feet.
1. Greenish shale	10
2. Soft greenish sandstone, including a band of ferruginous conglomerate, containing impressions of *Lepidodendra*	16
3. Gray marl, with nodules of blue limestone	6
4. Yellow and mottled limestone, (a handsome marble)	10
5. Blue, concretionary, cherty, silicious limestone, same as No. 35, section No. 1	50
6. Shelly argillaceous limestone, (same as No. 36 of section No. 1)	16
7. Yellow micaceous sandy shale, very soft	3
8. Coarse, soft white sandstone, sometimes a conglomerate	5
9. Red massive granite, to base.	

The other localities in the vicinity, where the Carboniferous strata are exposed, are on the Sandia, Placer, and Jemez Mountains, and in the valley of the Pecos, at and below Pecos Village. They underlie, it is true, almost all parts of New Mexico, but are only visible on the flanks of the mountains and in some of the valleys, which are cut through the overlying rocks. I had not an opportunity of obtaining a complete section of the Carboniferous group on the Sandia and Placer Mountains, as only a portion of the series is exposed in the localities which I examined. As far as observed, however, they seem there to be but little metamorphosed, and contain many of the fossils most characteristic of the Coal-Measure strata of Santa Fé and of the valley of the Mississippi. At Jemez, the rocks of this age rest upon the opposite sides of the red granite core of the mountain, are inclined at a high angle, and are highly fossiliferous. The features which they present there will, however, be described more in detail in a succeeding portion of this report.

The exposures of the Carboniferous strata, at and near Pecos Village, are of peculiar interest, for, although the section which they afford is less complete than at Santa Fé, the line of junction between the Carboniferous and Triassic series is more distinctly marked, and the upper beds of the former group are more fossiliferous. The strata forming the cliff at Pecos Village are the equivalents of the upper portion of the Santa Fé section, consisting of beds of limestone, separated by layers of shale and sandstone, the former containing, as characteristic fossils, *Athyris subtilita*, *Productus semireticulatus*, *P. scabriculus*, *P. Rogersi*, *Spirifer cameratus*, &c. The dip is here from the mountains toward the south and east, and, near the old Pecos church, all the Carboniferous series pass beneath the chocolate-colored sandstones and shales—the base of the Triassic formation—and disappear. The upper member of the underlying group is a brownish, rough, somewhat sandy limestone, of which portions are more purely calcareous. This bed contains a large number of fossils, as far as observed, without exception, such as are common in the Upper Carboniferous strata—Permo-Carboniferous of Meek and Hayden—of Kansas. These are a *Monotis*, not well preserved, but resembling *M. Hawni* (and, perhaps, as much, another found in the Middle and Upper Coal-Measures of Missouri and Kansas), *Athyris subtilita ?*, the same found in the Upper Carboniferous and Permian beds of Kansas, referred doubtfully to *A. subtilita* by Mr. Meek, and which is larger, broader, and more gibbous than what is known under that name in the Coal-Measures east of the Mississippi, yet accords well with the figures and descriptions of the type specimens by Professor Hall; spines of *Archæocidaris*, in great numbers, scarcely distinguishable from *A. aculeatus* of Shumard; a *Bellerophon*, very like, if not identical with, one found in the Upper Carboniferous and Permian of Kansas; a species of *Myalina* (*M. perattenuata*), and an undetermined *Avicula*. These fossils occur in great numbers, and there are, perhaps, other species, which I have not enumerated, contained in the bed. It will be seen that in this list of fossils there are none which are peculiarly Permian. The *Bakevellia*, *Pleurophorus*, *Axinus*, and the species of *Murchisonia*, which give character to the fauna of the upper magnesian limestone of Kansas, are here all wanting. It is evident, therefore, that the question whether this bed shall be regarded as of Permian age depends upon where the conventional line shall be drawn dividing the Permian and Carboniferous formations in Kansas. If that line be drawn at the base of No. 10 of Meek and Hayden's section, this stratum would be excluded from the Permian and connected with the Carboniferous series below. Should the Permo-Carboniferous beds of Meek and Hayden be included in the Permian, this would, of course, be Permian. If these beds were divided midway, this would probably fall into the Permian division, but it might be necessary to divide even this stratum, only 3 or 4 feet in thickness.

TRIASSIC FORMATION.

The Red Beds of the Gypsiferous series form a conspicuous feature in the geology of the neighborhood of Santa Fé, being very freely opened both in the valley of the Rio Grande and in that of the Pecos. In a previous report I have given a general description of the rocks of this formation as developed in this vicinity, and have compared the sections which they present with those of their equivalents in the Navajo country and other parts of New Mexico, where I have examined them. The question of their precise place in the geological series is also there discussed at some length, so that already much has been said, which, though essential to a full presentation of the facts relating to this group, need not be here repeated. A general résumé of this formation will also be given in a succeeding chapter. I have before remarked, in the description given of the geology of the country bordering the Santa Fé road, that the vertical interval occupied by the Gypsum series in Kansas is much less than in New Mexico. This fact will be at once obvious to the traveler coming from the East when he enters the valley of the Pecos. Where last seen on the Kansas, Little Arkansas, or Cow Creek, "the Red Beds" which represent this group have nowhere a thickness of more than 500 or 600 feet, while at Pecos village more than 1,000 feet of the series is exposed in a single section, and its entire thickness in the vicinity of Santa Fé cannot be less than 1,500 or 1,600 feet. By Mr. Marcou, this formation, considered as the equivalent of the Trias of Europe, is represented as attaining a thickness of 5,000 to 6,000 feet; but even in the Navajo country or on the San Juan, where it is apparently most fully developed, its entire thickness is not more than 2,500 feet. In the Pecos section the red sandstones and shales rest directly upon the Coal-Measure limestones, and the Permian magnesian rocks of Kansas are entirely wanting. It is possible, however, as I have before stated, that they are represented by the extreme upper portion of the calcareous beds and by a part of the overlying red sandstones and shales—the "Saliferous group" of my former report; the "*Bunter Sandstein*" or lower division of the Trias of Marcou. In the valley of the Pecos, both at Pecos Village and San José, I obtained from the Lower Red Beds vegetable impressions, which, if more perfectly preserved, would probably enable us to draw the lines of classification more sharply than has hitherto been possible. As it is, they give us reason to suspect that the lower portion of the Gypsum series should be regarded as of Permian age; and, by proving that these strata are not entirely without fossils, encourage us to hope that their place in the series may soon be accurately determined.

The mesa bordering the valley of the Pecos on the south forms a part of the great table-land which stretches away eastward from the base of the mountains, of which a portion has received the name of the Llano Estacado. Except where cut by the valleys it is continued throughout, and has, apparently, everywhere the same geological structure. The section afforded by its cut edge in the valley of the Pecos is as follows:

Feet.
1. Yellow and brownish foliated sandstones with alternations of red, purple, and gray shale, forming detached buttes on the mesa, without fossils 200
2. Yellow, massive sandstone, summit of cliff, without fossils 150
3. Red, white, or green, soft calcareous sandstones and shales with gypsum, without fossils 800
4. Red and green sandstones and conglomerates, separated by thicker beds of green, blue, and purple shales, with oxide of iron and copper, and with ferns, *Walchia?* and *Calamites* 200
5. Limestones and sandstones containing Carboniferous fossils, to bed of stream.

In this section I have supposed Nos. 1 and 2 to represent the Lower Cretaceous sandstone group. No fossils were discovered in them in this vicinity, but on the banks of Galisteo Creek, a few miles farther south, in the yellow sandstones which rest on the red gypsiferous strata, I found the leaves of angiospermous dicotyledonous trees, which prove them to belong to the Cretaceous system.

No. 3 of the section is apparently entirely without fossils, and consists of a series of alternations of deep or pale red and white—rarely greenish—indurated marls or soft, fine calcareous sandstones. No analysis has been made of these beds, but they probably contain as much sulphate as carbonate of lime. They are precisely similar to the strata forming the upper of the two plainly-marked divisions of the Gypsum series throughout Western New Mexico—what I have called in my former report the *Variegated marls*—and are distinguished by striking lithological characters from the "Saliferous sandstone group" which underlie them, and form No. 4 of the section.

This latter group is nowhere exposed in a section which could conveniently be measured, but its thickness is somewhere between 200 and 250 feet. A very good idea may be formed of its prevailing character from the following section taken at the village of San José; the first stratum being the highest:

Feet.
1. Coarse reddish or gray sandstone, frequently a conglomerate 8
2. Chocolate-colored or greenish foliated micaceous sandstone shading into shale; containing a band of compact dark-gray silicious limestone, weathering brown 20

		Feet.
3.	Foliated micaceous sandstone, generally gray, but often brownish-red, with very smooth surfaces; the red portions presenting precisely the lithological characters of the brown freestone of the Northern Atlantic States. The lighter portions more compact, containing many impressions of vegetable stems and small branches of *Walchia ?*...	11 .
4.	Chocolate and greenish micaceous shales	18
5.	Purplish-gray conglomerate, quite hard, containing much peroxide of iron...	10
6.	Purple and green shales	30
7.	Conglomerate, with masses of peroxide of iron and copper	9
8.	Purple and green shales to covered slope	20

At Pecos, on about the same level geologically with the stratum containing the vegetable remains of the preceding section, I found the surfaces of slabs of red sandstone marked with impressions of a large and handsome fern, evidently a *Pecopteris*, but too imperfect for specific determination or description. There is no doubt that, with more time than I had at command, fossil plants would be found in the valley of the Pecos, which would throw much light upon the geological age of the lower division of the Gypsum formation. Those which I obtained are insufficient to *decide* any of the questions which have been raised in regard to the parallelism of the beds containing them with those of other countries, while they may perhaps justly afford ground for a suspicion that the classification which refers *all* the Gypsum formation to the Trias may be in part erroneous. Calamites are ordinarily of little value in determining nice points of geological parallelism, and the specimens here obtained are few and imperfect. The same has been said of the ferns. The *Walchia* however, if undoubtedly such, would afford good evidence that the strata which contain it should be classed with the Permian of Europe, as that genus, as restricted by Brongniart, is confined to the Permian and older formations. But in the Trias, *Walchia* is succeeded and represented by *Voltzia*, a closely allied conifer, so similar that imperfect specimens of the two genera are not readily distinguishable; and until more and better specimens can be procured from the Pecos Valley, I should scarcely be justified in saying that the plant to which I have referred is a *Walchia* of Permian age, and not a *Voltzia*, an evidence of the Triassic date of the rock containing it. The specimens before me, however, have all the characters, so far as preserved, of the *Walchias*, but exhibit none of the cones, which would be decisive. The branchlets are closely approximated, pinnate and parallel, covered with small falcate or subulate, acute leaves, apparently more acute and less fleshy than the smaller leaves of *Voltzia heterophylla*, or even *V. acutifolia*. There is also, apparently, no tendency of the foliage to assume the dimorphous character so marked a feature in the *Voltzias*. If a *Voltzia*, it is evidently a new species, quite distinct from those of Europe. Until farther information can be obtained in reference to this plant, I am disposed to regard it as a *Walchia*, and as very similar in its general aspects to *W. Schlotheimii* of the schists of Lodeve. By Messrs. Unger and Endlicher the genus *Walchia* is not recognized, its species being placed by these authors, as formerly by Brongniart, in *Lycopodites*. Sternberg, and more recently Brongniart, have, however, regarded it as distinct, and the latter author compares it with the Norfolk Island pine (*Araucaria excelsa*).

CRETACEOUS FORMATION.

Except for the surface erosion, which has so greatly modified the topography of the region surrounding Santa Fé, we should still find the Cretaceous strata reaching high up on the slopes of the mountains and completely covering the underlying rocks, now so freely exposed, both on the mountain-sides and in the valleys of the streams. So deep and wide-spread has been the denudation, however, that, from the mountains proper, the Triassic and Cretaceous rocks have been wholly removed, and of the sedimentary series nothing but a part of the Carboniferous strata is left. The Triassic beds are generally soft and have offered little resistance to the mountain-torrents which have acted upon them, but they were once all covered with the massive, though not hard, sandstones of the Lower Cretaceous group, and, where these were not broken up by the upheaval of the mountain crests and cones, they have protected the Red Beds below, so that we find the latter in full thickness all around the bases of the mountain masses, still covered by the harder strata to which they owe their preservation.

The Upper Cretaceous rocks are also soft, and it is now necessary to go a long way from Santa Fé before anything like a fair representation of the upper portion of this series can be found. Indeed, east of the mountains the extreme Upper Cretaceous strata are only seen in place near the Mississippi and the Gulf of Mexico. In the valley of the Rio Grande none remain, and it is only after crossing the main divide, between the waters of the Atlantic and Pacific, and seeing the magnificent exposures of the Cretaceous series in the valley of the San Juan, that we can form a just conception of the grand scale on which the Chalk formation was originally built up in New Mexico, or of the enormous denudation which this region has suffered since it was raised above the surface of the ocean. The attention of every traveler over the great central plateau of our continent is attracted to the cañons which give character to the scenery, and when he learns that they are simply the effects of surface erosion, they become sources of unending wonder and interest; but, notwithstanding their magnitude and impressiveness as records of the lapse of countless ages, it is quite certain that they are referable to a single producing cause, viz., the slow, though constant, erosive action of running water. The proof of the truth of this assertion is given in my report on the geology of the country bordering the Lower Colorado, to which I have already frequently referred.

In the description of the Cretaceous strata, which came under our observation on our first expedition through New Mexico, I divided them into two groups, which I denominated Upper and Lower Cretaceous; that being the most simple and natural division of the strata exposed in Eastern New Mexico and the Indian Territory. I had at that time, however, no opportunity of examining the extreme upper portion of the formation, and it was only when, going west from Santa Fé, we had passed the divide between the waters of the Atlantic and Pacific, that we gained any knowledge of the upper thousand feet of the series. These we found to be made up of a group of rocks quite unlike, in lithological characters and fossils, the calcareous beds—Upper Cretaceous of my former report—of the banks of the Canadian. These true Upper Cretaceous beds will be described in detail in a subsequent chapter, and, as they do not

TRAP DYKE, POPE'S WELL,
S OF SANTA FE, NEW MEXICO

appear in the vicinity of Santa Fé, they require to be mentioned only as constituting the group which I have denominated Upper Cretaceous in the present report, and to distinguish them from the "Upper Cretaceous" of a former one, which I am compelled to regard as the middle portion of the series.

The Cretaceous formation, then, as exhibited in the vicinity of Santa Fé, consists of the two groups to which I have referred in the preceding pages as Lower and Middle, on a former occasion as Lower and Upper Cretaceous. Of these the first consists, as elsewhere in New Mexico, mainly of coarse yellow sandstones with impressions of angiosperm dicotyledonous leaves; the second, of calcareous shales and ferruginous, shaly, sandy limestones, with numerous marine fossils, such as *Ammonites*, *Nautilus*, *Inoceramus*, *Gryphæa*, fish-teeth, &c. Of these two groups the lower caps the cliffs bordering the valley of the Pecos on the south, forming the floor of the great plateau which stretches away southeast, where it becomes the Llano Estacado. It is not yet demonstrated that all the yellow sandstone formation of this plateau belongs to the Cretaceous formation, and that it is not in part, as claimed by M. Marcou, of Jurassic age. I should say, however, that in the vicinity of Santa Fé I was able to discover no Jurassic fossils; but, on the contrary, near Galisteo, in the yellow sandstone specifically noticed by M. Marcou, and regarded by him as Jurassic and identical with that of the Llano, I found impressions of dicotyledonous leaves, which prove it to be Cretaceous. In the vicinity of the mountains the stratification is considerably disturbed, and in many localities the Cretaceous rocks are broken through or removed by erosion; but, with local exceptions, they constitute the surface formation in all the area examined by our party east of the Sandia and Placer Mountains, and south and east of the mountains of Santa Fé.

The valley of Galisteo Creek has cut through the Middle and Lower Cretaceous rocks, and has freely exposed the Red Beds below. Going from the base of the Cerrillos to Galisteo Creek, after passing the eruptive material which composes this group of hills, the Middle Cretaceous shales are seen occupying a belt a mile or more in width on the north side of the stream. Beneath them are the yellow Cretaceous sandstones, underlying which are the blood-red sandstones and shales of the Trias. On the south side of the creek, ascending toward the base of the Placer Mountains, this section is again encountered. The Middle Cretaceous shales here contain beds of lignite several feet in thickness; at one point, by an eruption and overflow of trap, this lignite has been metamorphosed and converted into a compact and brilliant anthracite.

The boring made by Captain Pope, U. S. A., near Galisteo, in the hope of obtaining water that should spontaneously rise above the surface, was nearly all done in the Middle Cretaceous shales, which here have a thickness of at least thirteen hundred feet. The work was commenced in Tertiary tufaceous limestone precisely like that so frequently mentioned in Chapter I. After passing through twenty-five feet of this material the shales were struck, and they had not been passed through at the time the work was abandoned. It is to be regretted that the experiment had not been carried somewhat further, as it is highly probable that the Lower Cretaceous sandstones would soon have been reached, and, dipping down as they do from the Placer Mountains, it is at least possible that the water flowing through them would rise to the surface. A section of the rocks exposed east of Captain Pope's well is as follows, the thicknesses being estimated:

	Feet.
1. Concretionary tufaceous Tertiary limestone, cream-colored or white.......	25
2. Gray and yellow shales, with concretions of yellowish-brown limestone, 3 to 5 feet in diameter, with numerous casts of *Circeopsis crassa*, &c., traversed by bands of blue compact limestone, containing impressions of *Inoceramus*..	1,000
3. Grayish or yellowish sandstone	100
4. Gray or bluish shale, with bands of red, including thin layers of arenaceous limestone, containing, as characteristic fossils, *Ostrea lugubris, Gryphæa Pitcheri, Ammonites percarinatus, Inoceramus problematicus*	300
5. Brownish or yellow thick-bedded sandstone, with layers of shale containing impressions of dicotyledenous leaves.......................	350
6. White, fine-grained, calcareous sandstones.	
7. Red calcareous sandstones and marls.	

In this section Nos. 6 and 7 belong to the Trias, and are the equivalents of the red and white calcareous sandstones exposed in the valley of the Pecos and in Apache Cañon.

TERTIARY FORMATIONS.

Tertiary rocks are not a marked feature in the geology of the vicinity of Santa Fé, but they are visible in a great number of exposures, and usually form isolated patches of limited area, the remnants of more extensive deposits, now for the most part removed by surface-erosion, to which their yielding nature has offered little resistance. As is true of the patches of Tertiary lying along the eastern bases of the mountains, these beds are of very unequal thickness in different localities, and, in many instances, are mere local accumulations, filling depressions or excavations in the surfaces on which they were deposited. So far as my observation extended, they contained no fossils. In lithological characters they exhibit a remarkable resemblance to the Tertiary strata of the Arkansas basin; like those, consisting of beds of calcareous tufa, with bands of more compact tufaceous limestone and conglomerates, in which the pebbles are, for the most part, composed of volcanic materials, basalt, porphyry, trachyte, and scoria. I have little doubt that these beds have been stratified in fresh water, and that the period of their deposition was one in which volcanic forces were in vigorous action in the region where they occur. As will be noticed in the succeeding portions of our geological narrative, no similar deposits were discovered by our party in the region bordering the San Juan and Upper Colorado, though older Tertiaries, probably Eocene, occupy a limited district west of the Nacimiento Mountains.

CHAPTER III.

GENERAL VIEW OF THE GEOLOGY OF THE COUNTRY BORDERING THE UPPER COLORADO.

BIRDS-EYE VIEW OF THE COLORADO PLATEAU AND ITS SURROUNDINGS—MOUNTAIN CHAINS BY WHICH THE PLATEAU IS ENCIRCLED—ROCKY MOUNTAIN SYSTEM—ITS EXTENT AND GENERAL STRUCTURE—DIFFERENT FEATURES WHICH IT PRESENTS ON DIFFERENT PARALLELS—DIFFERENT RANGES OF THE ROCKY MOUNTAINS PROBABLY NOT OF THE SAME AGE—ROCKY MOUNTAIN REGION HAS SUFFERED ALTERATIONS OF ELEVATION AND DEPRESSION—THE CRETACEOUS EPOCH AN ERA OF SUBSIDENCE—THE TERTIARY OF ELEVATION—MOGOLLON MOUNTAINS PROBABLY NOT A DISTINCT SYSTEM—MOUNTAINS OF THE LOWER COLORADOS A PART OF THE SIERRA NEVADA SYSTEM—RELATIONS OF THE SIERRA NEVADA TO THE ROCKY MOUNTAINS—CERBAT MOUNTAINS—WASATCH MOUNTAINS—SAN FRANCISCO GROUP—RECENT VOLCANIC PHENOMENA OF THE GREAT CENTRAL PLATEAU—MOUNT TAYLOR—SIERRA TUCANE—SIERRAS ABAJO, LA SAL, ETC.—STRUCTURE OF THE COLORADO PLATEAU—DEVONIAN AND SILURIAN ROCKS OF THE GREAT CAÑON—CARBONIFEROUS FORMATION—TRIASSIC AND CRETACEOUS ROCKS—SIMILARITY OF STRUCTURE OF THE VALLEYS OF THE LITTLE COLORADO, SAN JUAN, GRAND, AND GREEN RIVERS—HIGH MESAS OF NAVAJO COUNTRY AND UPPER SAN JUAN.

A brief description of the general features of the structure of the country bordering the Colorado will be a necessary introduction to the more detailed analysis of the geology of the region west of the Rio Grande, explored by the San Juan expedition.

The country bordering the San Juan forms a part of one great geological district, of which the structure, though not alike throughout, considered in its totality, exhibits a remarkable symmetry. This district I have in part described in the fifth chapter of my report to Lieutenant Ives, and have designated by the name of the *Basin of the Colorado*. It is, in fact, geologically a basin; topographically, a great plateau. Could one be elevated to a sufficient height over the center of this region, and be gifted with superhuman powers of vision, he would see beneath him what would appear to be a great plain, bounded on every side by mountain ranges, and here and there dotted by isolated mountain masses, rising like islands above its surface. He would see, too, the profound chasm of the Colorado Cañon scoring with tortuous and diagonal course the plain, throughout the entire length of its greatest diameter; for nearly five hundred miles the stream flowing from 3,000 to 6,000 feet below the general level, and at all points bordered by abrupt, frequently perpendicular crags and precipices. Most of the surface beneath him he would perceive to be arid and desert-like; barren wastes of rock and sand; nowhere continuous forests or carpets of herbaceous vegetation;

only here and there dwarfed and scattered pines and cedars and threads of green along the streams; the surface marked with long lines of mesa walls, the abrupt, often vertical sides of broad valleys of erosion; over considerable areas the denudation of soft materials, of varied and vivid colors, having fretted the surface into wonderfully truthful imitations of Cyclopean cities, crumbled by time, or devastated by fire, giving double force to the sense of desolation which the scene inspired.

Such, in general terms, are the external features of the plateau country west of the Rocky Mountains, through which the Colorado flows. Perhaps no portion of the earth's surface is more irremediably sterile, none more hopelessly lost to human occupation, and yet it is but the wreck and ruin of a region rich and beautiful, changed and impoverished by the deepening channels of its draining streams; the most striking and suggestive example of over-drainage of which we have any knowledge.

To prevent misapprehension, it should be stated that, around the margins of the Colorado plateau, at the immediate bases of the mountains, the traveler will behold many scenes of beauty and fertility strikingly in contrast with the aspect of the country nearer the river. Here are limited districts deserving our highest encomiums; regions of green and flowery mountain valleys, of clear, cold, and copious streams; of magnificent forests; with an atmosphere of unrivalled purity, and a climate delightfully tempered. Here, too, are the mineral treasures of which the sedimentary rocks of the plateau furnish almost none; and here will be congregated the mining population, whose business it will be through future ages to extract for our use the mineral wealth with which many of these mountain ranges are stored.

Though valueless to the agriculturist; dreaded and shunned by the emigrant, the miner, and even the adventurous trapper, the Colorado plateau is to the geologist a paradise. Nowhere on the earth's surface, so far as we know, are the secrets of its structure so fully revealed as here.

I need hardly say that, with the exception of the isolated mountains to which I have referred, the rocks composing the plateau are sedimentary throughout. They include strata representing the entire Cretaceous formation, the Triassic, perhaps locally, though not yet identified the Jurassic, the Carboniferous, Devonian, and Silurian. In the different parts of its course the Colorado cuts through successively all these strata, and near the western margin of the table-land has worn a furrow 6000 feet deep in the underlying granite. The sections afforded by the cañons of the Colorado and its tributaries reveal in the most clear and unmistakable manner the superposition, thickness, and mineral character of the sediments forming the table-land to even the most hurried observer; and when, with time and patience, we shall have collected a full series of their characteristic fossils—there as elsewhere only locally abundant—we shall be able to write with unusual fullness and precision both the zoölogical and physical history of the epochs of their deposition.

A summary of the results of geological observations made while connected with two expeditions organized for the exploration of the course of the Colorado is briefly as follows:

The phenomena presented by the geology of the area drained by the Colorado—which embraces all Arizona, the western half of New Mexico, and much of Colorado and Utah—naturally fall into two great groups: first, that of the mountain ranges; second, that of the great plateau which they inclose. For convenience, these will be considered separately.

MOUNTAINS SURROUNDING THE COLORADO BASIN.

Nothing like a thorough exploration of the numerous and complicated mountain systems of the region under consideration has as yet been made, and years of patient study must be devoted to the subject before their intimate structure or relations to each other will be fully comprehended. Only a skeleton sketch of their extent, structure, and direction can now be honestly given, and the inferences drawn from the facts already observed will be liable to considerable modification in the light of future explorations.

The mountain chains and groups under consideration are as follows:
1. The Rocky Mountain system.
2. The Mogollon Mountains.
3. Cerbat and Aquarius ranges.
4. The mountains of Lower Colorado (Black and Mohave Mountains, &c.).
5. The Wasatch Mountains.
6. The San Francisco group (lately an active volcano).
7. The Mount Taylor (San Mateo) (lately an active volcano).
8. The Sierra Tucane (isolated mountain).
9. The Sierra Abajo (isolated mountain).
10. The Sierra La Sal (isolated mountain).
11. The Sierra La Late (isolated mountain).

By reference to the accompanying map it will be seen that the vast mountain-belt of the Rocky Mountain system, the great backbone of our continent, forms the eastern boundary of the Colorado basin, and, by its drainage, supplies by far the greater part of the flow of that stream. In the deep sinuosities of outline, occasioned by the interruption of many of the ranges of this great system, the courses of the San Juan, Grand River, and Little Colorado are laid. Between the Rocky Mountains on the east, and the Wasatch, Aquarius, and Cerbat ranges on the west, the Colorado plateau lies as a comparatively level plain, its northern and southern boundaries less accurately defined, and in part as yet unknown.

ROCKY MOUNTAIN SYSTEM.

In the preceding chapter and in another report, I have given my own observations on portions of this mountain system, and have expressed my views upon the indefinite and shadowy nature of the classification, according to which all portions of the immense and irregular mountain-belt which traverses the central portion of our continent are included in a single name and referred to a single epoch in geological history. So far as the limited explorations by geologists have extended, it is true that a general uniformity of composition and trend has been observed, and, as will be seen in the subsequent pages, I have now no new facts to report which indicate the necessity of its separation into several distinct systems. The evidence on this point is, however, for the most part negative. Many great ranges, now supposed to belong to the Rocky Mountains, have not been visited, and of those which have been examined almost none have been studied as closely as is desirable. If, as the facts in our possession seem to render probable, all the ranges now grouped together in the Rocky Mountain system have the same essential structure, the contemplation of this system as a whole is calculated to give us new and broader views of the action of the forces by which mountain-chains have been elevated. For example, confining our observation to our present field of inquiry, we have in Southern Utah and Northern New Mexico a broad, almost unbroken mountain-belt, extending from the western margin of the plains, westwardly to the western bases of the Sierra La Plata and Sierra San Miguel, a distance of nearly three hundred miles. This area is, with the exception of the valley of the Rio Grande, wholly occupied by mountain-ranges of great elevation, and the narrow valleys which divide them. On all the older maps the western half of this region is represented as occupied by the great ranges of the Sierra San Juan and Sierra La Plata, to which a nearly east and west trend was assigned. Our recent explorations, however, have given a new aspect to this mountain group. We found the western, like the eastern portion, to be composed of a number of prominent chains having a general north and south trend. The structure of these western mountains is similar to that of the ranges near Santa Fé, described in the preceding chapter, viz: an axis of red granite, flanked on either side by strata of highly inclined but almost unchanged Carboniferous limestone, containing most of our characteristic Coal-Measure fossils; above the limestones, entirely conformable, the red beds of the Gypsum series, (Triassic); upon this, also conformable, the different members of the Cretaceous formation. All these western mountain-ranges are comparatively short; terminating on the north in the open area traversed by Grand River and its tributaries; on the south reaching out, like so many fingers, into the plain country bordering the San Juan.

A transverse section of the Rocky Mountains, drawn a little north of west from Anton Chico across the Rio Grande, exhibits features as different from that just described as could well be imagined. Just north of this line the lofty ranges of the Santa Fé Mountains fall off abruptly and disappear. West of the Rio Grande, and in its immediate vicinity, lie the north and south ranges of the Valles, and the Nacimiento Mountain; altogether perhaps twenty miles in width. West of the Nacimiento the sedimentary plateau extends to and beyond the Colorado. On the line of this profile, or in its immediate vicinity, the Rocky Mountain ranges have dwindled to comparative insignificance.

In a profile drawn parallel with the last, a little farther south, the Rocky Mountain belt assumes far more respectable dimensions. East of the Rio Grande the Sandia Mountain rises as a frowning wall 7,000 feet above the valley; 12,000 above the sea. West of the river is the extinct volcano of San Mateo, to which I shall have occasion to refer again, then the Sierra Madre, northwest of which, *en échelon*, are the chains of the Sierras Tunecha and Cariso, both of which terminate south of the San Juan.

South of this line the mountains again narrow and diminish, and the headwaters of the Colorado Chiquito reach far over toward the Rio Grande.

Still further south, on and below the parallel of 34°, an almost unbroken succession of mountains stretch from the Sierra Blanca, the Sacramento, and Guadalupe Mountains, all the way across to the Colorado. Of those, those lying near the Rio Grande, both east and west, have apparently a structure similar to that of the ranges of the Rocky Mountains further north. West of these an immense area is occupied by the Mogollon Sierras, as yet almost unknown. Still further west are the ranges crossing the Lower Colorado, and belonging to the system of the Sierra Nevada. What is the relative space occupied by these different mountain groups; whether they represent one, two, or three distinct systems; and if distinct, what are their relative ages, are questions which future observations alone can answer.

In regard to the precise age of the Rocky Mountains, as before stated, we want more extended and minute observations before we can determine whether the elevation of all parts of the system was synchronous, and whether, if so, it is to be referred to a single epoch, or was continued through several geological periods. There are, however, some facts which lead me to conclude that the elevation of the different ranges now referred to this system was not in all cases synchronous, and that they are the result of the action of forces operating through all geological time, from the earliest Paleozoic period to the present. Still further—as a corollary to the last proposition—the Rocky Mountain region has suffered several alternations of elevation and depression. Much of the evidence on this subject is given in my report to Lieutenant Ives, page —. It is briefly as follows:

1. The Paleozoic strata, several thousand feet in thickness, which underlie the Carboniferous formation in the great cañon of the Colorado, are wholly wanting on the sides and summits of the mountain ranges which bound the Colorado basin, both on the east and west—Cerbat and Aquarius ranges, Santa Fé and Nacimiento Mountains, Sierras La Plata, Cariso, &c. On these ranges the Carboniferous strata, very little metamorphosed, rest directly upon the granite; the natural inference from these facts being that the mountains enumerated above existed, at least in embryo, previous to the deposition of the older Paleozoic rocks, and were elevated above the ocean from which the lower strata of the Colorado section were deposited.

2. The explorations of Dr. Hayden have demonstrated that the granitic axis of the Black Hills is flanked by the Potsdam sandstone, now exposed by upheaval, and overlaid by the Carboniferous and more recent strata; the evidence being conclusive that this portion of the Rocky Mountain system was beneath the waters of the primeval ocean.

3. In the fresh lava-streams of the Ratou Mountains, the Valles, in the Malpais near Fort Stanton, and about San Mateo, as well as in various other portions of the Rocky Mountain region, we have evidence that most violent volcanic action has been in operation distinctly within the present epoch, having been continued from the Middle Tertiary period, if not dating back still further.

4. As stated in the descriptions of the Arkansas Tertiary basin and the geology of the region about Cottonwood Spring, (Chapter I,) we have satisfactory proof that, previous to the deposition of the Lower Cretaceous strata, the central portion of the continent was above the ocean level, and that the Cretaceous sediments were mainly

deposited during a period in which a subsidence of several thousand feet took place. This is shown by the immense extent of the Lower Cretaceous sandstones, a littoral formation, the immediate *débris* of the land, containing only and abundantly the remains of land-plants; these sandstones being overlaid by a great thickness of marine strata.

5. At the close of the Cretaceous age a period of elevation began, which continued to the Drift epoch, when the continent was again depressed, to be again elevated, though not having as yet reached its former level.

The facts upon which these conclusions are based are briefly these: (*a.*) The Tertiary beds of the country bordering the Rocky Mountains on the east are mainly fresh-water deposits. (*b.*) They were precipitated upon surfaces which had suffered enormous subaerial erosion, filling troughs and basins excavated in the Cretaceous or Gypsum formations; the Tertiary strata being unconformable. (*c.*) The investigations of Messrs. Meek and Hayden have shown that in these Tertiary basins the lower beds sometimes contain estuary shells, the upper exclusively fresh-water species.

6. We may fairly infer from the facts given above that the great elevatory movement, which gave to the Rocky Mountain region the character it now exhibits, took place between the close of the Cretaceous period and that of the Miocene Tertiary. To this general rule, however, we cannot yet say that there are not marked exceptions.

MOGOLLON MOUNTAINS.

Perhaps no important mountain chains within the territory of the United States are so little known as these. No geologist has ever visited the region which they occupy, and I am not aware that any record has been made of the observations of the Army officers or others who have traversed it. In his synopsis of the mountains of North America, M. Marcou has referred the Mogollon ranges to a distinct system, and has assigned to them a trend very different from those of the mountains nearest them on either side. This classification has been, however, advanced on grounds wholly insufficient, and may be considered as purely imaginary. As I have stated in my former report, my own convictions are that future explorations will show that the ranges of the Mogollon and Sierra Blanca have a north and south or northwest and southeast trend, and are to be grouped with the Rocky Mountain ranges on the east, or those of the Sierra Nevada system on the west. My reasons for this belief are, that verbal statements of parties who have visited these mountains indicate their structure to be essentially that of the Rocky Mountains; *i. e.*, axes of red or grayish granite, flanked by Carboniferous limestones with their characteristic fossils; some of which, such as *Productus semireticulatus*, have been brought in. In addition to this, it may be said that ranges of mountains, with an east and west trend, would be a strange anomaly in the topography of New Mexico. Such a thing I have not yet met with in any portion of the central or western parts of our continent which I have visited.

MOUNTAINS OF THE LOWER COLORADO.

These ranges, which form the southwestern boundary of the table-lands, seem but continuations of the metalliferous chains of Sonora, passing with a northwest trend up into Nevada and California, there blending with the Sierra Nevada. In trend and structure they seem to accord with that system, and in the present state of our knowledge would naturally be included in it. In composition they generally exhibit a marked difference from the ranges of the Rocky Mountain system. They are composed in a much greater degree of purely eruptive rocks, whole ranges being formed of trachytes, tufas, porphyries, amygdaloids, &c., in endless variety. Their granites are generally white or gray. Metamorphic rocks are abundant among them, consisting of gneiss, mica-slate, clay-slate, talcose-slate, and limestone, the latter highly metamorphosed and crystalline, forming white, blue, gray, and clouded marbles; so far as observed, wholly destitute of fossils. They are rich in valuable minerals; large quantities of gold, silver, copper, lead, and iron having already been discovered in them. The Black Mountains may be regarded as the most northerly, as well as the most important, of these ranges which cross the Colorado. This chain crosses below the mouth of the Virgen, and thence seems to trend away northwesterly toward Washoe. It may be anticipated that the stores of metallic wealth so characteristic of these ranges will be discovered in the unexplored region into which they are prolonged after crossing the Colorado.

The question of the relative age of the Colorado Mountains, and hence of the Sierra Nevada and Rocky Mountains, is one of great geological interest, and yet one on which at present we have almost no light. The prevailing mineralogical characters of the two systems are, as has been said, considerably alike, and yet it remains to be proven that in their southern prolongations they do not blend in one.

I have suspected that the metamorphic limestone of the Sierra Nevada is of Carboniferous age, and that it holds a position corresponding to that of the Rocky Mountains. It is, however, so generally metamorphosed that all traces of fossils have disappeared. By reference to my report to Lieutenant Williamson, (P. R. R. Rep., vol. VI, Geol. Rep., p. 27,) it will be seen that near Mount Shasta a Paleozoic limestone of great thickness is exposed, which is highly fossiliferous. By Dr. Trask, who has examined it, it is regarded as Carboniferous. A further examination of this interesting locality may, perhaps, give us the information which we so much desire.

CERBAT MOUNTAINS.

These mountains, with their associates, the Aquarius and Aztec ranges, are so fully described in my first report on the geology of the Colorado country, that nothing need now be said of them further than what is necessary to give them their proper place in the wider view which later observations permit me to give of the Colorado Basin; of this basin these mountains form the western margin. Against their sides the older Paleozoic rocks seem to abut, and on their flanks the Carboniferous rocks rest, just as on the slopes of the Rocky Mountains, three hundred miles eastward.

In trend and composition these mountains seem to share the characters of the Sierra Nevada and Rocky Mountain systems. Their granites are gray, and the sedimentary rocks rest upon them nearly unchanged; the metamorphic slates and limestones of the Colorado ranges not having been discovered. Their trend is slightly west of north, nearly parallel with that of the Sierra Madre, their *vis-a-vis*.

WASATCH MOUNTAINS.

At present it is impossible to say what is the extent, or very definitely what is the structure of the great mountain groups bordering the Great Salt Lake and extending thence southward toward the Colorado. Of these the more conspicuous ranges, lying east and south of the lake, have been designated by the name of Wasatch. From the explorations of Captains Gunnison, Whipple, and Fremont, we learn that a series of mountain ranges extend south and west from these to and beyond the Vegas de Santa Clara. In this region they form the northwestern boundary of the Colorado plateau, holding the same relation to that great area of stratified rocks as do the Aquarius and Aztec ranges farther south. Their flanks are covered with Carboniferous limestones, turned up and broken through by their granitic axis. How broad the mountain belt may be which exhibits this character we do not yet definitely know. We are informed, however, that there are several distinct ranges having a trend north and south, or a little east of north by west of south. Going westward these ranges merge insensibly in the "lost mountains" of the Great Basin, some of which retain, in a greater or less degree, the structure of the Wasatch ranges, while others are composed mainly of trappean rocks, having the composition and ragged, picturesque outlines of the cockscomb sierras of the Lower Colorado. All this portion of the continent is thickly set with mountain groups or ranges, forming a labyrinth whose mysteries years of patient effort will hardly suffice to penetrate and reveal. This region has been recently traversed by Captain Simpson, United States Topographical Engineers, with interesting though as yet unpublished results. Among the collections made by Mr. H. Engelman, the geologist of the party, are a few Devonian fossils, such as *Atrypa reticularis* and several species of *Spirifera*, described by Mr. Meek (Proc. Acad. Nat. Sci. Phila., July, 1860), the first instance where fossils of this age have been found so far west.

Up to the present time we have no well-marked geological criteria by which to distinguish the Wasatch ranges from those of the Rocky Mountains, and it is possible that future explorations will show that the Colorado Basin is completely encircled by the widely separated chains of the same vast mountain system.

SAN FRANCISCO GROUP.

Of the San Francisco Mountain and its associates, Bill Williams, Mount Kendrick, and Mount Sitgreaves, a detailed description is given in the seventh chapter of my report to Lieutenant Ives, United States Topographical Engineers. By reference to that description and the accompanying geological map it will be seen that these mountains are great volcanic foci, the eruptions from which have covered all the adjacent country with lava. The precise date of the commencement of the volcanic action in this region cannot, perhaps, be accurately determined, but it is evident that the greater portion of the erupted material was thrown out, geologically speaking, at a comparatively recent epoch, at a time when the topographical features of that vicinity were in all essential particulars the same as now; when the high plateau from which these mountains rise was already a plateau elevated several thousand feet above the sea. Its surface-rock was then Carboniferous limestone, from which the overlying formations had been entirely removed, and in which lines of drainage had been excavated, having the general direction and character of the present stream-beds. There is evidence that the cones of the mountains themselves, and the floods of lava which surround them, have been formed by a series of eruptions, and that the latest of these paroxysms occurred within a few years.

As I have previously remarked, the eruption of the material composing and surrounding these volcanoes has produced comparatively little disturbance of the sedimentary rocks upon which they rest. We have as yet no evidence that they form part of any well-marked line of upheaval, nor is there any obvious connection between these mountains and any of the chains which surround them, or with any of the other volcanic vents which are scattered over the great central plateau. My attention was particularly directed to this point by Baron Humboldt, through Mr. Möllhausen, before visiting New Mexico; and I was particularly requested to examine the country between the San Francisco Mountain and San Mateo, to detect, if possible, some connecting link, such as lines of upheaval or of volcanic vents. I was, however, able to discover no proof whatever of any relationship between the two other than the perfect correspondence which their local phenomena present. It is true that east of the Little Colorado, just south of the Moqui Villages, is a series of buttes composed of comparatively recent volcanic matter, which made its exit from a number of vents in that vicinity; but the sedimentary rocks are scarcely at all disturbed, even in the intervals between these trap buttes, and the country on either side is entirely free from dikes, faults, or displacements of any kind which would indicate the action of disturbing forces along the line connecting San Francisco Mountain and San Mateo.

It is a somewhat remarkable fact that volcanic vents similar to those under consideration, though of less magnitude, are scattered over the entire area of the central table-lands, from Mexico far up into the British possessions. About many of these the evidence abounds that their fires have only been quite recently extinguished, and yet in none, so far as we know, are they now burning. The cause of this simultaneous cessation of an action, lately so wide-spread and vigorous, becomes an interesting subject of inquiry.

SAN MATEO (MOUNT TAYLOR).

This is the second in importance of the great extinct volcanoes of the central portion of our continent which have come under my observation. It has an altitude of between 11,000 to 12,000 feet, perhaps a thousand feet less than that of the San Francisco Mountain. It stands quite alone, and has no apparent connection with any other peak or range. Like most isolated mountains, it is composed of erupted material, and seems to have been wholly formed by the accumulation of ejected matter around a volcanic vent. As has been remarked of the San Francisco Mountain, this volcano has been in vigorous action at a very recent period. The lava-streams of its latest eruptions present precisely the same appearance as those of Vesuvius, when but just cooled; and it is difficult to believe that they have been exposed to the action of the atmosphere even for so much as a hundred years.

The existence of great volcanos, like San Francisco Mountain and San Mateo, in full blast, many hundred miles from the sea, is a powerful argument against the theory which restricts all volcanos to the vicinity of large bodies of water.

SIERRA TUCANE (NAVAJO MOUNTAIN).

This mountain is situated near the junction of the San Juan and Colorado Rivers, and was, therefore, not reached by either of the expeditions with which I have been connected. As seen from a distance, it seems to be a mountain of very considerable elevation, either solitary or associated with a few subordinate peaks, forming a group of limited extent. What its structure is we can, of course, only conjecture, but from its isolated character we may be quite sure that it is composed of erupted material; and it should probably be grouped with the North Side Mountains, the Sierra Abajo, Sierra La Sal, La Late, &c., which are scattered like islands over the surface of the plateau. The description of these latter groups, as well as that of the Rocky Mountain ranges lying on or near our trail, will be given in the succeeding chapters devoted to the geology of our route.

THE COLORADO PLATEAU.

In the preceding pages, where I have referred to the area under consideration, I have used indiscriminately the terms plateau and basin; the one having reference to the prevailing character of the surface, the other to the geological structure. Both terms are sufficiently appropriate; for, when viewed as a whole, it has a distinctly plateau character, formed by a series of table-lands, which rise step by step from the Carboniferous limestone to the summit of the Cretaceous formation, and from the broad valleys of erosion, in which its cañons are scored, to the summits of the divides between its draining streams. In the geological portion of the report of the Colorado Expedition will be found both a general and a detailed description of the topography and structure of the central and southern portions of the Colorado Plateau. The observations made on our recent explorations enable me to complete, in a great degree, the sketch, much of which was then only given in outline; to make important additions to the information then gained of both the geographical and vertical extension of the sedimentary strata which are there represented, and, by satisfactory proofs, confirm views before only conjectural.

Adding to the facts then given those more recently observed, we find that the generalities of the structure of the Colorado plateau or basin are as follows:

On both the eastern and western sides, Carboniferous strata, the equivalents of the Coal-Measures in age, are seen resting on the granitic axes of the bounding mountains; dipping at first rapidly, then more gradually, toward the center of the basin or trough. On the eastern side the Carboniferous strata are exposed only in a narrow belt along the mountain-sides, almost immediately passing beneath the Triassic and Cretaceous strata, which there have an aggregate thickness of 5,000 feet or more. On the western side, on the contrary, the first easterly dip of the Carboniferous rocks is succeeded by a gentle rise toward the east; a broad arch being formed, of which the eastern slope reaches as far as the Little Colorado. Up to this point the more recent formations have been removed from the Carboniferous, and this occupies a broad belt of country, indicated in the geological map, accompanying the report of Lieutenant Ives. As we go northward this Carboniferous belt rapidly narrows, and on the flanks of the Wasatch Mountains it exhibits simply a line of outcrop, as on the opposite ranges of the Rocky Mountains. Along the Little Colorado the Carboniferous limestones dip beneath the overlying rocks, and are lost to view in all the interval between that point and the Rocky Mountains. On the east side of the Little Colorado, its valley is bounded by a mesa composed of the Triassic marls and red sandstones, which form a distinct step in the table-lands, reaching eastward for many miles, with a still greater extension north and south. Above this, on the east and north, the Lower Cretaceous rocks form a third plateau, along its margin cut into detached mesas and mesillas by valleys of excavation. Farther east and north these mesas combine, and the Cretaceous rocks in an unbroken sheet underlie the whole country.

The broad eroded valleys of the San Juan, of Grand and Green Rivers, and the Upper Colorado generally, exhibit precisely the same structure as that of the valley of the Little Colorado. The Carboniferous limestones are exposed in the cañons of these streams, while the broader valleys through which they flow are excavated in the red Triassic rocks; large surfaces of which are exposed on the banks of all these streams. The process of erosion has there, as on the Little Colorado, everywhere left the most surprising monuments of its action; domes, castles, walls, spires, which by their vivid colors and fantastic outlines attract the attention and excite the wonder of every explorer who beholds them. Above the Triassic rocks the Lower Cretaceous sandstones—massive beds of comparatively resistent material—cap mesas which stretch away to a great distance both east and west of the Colorado. They form the floor of the great sage-plain lying between the Sierra La Plata and Sierra Abajo. South of the Sierra La Plata they are covered by the Middle and Upper Cretaceous beds forming the Mesa Verde—the third great step in the table-lands above the Carboniferous—which on the east connects with the plateau bordering Cañon Largo and extending to the base of the Nacimiento Mountain. High table-lands are visible west of the Colorado, where it is formed by the junction of Grand and Green Rivers, evidently corresponding to the Cretaceous mesas just mentioned, but whether they correspond precisely to it in geological structure can only be determined by further explorations.

The country bordering the Upper Grand and Green Rivers, as described by Dr. Schiel (Pacific R. R. Rep., vol. 2), by Mr. Egloffstein and Colonel Henderson, who have kindly communicated to me their observations, has essentially the same structure with that bordering the Little Colorado and the San Juan. The Triassic rocks are freely exposed in the valleys of erosion, while table-lands floored with Cretaceous strata occupy the greater portion of the intervals between the mountain chains. This margin of the Colorado basin is very irregular, and its outline has not been accurately traced.

Between the Little Colorado and the San Juan the country is almost exclusively occupied by Cretaceous rocks. The Lower Cretaceous sandstones are here largely developed, containing numerous impressions of leaves of land-plants and heavy beds of lignite, which have attracted the attention of all the exploring parties who have entered this region, and have been mentioned in their notes as beds of bituminous coal. The higher table-lands between the San Juan and Little Colorado have an altitude of about 8,000 feet, and are composed of the upper members of the Cretaceous formation, corresponding in all respects with the Mesa Verde north of the San Juan, with which they were at one time undoubtedly continuous; the immense void which now separates them having been removed by erosion. This high table-land—the "white mesa" of my former report—seems to reach westwardly to and beyond the Great Colorado, but its western boundaries have not been accurately determined. Where this mesa is cut by the Colorado that stream is supposed to have an elevation of less than 2,000 feet above the level of the sea. The awfully grand precipices—over a mile in height—which overhang it, I have described in my former report on the geology of this region.

On the eastern margin of the Colorado plateau, especially in that part of it which borders Cañon Largo, and forms the western base of the Nacimiento Mountain, a series of variegated gypsiferous strata overlie the Upper Cretaceous beds of the Mesa Verde, and occupy a considerable superficial area. These strata seem to be conformable to the Cretaceous rocks below, and may form the summit of this series, or, as I have suggested in another chapter, they may be Tertiary. If so, they belong to an older division of the Tertiary series than the chalky beds of Santa Fé and the plains, and represent a group not elsewhere seen in any part of the Colorado plateau. Whatever their age, these strata form the geological summit of the plateau series of sediments.

CHAPTER IV.

GEOLOGY OF THE ROUTE FROM SANTA FÉ TO THE SIERRA LA PLATA.

STRUCTURE OF THE VALLEY OF THE RIO GRANDE—THE VALLEY OF THE CHAMA—ABIQUIU-COPPER MINES—FOSSIL PLANTS—RUINS OF LOS CAÑONES—ABIQUIU PEAK—PLATEAU COUNTRY BORDERING THE UPPER CHAMA—ARROYO SECO—TRIASSIC MARLS—NAVAJO SPRING—CRETACEOUS SANDSTONES AND PLATEAU—BANKS OF THE NUTRIA—MIDDLE CRETACEOUS BEDS—VADA DEL CHAMA—SECTION OF VALLEY OF THE CHAMA—HIGH MESA OF UPPER CRETACEOUS ROCKS—LAGUNA DE LOS CAVALLOS—DIVIDE BETWEEN THE WATERS OF THE RIO GRANDE AND SAN JUAN—GENERAL VIEW OF THE STRUCTURE OF THE SURROUNDING COUNTRY—MOUNTAIN CHAINS—BELT OF FOOT-HILLS—TABLE LANDS—RIO NAVAJO—CERRO DEL NAVAJO—SIERRA DEL NAVAJO—RITO BLANCO—THE PAGOSA—SIERRA SAN JUAN AND ASSOCIATED MOUNTAIN RANGES—CRETACEOUS ROCKS AND FOSSILS—THE PIEDRA PARADA—RIO PIEDRA—BROKEN MESA—VIEW FROM HIGH DIVIDE—RIO DE LOS PINOS—SIERRA DE LOS PINOS—RIO FLORIDO—VALLEY OF THE ANIMAS—RUINS ON THE ANIMAS—CROSSING OF THE ANIMAS—STRUCTURE OF THE MOUNTAINS DRAINED BY THE ANIMAS—RIO DE LA PLATA—DELIGHTFUL CAMP—CRETACEOUS ROCKS AND FOSSILS—SIERRA DE LA PLATA—METALLIFEROUS VEINS OF THE SIERRA DE LA PLATA.

VALLEY OF THE RIO GRANDE.

The structure of the Rio Grande Valley seems to be essentially the same throughout its entire extent—that is, as far as it is really a valley, viz., from its northern extremity to El Paso. Throughout all this interval it is a synclinal trough, lying between imperfectly parallel ranges of mountains. At El Paso the river breaks through its eastern wall, and, thence to its mouth, follows a devious course determined by the local obstacles which it meets, no longer modified by the meridional topography of the Rocky Mountain system. Opposite and above Santa Fé the trough in which the river flows is bounded on the east by the lofty ranges of the Santa Fé Mountains and their northern representatives, which extend in an unbroken series to the Parks; on the west, immediately opposite Santa Fé, by the bold and picturesque chains of the Valles. These mountains have but a limited extent, falling off suddenly on the north, and leaving a low pass, which is traversed by the Chama. North of the Chama they are succeeded by the mountains of Conejos, which connect with the wide-spread and tangled maze of high sierras, to which I have referred in the preceding chapter; mountains somewhat vaguely designated on different maps as Sierras San Juan, Sahwatch, &c. By the Mexican mountaineers, all the mountain mass, drained by the western headwaters of the Rio Grande, is known under the name of the Sierra El Wanico.

On both sides of the valley the Carboniferous strata may be seen exposed in numerous localities, dipping rapidly inward toward the river; resting conformably upon these, the red beds of the Triassic series, here soft, sandy, and extensively eroded. Over a large part of the valley surface the drift from the adjacent mountains is spread so thickly that the rocky substrata are wholly concealed. It is possible, therefore, that in some localities the Cretaceous rocks hold their relative position there, as elsewhere, upon the Trias. I cannot say, however, that I have ever seen the Cretaceous strata in the immediate valley of the Rio Grande, except on the slopes of the Organ Mountains, above El Paso.

Between Santa Fé and the mouth of the Chama the country is much broken and generally sterile. Rounded gravel hills, dotted with scrubby trees of cedar and piñon, and eroded buttes of pale red, pulverulent sandstone, everywhere meet the eye and give character to the scenery. Among these, wind threads of fertility, following the courses of the streams, marked by lines of cottonwood, by meadows of coarse grass, and, in some localities, by fields of grain. On the west side of the river the scenery is bolder, the surface more broken and unproductive; the character which it exhibits having been given, for the most part, by floods of lava poured out from the Valles, now remaining in sheets and masses of black and ragged trap. Reaching up toward the mountains are many valleys of erosion in which the parti-colored strata of the Triassic series are visible, even at a distance of many miles.

VALLEY OF THE CHAMA.

The course of the Chama, as before stated, lies in a natural gap in the mountains bordering the Rio Grande on the west. Below Abiquiu its valley has essentially the character of that of the Rio Grande, of which it may be indeed said to form a part. On the southwest it is bounded by the slopes and the trap mesas of the Valles, and on the north by the gentler declivities of the mountains of Conejos. At Abiquiu these boundaries closely approach each other, and the river seems to have burst through the low axis of elevation connecting the Valles with the northern mountains. On the south side the trap mesas come flush up to the stream, and, just below the village, overhang it in a cliff 800 feet in height. On the north side are high and broken hills of erupted rock, formed by a series of dikes crossing each other at different angles; the principal one having a trend nearly north and south, from which diverge one with a northeast and southwest trend, and another running a little north of west by south of east. These minor dikes are also much broken and forked. The gate through which the river passes this axis of elevation is exceedingly bold and picturesque; its beauty being enhanced by a high and ragged butte of rock, which stands disconnected from either side, partially blocking up the gap. It should also be mentioned that a similar line of displacement crosses the river below Abiquiu, in the form of a sharp interrupted ridge, known throughout that region as the Cuchillo or

Knife. By both these axes the sedimentary rocks are much disturbed and metamorphosed.

On the north side of the river at Abiquiu, just beyond the ancient ruins which crown the bluff, is a little valley cut from soft white and blue conglomerate, sandstones, and tufas, which, though destitute of fossils, I have suspected to be of Tertiary age. This deposit is entirely local, and seems to have filled a basin or valley, as the fresh-water Tertiaries of the interior of the continent so frequently do. The strata have a thickness of perhaps 150 feet, and have been worn by erosion into most striking imitations of spires, churches, pyramids, monumental columns, and castles. At Jemez, a few miles south of Abiquiu, the picturesque buttes, which stand isolated in the open valley, are composed of precisely similar materials. These latter are evidently remnants of a mass which once filled the valley about them, nearly all of which has been removed by erosion. They are to be classed with the other patches of fresh-water Tertiary in the vicinity of Santa Fé; local deposits made after all the great topographical features of the surrounding country had received nearly their present forms. As the most perfect parallelism seems to exist between the castellated buttes of Abiquiu and Jemez, I am disposed to refer them to the same epoch.

Above Abiquiu the Chama flows through a country quite different from that which I have described. West of the Valles, the Nacimiento Mountain terminates abruptly, leaving a large area of open country between it and the mountains which may be supposed to be its representative on the north. This area, topographically and geologically, is but a portion of the great Colorado plateau; there being nothing but a low line of elevation—the prolongation of the Nacimiento axis, by which the strata are not often broken through—to separate it from the table-lands bordering Cañon Largo and the Upper San Juan. After leaving the mountains in which it takes its rise, the valley of the Chama is, therefore, as far as Abiquiu, a valley of erosion, and is bordered on either side by the cut edges of the different steps of the plateau. Immediately above Abiquiu, the sides of the valley are composed of the Triassic formation. A few miles further west, the Lower Cretaceous sandstones cap the table-lands and floor a plain, the precise counterpart, except in extent, of the great sage-plain west of the Sierra de la Plata. At the Vada del Chama, still higher up the stream, we reach the base of a wall, more than a thousand feet in height, composed of the Middle and Upper Cretaceous strata, corresponding, and perhaps connecting, with the table-land bordering Cañon Largo, of which a full description will be given hereafter.

ABIQUIU COPPER MINES.

In a former chapter I have referred to the deposits of copper found in the sedimentary strata in various portions of New Mexico, and have enumerated several localities—San Miguel, Jemez, &c.—where this copper exists in considerable abundance, and where mines were formerly extensively worked to obtain it. The old mines of Abiquiu belong to this category. To the residents of the vicinity they are objects of much interest and some wonder, and having had our curiosity excited by their glowing accounts of them, while our party was at Abiquiu we paid them a visit, under the guidance of Mr. Albert H. Pfeiffer, resident Indian agent, whose intimate knowledge of the country, joined to his unextinguishable enthusiasm and good nature, made him an invaluable companion in our explorations during the time that he accompanied us. As these deposits of copper are matters of some geological interest, I take the liberty of transcribing from my journal the description of our visit to the "*Cobre*" of Abiquiu.

"*July* 17.—Started this morning, with Mr. Pfeiffer and several members of our party, for the copper mines, situated some nine miles north of Abiquiu. As we rose from the valley, we were gratified by the most charming view we had yet beheld in New Mexico. The alluvial bottom-lands, covered with groves of vivid green cotton-woods, alternating with fields of wheat and corn, interspersed among which were the white-washed adobe houses of the residents, each with its walled corral, its garden, and its clumps of apricot-trees, formed a scene of fertility and rural beauty rare enough in a country whose sterility is proverbial. Above the valley rose the frowning battlements of the trap mesas, which sweep around the foot of the Valles, and the rough and rocky slopes stretching up to their lofty and picturesque summits. In another direction were above, the peculiar outline of Abiquiu Peak, and below, the rocky gate from which the river issues.

"Leaving the Chama, we passed up the eroded valley of an intermittent tributary. This is excavated in the Triassic series, and its sides exhibit bands of brilliant color, red, orange, blue, white, &c., as vivid as could be drawn from an artist's color-box. In some localities the red sandstones—usually soft and fine-grained—are replaced by coarse conglomerates or masses of cemented bowlders, generally of large size. These bowlders are composed of quartzose and syenitic rock, hard and smoothly rounded. They indicate stronger currents and more violence of action, during the deposition of the Trias, than in any other locality where I have observed it; also, closer approach to the source of the material of which these beds are composed. Ascending the arroyo, toward its head, we found the strata rising rapidly toward the north, and cut through so as to expose the saliferous sandstones—the lowest member of the Trias—in sections of at least 200 feet. This group here consists of thick-bedded, chocolate sandstones, like those of New Jersey and the Connecticut Valley, except that here and there they showed large patches of white, interstratified with green and brown shales. Here, as on the Little Colorado, this formation contains much saline matter, as shown by numerous salt springs and a white saline efflorescence on the surfaces of the rock itself. The *Cobre* is situated in the face of the cliffs, bordering an eroded valley drained into the Chama below Abiquiu. These cliffs are composed at base of the saliferous sandstones and interstratified marls, some 250 feet in thickness; above these, blood-red marls and calcareous sandstones, 200 feet thick; the whole crowned by coarse yellow sandstones, having a thickness of about 150 feet; a section corresponding to that on the Pecos, but exhibiting a much less thickness of the red marls and calcareous sandstones. The copper occurs in the base of the yellow sandstones just above the marls. To reach the most important of the ancient mines of this vicinity, we climbed up the face of the southern cliffs of the valley, over the red sandstones and marls, till we reached the coarse yellow sandstones which overlie them. Here we found an entrance, five by six feet in dimensions, which led to a series of galleries, having a combined length of perhaps a hundred yards. The work exhibits considerable skill in the use

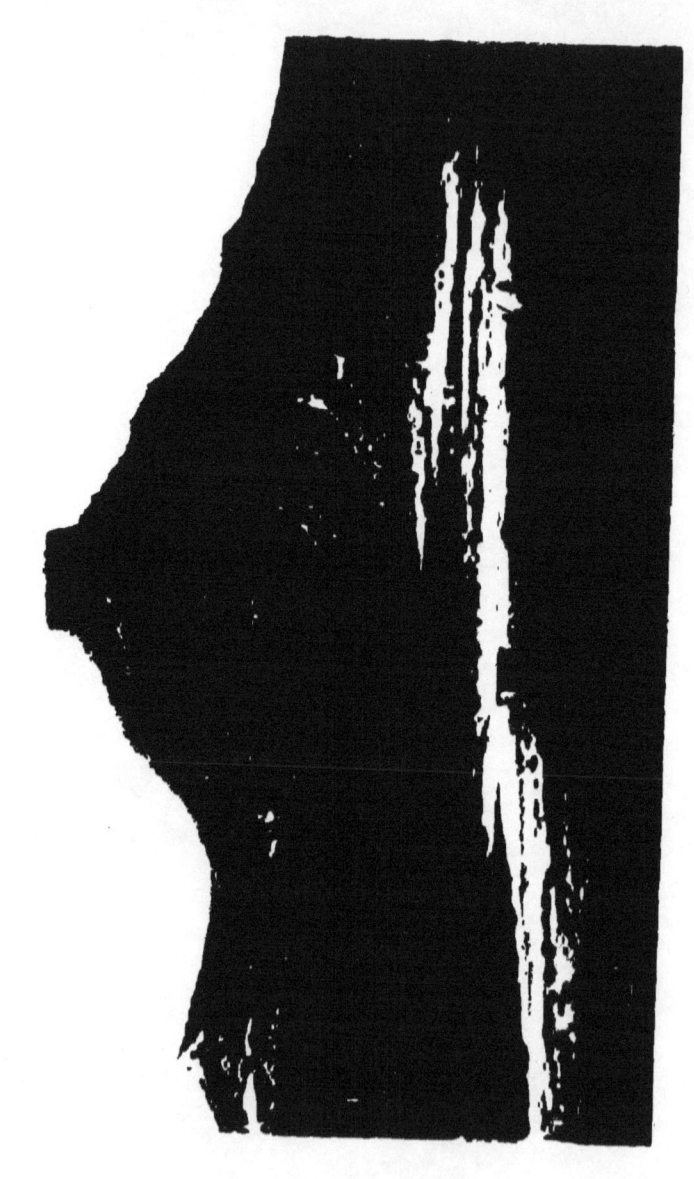

of tools, and a familiarity with the business of mining. The roof is carefully braced where weak, and old galleries are closed by well-laid walls of masonry. From the style in which the excavation is done, and from the perfect preservation of the woodwork, I attribute this and other similar mines in this region to the earlier Spanish explorers. The rock which contains the ore is very coarse, frequently a conglomerate, with bands of light-gray clay. The copper is distributed with considerable uniformity through a layer four or five feet in thickness. It occurs in the form of sulphide of copper and iron, (erubescite,) and green carbonate, replacing trunks of trees and fragments of wood, and in concretions and botryoidal masses scattered among the pebbles of quartz, or as minute points of carbonate specking the shales. It has evidently been deposited from solution, investing and replacing the wood precisely as the sulphide of iron is prone to do.

"The most interesting incident of our visit to this copper-mine was the discovery in the shale roof-stone of thousands of impressions of plants, of which abundant specimens were procured. They are mostly cycadaceous—*Otozamites* and *Pterozamites*—with a few conifers (*Brachyphyllum* and *Voltzia?*). The species are probably new, and will not afford the means of determining with precision the age of the stratum containing them, but the discovery is of great geological interest, as showing the wide distribution of the cycadaceous flora of the Triassic and Jurassic epochs, and gives additional confirmation of the generalization of Brongniart, who characterized this epoch in the botanical history of the world as the reign of Gymnosperms."*

On the 19th of July we left Abiquiu for the ascent of the Abiquiu Peak. My notes of the trip are as follows:

"Left camp at 7 a. m. The train, moving on to the Arroyo Seco, passed up the Chama to a point just above Abiquiu, and then turned to the left and ascended, by a long and difficult road, the high mesa which overlooks the valley on the south side. This mesa is here full a thousand feet above the Chama, and is connected with that of which the broken edge forms a bold headland below the town, known as Abiquiu Cliff. The upper part of this mesa is composed of trap, below which are exposed several hundred feet of the variegated marls (Trias), and the white tufaceous Tertiary beds, all quite soft, and, in many places on both sides of the Chama, very fantastically eroded. The mesa over which we passed extended, with a nearly level surface, several miles toward the peak. It is covered with groves of piñon, separated by prairies uniformly coated with grama grass, now very short and dry. Arriving at the western border of this mesa, we looked directly down into the narrow but fertile valley in which is nestled the little Mexican village of Los Cañones. Descending by a steep and tortuous path, we left our mules at the bottom and climbed a detached *mesilla* which stands at the junction of the two branches of the valley, and on which is situated an ancient and ruined pueblo, once a stone-built town of considerable size. Even its name is now lost, and of the inhabitants whose busy hands constructed its walls, and whose feet in suc-

---

* Descriptions of these plants will be found in another chapter, where it is shown that the most conspicuous species (*Otozamites Macombii*) is the same with one found in the Triassic strata of Los Broncos, Sonora, where it occurs in company with *Pecopteris Stutgardiensis*, *Tæniopteris magnifolia*, and other well-known Triassic plants of Virginia, North Carolina, and Europe. We have, therefore, in these plants evidence of the Triassic age of *all* the variegated gypsiferous rocks of northern New Mexico; for the Lower Cretaceous sandstones immediately overlie the plant-bed of the *Cobre*.

cessive generations wore so deeply the threshold of its entrance, no tradition now remains. The mesa on which it stands is some 500 feet in height, is composed of a cellular trachyte, and the top is only to be reached by a narrow and difficult path. The houses are now in ruins, but were once numerous, and all built of dressed stone. Within the town we noticed a dozen or more *estuffas* excavated from the solid rock. They are circular in form, 18-20 feet in diameter by 10 or 12 in depth. They all exhibited evidence of once having been covered with wooden superstructures. In most of them, four excavations on opposite sides would seem to have been used as the sockets for the insertion of wooden posts, and in one is a niche cut in the side, with a chimney leading from it; probably the place where the sacred fire was kept perpetually burning. The style of architecture in which this town was built, as well as the *estuffas*, show that its inhabitants belonged to the race of Pueblo Indians; a race now nearly extinct, but once occupying every habitable portion of New Mexico.

"Spending the night at Los Cañones, we started this morning very early for the ascent of the peak. This we mostly accomplished on mule-back; passing over a succession of hills composed of the variegated marls—containing beds of gypsum of great thickness—covered with a forest of piñon and cedar. When we had arrived within 500 feet of the summit, we left our mules and commenced the ascent on foot. This part of the mountain is very steep, and the upper 200 feet is a perpendicular wall of trap-rock. The summit we found to form a *cuchillo*, a narrow, knife-like ridge, bounded on every side by vertical precipices. Its height above the sea is about 9,000 feet. The extreme summit is covered with piñon, and the slope with yellow pine, Douglass spruce, the western balsam-fir, and the quaking-asp. The view from the summit was particularly fine, sweeping a circle of fifty miles radius, except toward the Valles, which are very near, and fill the southeastern horizon. On the east we looked down the valley of the Chama, across that of the Rio Grande, and our view in this direction was bounded by the high and unbroken ranges of the Santa Fé Mountains. Northeast the Taos Mountains and the Spanish Peaks were plainly visible. On the north the foreground was filled with the low and near mountains of Conejos, beyond which, north of west, we could just discern the picturesque summits of the Sierra San Juan, and Sierra de la Plata. In the northwest we overlooked the course of the Chama for many miles, and the comparatively level and open country through which it flows. Almost beneath us was the junction of the Puerco and Chama, in a broad valley of excavation, as red as blood, from the exposed surfaces of the eroded marls; farther west, higher table-lands, composed of the yellow and blue rocks of the Lower and Middle Cretaceous.

"Descending from the mountain, we regained the trail of our party at Arroyo Seco. There we were surrounded by a series of buttes of most varied and fantastic forms, worked out by erosion from the marl series of the Trias. Their colors are exceedingly brilliant, crimson and orange being the most conspicuous. The vivid green and level valley is framed by these colored cliffs, forming a most beautiful and impressive picture."

At Arroyo Seco the trail we were following leaves the river and enters a cañon, which cuts the plateau bordering the valley from base to summit. Most of the section exposed in its walls is composed of the Triassic marls, which includes beds of gypsum

NEAR VADO DEL CHAMA.
UPPER CRETACEOUS MESA

in some places 150 feet thick. Above the marls are the yellow sandstones—the base of the Cretaceous—which floor the plateau on either side. Pursuing a northerly direction, we gradually rose through the Trias, and at Navajo Springs reached the base of the Cretaceous sandstones. Continuing our ascent, two or three miles farther on we reached the base of the cañon, and emerged upon the plateau of which I have before spoken. This plateau extends northward to the Vada del Chama, where it begins to be broken by the foot-hills of the mountains. Westward it reaches to and beyond the source of the Chama, and is broken through and locally disturbed by the upheaval of the Gallinas Mountain, which seems to be situated on the Nacimiento axis. Over this plateau the Lower Cretaceous sandstones form the general substratum, but here and there are rounded knolls, composed of the dark shales and blue shaly limestones, the lower part of the middle division of the Cretaceous formation, here, as at a thousand other points on our route, characterized by the presence of *Gryphea Pitcheri, Inoceramus problematicus, Ostra congesta,* &c. The more level portions of the plateau are covered with sage bushes, with here and there more moist and fertile spots, sustaining grasses and annual plants, conspicuous among which is the wild sunflower (*Helianthus*). The knolls are usually covered with groves of piñon. As a whole, this plateau country has little agricultural value, although there are portions of it which will afford good grazing for stock.

Between the Cebolla and Nutria, the Middle Cretaceous rocks occupy a considerable area, and attain a thickness of perhaps a hundred feet. They present precisely the same lithological characters and fossils as do their equivalents on the banks of the Canadian and Ocaté, east of the Rocky Mountains, viz., thin layers of hard dark-blue or ferruginous limestone alternating with layers of bitumino-calcareous shales.

At the Vada del Chama we again encamped on the banks of this stream in a very beautiful region, one of considerable fertility and of great geological interest. On the east side of the river are high and broken hills—the foot-hills of the mountains—covered with forests of splendid pine timber. These hills are mainly composed of the Lower Cretaceous sandstones, having a thickness of nearly 300 feet. Here, as farther west, they contain beds of lignite, and the impressions of dicotyledonous leaves. They are considerably broken up, but have a general and rapid dip toward the southwest. On the opposite side of the valley is a mesa, with bold, nearly perpendicular faces over 1,000 feet high, composed of the Middle and Upper Cretaceous rocks lying nearly horizontal. Between these elevated banks lies the excavated valley of the river, with its narrow but fertile bottom-lands, its winding stream of pure cold water, its groves of cottonwood, and its grassy meadows spangled with flowers. The structure of the valley will be more readily comprehended from the accompanying section than from any detailed description I could give of it.

Transverse section of the valley of the Chama at the Vada.

	Feet.
1. Yellowish brown sandstone (Lower Cretaceous)	125
2. Brown and black shales, often dark olive, with beds of lignite	50
3. Sandstone similar to No. 1	70

	Feet.
4. Black shales with bands of light-dove-colored limestone...............	150

The upper of these shale-beds is greenish-brown, with bands of foliated sandy limestone, containing immense numbers of fragmentary or entire fossils. These are principally *Inoceramus problematicus*, *I. fragilis*, *Ostrea congesta*, *Baculites anceps*, *Scaphites Warreni*, *S. laviformis*, &c.

| 5. Bluish-black shales, with concretions and bands of limestone containing a large undulated *Inoceramus*, the broken fragments of which are thickly set with *Ostrea congesta* .... | 1,000 |

The lithological characters of this division are nearly the same throughout, but the limestone bands and fossils are nearly restricted to the lower portion. The layers of limestone are from 6 to 12 inches in thickness, quite pure and compact, blue in color, but weathering reddish yellow, and breaking on exposure in vertical prisms, like starch.

| 6. A light dove-colored sandy limestone or calcareous sandstone, weathering yellow, massive toward the top, foliated below, without fossils.......... | 200 |

7. This, the cap-rock of the high mesa, is a higher member of the Cretaceous series than has before been met with in New Mexico. Our subsequent observations showed it to be the base of the third great division of this formation as developed on the Colorado Plateau.

8. Gravel hills, valley drift.

At the Laguna de los Cavallos we reached the summit of the divide between the waters of the Pacific and the Atlantic, at the height of 7,600 feet. No conspicuous elevation marks the summit, but the strata are somewhat broken by a line of displacement, apparently a continuation of the Nacimiento axis. The country about the Laguna may be taken as a type, both as regards its general aspects and its geological structure, of all that bordering our route while we were skirting the bases of the mountain ranges, the drainage of which supplies the flow of the San Juan River and its tributaries. This region includes three topographical belts or districts in which the physical features exhibit the most striking contrasts, viz., the mountains, the foot-hills, and the table-lands. The mountainous district includes a large number of lofty chains, having a north and south trend and the general characteristics of the Rocky Mountain system, connected by thousands of interlocking spurs, or separated by narrow valleys, traversed by clear, cold, and rapid streams. These ranges terminate southward *en échelon*, and, when viewed from a distance, present the appearance of a continuous sierra, having a northwest and southeast trend. The outlines of these mountains are bold and picturesque; their highest summits having an altitude of 12,000 or 13,000 feet, entirely bare of vegetation, and showing, here and there, patches of perpetual snow; their slopes covered with forests of spruce and fir above, of yellow pine below; many of their gorges set with thickets of scrub-oak and quaking-asp.

Along the base of the mountains stretches a belt of foot-hills, a region of which the surface is broken into rounded or abrupt hills, from 100 to 1,000 feet in height, generally composed of sedimentary rocks, very much disturbed, often pitched about in the greatest confusion. These hills are covered with noble forests of yellow pine, with open intervals where grama and bunch grass grow with great luxuriance. Between the hills are charming mountain valleys, carpeted with fine grass, in the summer season perfect gardens of flowers, through which meander cool and sparkling mountain streams, fringed with thickets of willow, or shaded by groves of the narrow-leaved cottonwood. Through this delightful region our route lay, going from Santa Fé toward the Colorado. On our return we traversed the third of the districts I have enumerated, that of the table-lands. Where unaffected by the disturbing forces which have elevated the mountain chains, the sedimentary rocks lie nearly horizontal, forming a wide plateau deeply cañoned by the streams which take their rise in the mountains.

Although the generalities of the country of the foot-hills, with which we at present have to do, may be given in few words, perhaps a more detailed description will be needed to convey all the information that may be sought of a region destined to become the home of many of our countrymen, and, therefore, of considerable economical and political importance. For the purpose of satisfying the want I have anticipated, I shall, from time to time, copy from my journal such detailed descriptions of local scenery or structure as may seem best fitted to complete the picture I have already sketched. From my notes made at our camp on the Rio Navajo, sixteen miles west of Laguna de los Cavallos, I take the following extracts:

"From the Laguna our route westward passed through a beautiful and fertile country, the trail winding among hills composed of Upper Cretaceous rocks, covered with trees of yellow pine, often attaining large size. On the south is a high mesa, with picturesque broken edges, a continuation of that east of the Laguna bordering the valley of the Chama. On the north is a similar wall in which the strata are more highly inclined. Beyond this is another valley or series of valleys which border the bases of the mountains connected on the east with the Tierra Marin, a charming spot at the forks of the Chama, where the Mexicans had formerly a settlement, now abandoned on account of the depredations of the Indians. The drainage toward the west begins a mile west of the Laguna, and the Rio Navajo is the first of the tributaries of the San Juan. This is a small but rapid stream which rises in the Sierra del Navajo, of which the southern extremity is but a few miles distant from our camp. This range apparently forms the divide north of the Laguna, the drainage of its eastern slope falling into the Chama, its western forming the Rio Navajo. The material washed down from the Sierra del Navajo is mostly eruptive in character, trap, trachyte, and porphyry, and the outlines of this extremity of the range show that it is mainly composed of rocks of this character. Just above our camp the river issues from a magnificent wooded gorge, which it has cut through the chain of Cretaceous hills that I have mentioned as bordering our route of to-day on the right. A little below our camp is an isolated mesa, an outlier of the great table-lands which spread out to the south. This mesa, called by our guide the Cerro del Navajo, has a superficial area of perhaps 100 acres, a relative altitude of 1,500 or 1,600 feet, and an absolute altitude of about 8,500 feet. It is entirely composed of the Middle and Upper Cretaceous rocks, lying nearly horizontal, and stands a stupendous monument of the erosion which this region has suffered.

10 s f

* * * As we approached Rito Blanco we entered a narrow ravine or cañon cut in the Upper Cretaceous rocks—yellow sandstones and gray shales—which rapidly deepens till, at its junction with the Rito, its bounding hills have an altitude of a least 1,000 feet.

"This cañon is very picturesque; the sides covered with yellow pine, Douglas' and Menzies' spruces, the latter now for the first time seen in New Mexico. It grows here very beautifully, somewhat more spreading than in Oregon, the foliage very dense and silvered. Among the evergreens are slopes on which grow thickets of wild cherry, serviceberry, and gooseberry, all now in fruit. In the bottom are bushes of black currant, also fruiting, all these berries are called *manzinitas*—little apples—by the Mexicans, but the serviceberry is particularly distinguished by this name by those who would be exact. The California *manzinita* has better claim to the name, and is a very different plant. The cliffs of Rito Blanco are frequently precipitous, but so widely separated as to leave a pretty valley between. They are wholly composed of Cretaceous strata, mainly of the middle division, with a capping of the yellow sandstones and marls of the upper member of the formation."

Pagosa, July 28.—"Left Rito Blanco early this morning, passing through a country similar to that of yesterday. At 9 o'clock, came down a pretty ravine to the San Juan, here 30 yards wide, 3 feet deep, very rapid. At this point it enters a cañon, cut in the Upper Cretaceous sandstone, which has a strong local dip toward the north. Above this cañon is a delightful valley, running up to the foot-hills of the San Juan Mountains, which are here very beautiful in form, and lofty, as patches of snow are visible upon them. The river San Juan here issues from the narrow valley between the Sierra San Juan and Sierra del Navajo, where it takes its rise, and this is apparently the first interval of level land through which it flows. In the upper part of this valley is the *Pagosa*, one of the most remarkable hot springs on the continent, well known, even famous, among the Indian tribes, but, up to the time of our visit, never having been seen by the whites. It can hardly be doubted that in future years it will become a celebrated place of resort, both for those who shall reside in the surrounding country, and for wonder-hunting health-seeking travelers from other lands. There is scarcely a more beautiful place on the face of the earth. The valley is three miles long by one broad; a verdant meadow of the finest grass, thickly strewed with flowers, through which winds the bright and rapid river, margined by clumps of willows, and most graceful groups of cotton-wood. On every side are hills covered with gigantic pines or the slender Oregon spruces, and on the north, far above these, rise the forest-clad slopes and craggy crests of two great Sierras. The Pagosa is at the edge of this prairie. As the river leaves the great wooded gorge embraced between the San Juan and Navajo Mountains, and comes out into this beautiful amphitheater, it sweeps round in a curve, inclosing some 20 acres. From all parts of this space, which is evenly turfed over, the surface rises very gently to the center. Here is a great basin, oval in form, 40 by 50 feet in diameter, its walls of white rock, of unfathomable depth, in which the deep-blue water seethes and surges as in a boiling caldron, giving off a column of vapor which in damp weather is visible for miles. The water, though hot, is not at the boiling-point, and the ebullition is produced by

SCENE NEAR SAN COSMODO EXIT.
VICINITY.
H. W. GOODWIN

the escape of gases, which are generated in enormous quantities. The temperature at the side of the basin is 140°; in the center, perhaps something higher. The gases with which the water is charged consist, in part at least, of carbonic acid and sulphuretted hydrogen; the former giving it an effervescence, like that of soda-water, and the same pungent taste. The sulphur is also perceptible by taste and smell; a strong sulphurous odor, which is distinguishable at some distance, being exhaled from the spring. When cooled, the water has a strong mineral taste, though rather agreeable than otherwise. It was freely drank by all our party while in this vicinity with no unpleasant effects, but, on the contrary, a decided sharpening of the appetite. No analysis has yet been made of it, but it is evident that the large amount of saline matter it contains is of somewhat complex composition, and such as gives it a character unlike that of the water of any other mineral spring with which I am familiar. To make a rude comparison, the water of the Pagosa might be imperfectly imitated by mixing Blue Lick and Congress water and heating the compound to 140°. The flow of water from the Pagosa is very large, and it finds its way into the San Juan by several subterranean channels. The deposit from it is very copious, generally snow-white, but in many places bright pink or green in color. It floats in crusts which revolve upon the surface of the basin I have described, and which envelop the bodies of water-beetles, frogs and snakes that have incautiously plunged into it. When first precipitated this deposit consists, in a great degree, of chloride of sodium, but mingled with this are silicates—probably of soda, lime, and potassa—which form a hard and indestructible white rock. In the lapse of ages an immense amount of this material has been thrown out from this spring. All the low, broad mound, which I have mentioned as surrounding the basin, is composed of it, and over an area of ten to twenty acres it has a thickness of at least twenty feet. This is shown on the banks of the San Juan, which is for some distance bordered by walls of this material, having an altitude of twelve to fifteen feet.

The geology of all this region is Cretaceous. The upper members of the series are exposed in all the hills surrounding the Pagosa; and it is evident its waters issue from the bitumino-calcareous shales forming its middle division. These shales are of marine origin, have a thickness of over 1,000 feet, contain many animal remains, and are highly charged with salts and sulphur; in all these respects resembling the Hamilton group of the New York geologists. I think it is true that mineral springs more frequently flow from rocks of this character than any other, and I have been led to suppose that the water of such springs derives its peculiar character immediately from the rock from which it emanates. It is certain that hot water, forced through these strata, would dissolve and carry off many of their constituent elements, and would become the agent by which an extensive range of chemical combinations would take place. In the case of the Pagosa, the hot water is doubtless derived from a great depth, yet it is entirely possible that the gases and salts which it contains are all derived from the superficial strata through which it passes.

THE SIERRA SAN JUAN.

This name has been applied by geographers to several distinct mountain ranges which really exist in this portion of the continent; or, more generally, to a great imaginary chain, which was assigned an inordinate extent and a trend altogether hypothetical and abnormal. It is to be hoped that one result of our expedition will be to bring something like order out of the confusion of ideas which has prevailed in regard to the intricate mountain ranges of this region. As has been before intimated, these ranges, though numerous, exhibit no exceptional features, and are comparatively simple and harmonious in structure and trend; while it is true that the great mountain belt north of the San Juan River, with its higher chains, their thousand interlocking spurs and narrow valleys, form a labyrinth whose extent and intricacy will at present defy all attempts at detailed topographical analysis. It is equally true that a general topographical character has been given to all of this region by a comparatively few lines of lofty summits, which have nearly a north and south trend, and seem to form an integral portion of the Rocky Mountain system. This great truth may be learned at a glance by the drainage of this country; this all flows through streams which have approximately a north and south direction. On the south, the tributaries of the San Juan, the Navajo, the Blanco, the Upper San Juan, the Piedra, the Pinos, the Florido, the Animas, the La Plata, and the Mancos, all flow southward; and most of them issue from the north and south valleys, lying between the parallel ranges to which I have so frequently referred. On the north side of this mountain-belt similar topographical features present themselves. The tributaries of Grand River, which sweep the bases of the northern extremities of these ranges, almost without exception issue from valleys which have approximately a north and south direction; hence, it is plainly apparent that one great fundamental idea pervades the topography of all this region, and that one great force has given shape to all its principal topographical features.

Most of the prominent ranges visible from our route have received from the Indians and Mexicans distinct names, by which they are well known to those who know the country; for example, the chain north of the Laguna, of which the southern extremity is drained by the Chama and Rio Navajo, is called the Sierra del Rio Navajo or the Sierra del Navajo. From between the spurs of this sierra flows the Rito Blanco (Little White River), so called from the milky color given to its waters by the Cretaceous shales. From the valley separating the upper part of this sierra from the Sierra San Juan, which does not extend so far south, issues that branch of the San Juan River which retains its name. West of the San Juan Mountains, as we shall see as we progress with our geological narrative, the Rio de los Pinos issues from the valley between the Sierra San Juan and the Sierra de los Pinos; beyond the Sierra de los Pinos, the great valley of the Animas; then the Sierra de la Plata, west and north of which lies the Sierra San Miguel; west and south of the latter chain, the broad expanse of the Colorado Plateau. From this sketch, it will be seen that the great east and west chains of the Sierra San Juan and Sierra de la Plata, which form so conspicuous features on some of our maps, have really no existence, and need therefore no longer vex us as incongruous elements in the orology of our country.

Like the Santa Fé Mountains, the Sierra San Juan terminates abruptly southward, standing out as a bold headland on the margin of the sea-like plateau. The altitude of its highest summits must be nearly 13,000 feet, as snow lies on them in

THE PAGOSA & SAN JUAN RIVER.
LOOKING EASTERLY

Capt. J. N. Macomb Exp. in New Mexico & Utah.

Plate IV.

places throughout the year, while from the Sandia and Santa Fé Mountains—over 12,000 feet in height—it entirely disappears in midsummer. Only a small portion of the range came under our observation; but enough was seen to show that its structure was essentially the same with that of the other chains belonging to the same series which we were able to examine more fully. The southern extremity is mostly eruptive in character, consisting of basaltic trap, porphyry, and trachyte, some of the latter containing crystals of feldspar of large size. As usual, the summits composed of these materials present very varied and picturesque outlines. In the opposite chain of the Sierra del Navajo are some castellated summits, which, as seen through a powerful glass, presented an appearance exceedingly imposing and beautiful. Among these are precipices, ornamented with imitations of columns, arches, and pilasters, which form some of the grandest specimens of nature's Gothic architecture I have ever beheld. When viewed from some nearer point they must be even awful in their sublimity.

The Cretaceous strata at the base of the San Juan Mountains are highly fossiliferous, and yielded me a large number of species. The ferruginous, sandy limestones and shales near the base of the middle division of the Cretaceous series, where exposed just north of the Pagosa, are almost made up of the shells of *Ostrea, Inoceramus, Ammonites,* &c. This is the horizon from which the oysters, gryphaeas, fish-teeth, &c., were collected in such abundance on the Canadian, at Galisteo, at the ford of the Chama, and various other points on our route. These fossils are limited to the first hundred feet of the shale-beds above the Lower Cretaceous sandstones; the most abundant at the Pagosa are *Ostrea lugubris, O. uniformis,* Meek, n. sp., *Inoceramus problematicus,* and *I. fragilis.* I also found here an interesting series of the teeth of *Ptychodus Whipplei,* described at length in the chapter on Paleontology. Above the beds in which these fossils are found, the black bituminous shales contain large, generally broken, shells of *Nautilus* and *Inoceramus,* thickly set with *Ostrea congesta.*

All the interval between the Pagosa and Rio Piedra is occupied by Cretaceous rocks. Over large surfaces the Lower Cretaceous sandstones are laid bare, generally much disturbed, and somewhat changed. The only fossils discovered were indistinct vegetable impressions, among which the most conspicuous is a tuberculated fucoid (*Halymenites*) common in the Cretaceous sandstones of all this region. Here, as at the Tierra Marin, these rocks are cut by joints into blocks of nearly uniform size. Of those joints the most strongly marked have a bearing approximately north and south; the others cross these nearly at right angles. In the great number of localities in New Mexico where I observed jointings of these rocks, I found them to have similar directions, and to be in no case influenced by local disturbances, nor having any obvious connection with the prevailing dip. This rule is of so general application that I have been driven to refer the jointing of all the rocks of this region to one great common cause. This has seemed to me probably magnetic, but may possibly be connected with the action of the forces which have given to all the great lines of elevation a general north and south trend.

On the Nutria Frances, a small tributary of the Rio Piedra, the black shales of the Middle Cretaceous are exposed in various places. They here contain large *Ino-*

cerami, *Nautili*, and fish-scales. The Piedra Parada, a well-known landmark, which has conferred its name upon the Rio Piedra, is a chimney-like column of rock, rising with its base to the height of eight or nine hundred feet above the surrounding country. It is itself composed of the Upper Cretaceous sandstone, resting upon a base of dark shales, (Middle Cretaceous,) and is a remnant of a plateau now almost entirely removed by erosion.

The valley of the Rio Piedra is, in physical aspect and geological structure, the counterpart of that of the Rito Blanco, already described; the only noteworthy point of difference being that the Upper Cretaceous sandstone here contains beds of lignite of considerable thickness, though of limited lateral extent. The disturbances which the Cretaceous strata have suffered in this region are very well shown in the immediate vicinity of our camp on the Piedra. On the east side of the river the plateau, with which the Piedra Parada was once connected, stretches away south for several miles, with a rapid dip in that direction. On the west side is a mesa of which the cut-edge rises abruptly from the margin of the stream to the height of over twelve hundred feet. This mesa is composed of precisely the same materials as that bounding the valley on the east, but its strata are almost perfectly horizontal. Just above our camp this mesa is broken short off by a line of fracture running nearly east and west; its component rocks, set nearly on edge, forming a wall which rises to the height of eighteen hundred feet above the river. Between this disrupted mass and the mesa from which it has been broken is a low pass through which our trail ran.

Soon after leaving the Rio Piedra we began to ascend rapidly and soon rose on to a high divide between the Piedra and Rio de los Pinos. This divide seems to be an axis of elevation, running southward from the mountains between the Piedra and Pinos. It is composed of Cretaceous rocks irregularly broken up, generally inclined at a high angle. It has an altitude of about sixteen hundred feet above our camp on the Piedra. The view from its summit is peculiarly grand and interesting; eastward the Navajo and San Juan mountains bound the horizon, terminating southward in the Cerro del Navajo. On the south and west sides of these ranges the rivers we have recently passed take their rise, and their valleys may in part be followed by the eye. None of the summits visible in this direction are covered with perpetual snow, but all bear patches in the higher valleys.

Nearer us than the mountains was a labyrinth of hills, spread out before us as on a map. These seem to have been generally formed by a series of breaks in the Cretaceous rocks, and, so far as we could see, are all composed of these materials.

Toward the west our view was quite different. In that direction we looked down on what seemed an extensive plain, extending northward to the base of the Sierra de la Plata, now for the first time distinctly seen, and on the south bounded by high mesas, through an opening in which, the gap of the Rio las Animas, was visible the high chain of the Carriso Mountains south of the San Juan. This plain before us we subsequently found to be a basin-like space, lying between the mountains on the north and the table-lands south; a depressed area, completely inclosed in high lands, except where these are cut by the narrow gorges through which the waters of

the Animas and the Pinos have forced their way to join the San Juan. It is, in fact, an expansion of the valley of the Animas, has been mainly excavated by its current, and is everywhere covered with beds of transported material washed down from the mountains.*

As we descended into the valley and thus opened it more to the north, we gained sight of a chain of mountains in that direction, which our guide calls Sierra de los Pinos. These are quite lofty, and consist, as I discovered from the drift brought down from them, of quartzites, silicious slates, limestone, and granite, with some trap, but with a prevalence of metamorphic over erupted rocks. The Rio de los Pinos is a clear, cold, trout-stream, full as large as the San Juan at the Pagosa. The bottom-lands are wooded with willows, cottonwood, alder, &c., and scattered trees of yellow pine, the latter of which mark its course in the open sage-covered country through which it flows, and have naturally suggested the name which it bears.

The interval between the Rio de los Pinos and Rio Florido is underlaid by the Middle Cretaceous shales; is gently rolling in outline, its more level surfaces covered with sage (*Artemisia tridentata*), its rounded hills with cedars or scrub-oak. Here and there are meadows of good grass, with a strong growth of annual plants. On the whole, however, the country is less picturesque and less productive than that lying south and east of it.

The Rio Florido, or River of Flowers, is so named from the flowery meadows which line its banks; meadows which, so far as we could see, are no broader, greener, or more flowery than those which border the other rivers of this region. It is, however, a bright, handsome stream, similar in character to the Pinos, and about half as large. It is probably not more than thirty or forty miles in length; rises in the foot-hills of the Sierra de los Pinos, and joins the Animas some fifteen miles southwest from where we crossed it. The bowlders which it has brought down from its sources are quite varied in character, and probably give a very fair representation of the geology of the mountains which it drains. Of these many are composed of coarse red granite, much like that of the Santa Fé Mountains, black and white porphyry, closely resembling that which is so abundant at the gold-mines in the Placer Mountains; blue limestone, containing many of the characteristic Coal-Measure fossils so common at Santa Fé, such as *Productus semireticulatus*, *P. nodosus*, *Spirifer cameratus*, *Chonetes mesoloba*, &c.; with these are masses of red and white sandstone, probably Triassic.

The course of the Florido lies altogether within the basin-like area of which I have before spoken. The extent and character of this area were fully learned in an excursion which I made from our camp on the Florido, about forty miles down the Animas, to visit some extensive and interesting ruins situated in the valley of that stream some twenty miles above its mouth. From my notes of this trip I make the following extracts:

"*August 4th.*—Left camp early with Pfeiffer, the Indian agent, Messrs. Fisher and Dorsey, and several Indians, to visit the ruins reported to exist at a certain point on the banks of the Animas; crossed over in a direct line to the Animas, a distance of about ten miles. All this interval is occupied by a gravel mesa, of which the surface is

---
* Since named Animas Park.

gently rolling, generally covered with grass or sage-bushes, with scattered trees of piñon and cedar. Reaching the Animas we found it flowing in a valley one to three miles wide, bounded by gravel terraces, of which there are two, sometimes three, distinctly visible. Near the mouth of the Florido the first terrace, which is near the stream, has an altitude of about 50 feet; the second, 260 feet higher; the third, the general surface of the plain which we crossed, 200 feet higher still. All these terraces are, I suppose, of local origin, having been left by the sinking of the bed of the stream consequent upon the cutting down of the gorge it has opened in the table-lands south. Between the junction of the Florido with the Animas and the valley of the San Juan, the table-land seems to be continuous, but has its greatest altitude along its northern margin. Immediately after receiving the Florido the Animas enters a deep and narrow cañon, in which it flows for several miles; the walls of this cañon are 1,500 to 1,600 feet in height; in places nearly vertical; the rocks exposed are principally sandstones, of which the prevailing color is a light brownish-yellow, sometimes becoming a pale red. These sandstones belong to the Upper Cretaceous series, which is here more fully exposed than anywhere in that portion of our route already passed over. Through the cañon the river is very rapid and much obstructed by rocks, and cannot be followed on horseback; below this the valley widens and the declivities of the bluffs which bound it become more gentle; the bottom-lands are from a mile to two miles in width, and quite fertile; the river is bordered by thickets of willow and buffalo-berry, with groups and sometimes groves of cottonwood. It is in this part of the valley that the ruins are situated. The principal structures are large pueblos, handsomely built of stone, and in a pretty good state of preservation. The external walls are composed of yellow Cretaceous sandstone, dressed to a common smooth surface without hammer-marks; in some places they are still 25 feet in height. As usual in buildings of this kind, the walls were unbroken by door or window to the height of 15 feet above the foundation. The interior shows a great number of small rooms, many of which are in a perfect state of preservation, and handsomely plastered. These larger structures are surrounded by mounds and fragments of masonry, marking the sites of great numbers of subordinate buildings; the whole affording conclusive evidence that a large population once had its home here. The fragments of highly ornamented and glazed pottery which cover the surface in the vicinity of these buildings, as well as the peculiar style of architecture in which they are constructed, show that the people who built and occupied these structures belonged to the common aboriginal race of this region, now generally known as the Pueblo Indians.

"After our return from the ruins on the Animas, our party moved over and encamped on that stream, at the point where it is crossed by the old Spanish trail. It is nearly a hundred yards wide, deep and rapid, and, at the present stage of water, not easily forded. It here issues from the hills and enters the basin before described. Above this point it flows through a broad mountain valley not yet explored, but of which the general features are given by the two great mountain groups which border it on the east and west—the Sierra de los Pinos and Sierra de la Plata. Of these the Sierra de la Plata is the most conspicuous feature in the scenery, a broad and lofty mountain belt stretching continuously northward as far as the eye can reach.

"The drift from the mountains drained by the Animas shows that their structure is essentially that of the Santa Fé Mountains and the other principal ranges of the Rocky Mountain system. In this transported material are blocks, often weighing several tons, of red granite, similar to that of Santa Fé; gray granite, not unlike that forming the base of the section in the Colorado Cañon at the mouth of Diamond River, described in my former report; Carboniferous limestone, with many of the fossils found at Santa Fé and in the Coal-Measures of the Mississippi Valley; black and white porphyry, trachyte, trap, and metamorphosed red sandstone. No traces of Silurian or Devonian rocks were discovered. The hills just above our camp are composed of red sandstone and conglomerate (Triassic), very much disturbed."

Below the crossing of the Spanish trail the valley of the Animas is susceptible of cultivation to the junction of the Florida, though the belt of arable land is narrow, and, in part at least, can only be cultivated by irrigation.

In regard to the origin of the broad valley or basin which borders this part of the course of the Animas, I think we may safely say that its features were given by the disturbances which this region has suffered; that, in the breaking up of the table-lands, a basin-like depression was left, into which the Animas flowed, and which it partially filled with gravel and bowlders brought down from the mountains above. Subsequently, the enclosing walls of this area were cut down, along the natural line of drainage, until the river reached its present level, and what was its bed at different epochs, now forms gravel terraces high above it.

The geology of that portion of our route lying between the Animas and the Rio de la Plata is precisely similar to that of most of the country previously passed through; the only rocks exposed are those of the upper portion of the Cretaceous formation, which compose broken hills flanking the eastern and southern slopes of the Sierra de la Plata. Among these hills the trail winds, following the courses of the picturesque and fertile, though narrow, valleys which separate them. From the headwaters of a small tributary of the Animas we crossed over a divide which rises to the height of about 1,000 feet above our Camp 17; thence descending nearly as much, we struck the La Plata just where it issues from the mountain-gorges in which it takes its rise. Of our camp on the La Plata I find the following description in my notes: "The Rio de la Plata is a beautifully clear, cold, mountain-brook; like the Animas and other streams we have recently crossed, well-stocked with trout. The valley in which it flows, as it issues from the mountains, is exceedingly beautiful, and our camp one of the most delightful imaginable. Our tents are pitched in the shade of a cluster of gigantic pines, such as are scattered, here and there, singly or in groups, over the surface of the valley, separated by meadows thickly coated with the finest gramma grass. Stretching off southward, a wall of verdure, tinted with the fresh and vivid green of cottonwoods and willows, marks, while it conceals, the course of the sparkling stream whose murmuring flow comes softly to the ear. On either side of the valley rise picturesque wooded hills, which bound the view both east and west; between these on the south an open vista reveals, far in the distance, the blue chains of the Sierra del Carriso and Tunecha. On the north the bold and lofty summits of the Sierra de la Plata look down upon us in this pure atmosphere with an apparent proximity almost startling. Patches of snow are visible upon them, which, by their wasting, supply the flow of the Rio de la Plata, which rises in the gorges beneath them."

The geology of the vicinity is similar to that of much of our route already passed; the prevailing rocks are Upper Cretaceous, which compose the hills bordering the valley; the thick mass of sandstone, which forms the Piedra Parada, caps these hills and has a rapid dip away from the mountains; this is succeeded below by a series of gray and yellow foliated sandstones or sandy shales, containing immense quantities of fucoidal stems, so many indeed that these casts make up the greater part of the deposit. They are a half-inch in diameter, the surface covered with indistinct annular markings. Beside the fucoids, these beds contain the well-known Cretaceous fossil, *Ammonites placenta*, and in lenticular masses of limestone immense numbers of *Baculites anceps*, *Cardium bellulum*, Meek, *Astarte Shumardi*, M., *Aporrhais Newberryi*, Meek, &c.

Several of these fossils are common in the Upper Cretaceous beds of Nebraska (Nos. 4 and 5 of Meek and Hayden's section of the Cretaceous rocks of Nebraska), and afford satisfactory confirmation of the parallelism before suggested between the rocks of this region and those of more eastern localities. The Baculites are so numerous as to form in some places half the bulk of the rock. Of these, the greater number are ornamented with nodes, in the manner of *B. asper* (Roemer), with which they may be identical. The smooth ones resemble *B. ovatus* and *B. compressus*. They vary much in form, some being nearly cylindrical, others much compressed, with every possible variety between these extremes. All, however, as it seems to me, belongs to one species.

From the summit of the hills, near camp, we have a fine view of the country south of us to the San Juan. All this interval is occupied by a mesa composed of the Upper Cretaceous rocks, deeply scored along the lines of drainage. The dip of the rocks composing this plateau is here southward, and very rapid; farther from the bases of the mountains they seem to lie nearly horizontal.

The southern end of the Sierra de la Plata is composed mainly of light-colored porphyry and other forms of erupted rock. It also consists in part of granite, with mica and clay-slate, traversed by extensive veins of quartz and epidote, which are metalliferous, containing magnetic iron, and sulphides of iron, copper, and lead; doubtless, also, in certain localities, silver and gold; at least there is better promise of the discovery of the precious metals in these mountains than in any others we have visited since leaving the Rio Grande.

The name given by the Spaniards to this great sierra, Silver Mountain, would seem to indicate that at some time silver had been found there, but I cannot learn that any definite knowledge is possessed by the Mexicans or the Indians of the existence of metallic veins such as would justify their choice of a title so significant.

CHAPTER V.

GEOLOGY OF THE SAGE-PLAIN AND VALLEY OF THE UPPER COLORADO.

GENERAL FEATURES OF THE NORTHERN PORTION OF THE COLORADO BASIN—ASPECTS AND STRUCTURE OF THE SAGE-PLAIN—MESA VERDE—ENORMOUS DENUDATION OF THE COLORADO PLATEAU—CROSSING THE SAGE PLAIN—RIO DE LOS MANCOS—RIO DOLORES—SECTION OF LOWER CRETACEOUS ROCKS—RUINS ON THE DOLORES—SIERRA SAN MIGUEL—SUROUARA—TIERRA BLANCA—GUAJELOTES—CAÑON PINTADO—TRIASSIC ROCKS—SAURIAN BONES—LA TENEJAL—ERODED BUTTES—CASA COLORADO—OJO VERDE—SIERRA LA SAL—EXCURSION TO GRAND RIVER—CAÑON COLORADO—PLATEAU BORDERING THE COLORADO RIVER—ERODED MONUMENTS—LABYRINTH CAÑON—RUINED BUILDINGS—SUMMIT OF THE CARBONIFEROUS FORMATION—SECTION OF TRIASSIC ROCKS—REMARKABLE COUNTRY ABOUT THE JUNCTION OF GRAND AND GREEN RIVERS—SINGULAR ERODED BUTTES AND PINNACLES—NETWORK OF CAÑONS—CAÑON OF GRAND RIVER—SECTION OF CARBONIFEROUS STRATA—TRANSVERSE SECTION OF THE COLORADO VALLEY—RETURN TO SAGE-PLAIN—JOURNEY SOUTHWARD TO THE SAN JUAN—SIERRA ABAJO.

Between the Rio de la Plata and the Rio de los Mancos we skirted the base of the extreme southern point of the Sierra de la Plata. These mountains terminate southward in a long slope, which falls down to a level of about 7,500 feet above the sea, forming a plateau which extends southward to the San Juan, the *Mesa Verde*, to which I shall soon have occasion again to refer. This mesa terminates on the west by an abrupt nearly vertical precipice from 1,200 to 1,500 feet in height. Between the mesa and the mountains is a natural pass or *puerta*, through which the Spanish trail leads where it crosses the divide. On the west this *puerta* opens to the right and left; bounded on the north by the retreating southwesterly slopes of the Sierra de la Plata, on the south by the wall-like edges of the *Mesa Verde*. As we stood on its threshold we looked far out over a great plain, to the eye as limitless as the sea; the monotonous outline of its surface varied only by two or three small island-like mountains, so distant as scarcely to rise above the horizon line. Here we were to leave the lofty sierras of the Rocky Mountain system, which had so long looked down on our camps and marches, the picturesque scenery of the foot-hills, their flowery valleys and sparkling streams, the grateful shade of their noble forests, and take our weary way across the arid expanse of the great western plateau; a region whose dreary monotony is only broken by frightful chasms, where alone the weary traveler finds shelter from the burning heat of a cloudless sun, and where he seeks, too often in vain, a cooling draught that shall slake his thirst. To us, however, as well as to all the civilized world, it was a *terra incognita*, and was viewed with eager interest, both as the scene of our future explorations and as the possible repository of truth which we might gather and add to the sum total of human knowledge.

An outline sketch of this portion of the Colorado Plateau has been already given in Chap. III, and but little more need be said to make its general features clearly comprehended. The plain which stretches westward from the Sierra de la Plata—indicated on the accompanying map, where it is called the Great Sage-plain—is part of an immense plateau which once stretched continuously far beyond the course of the Colorado. How it has been divided by the cañons of the draining streams, and how, by erosion, its plateau character has been so modified as to be locally lost, will fully appear in the progress of our geological narrative; yet no one who observes the orderly and unbroken arrangement of its underlying rocks, the perfect correspondence of the sections on opposite sides of the profound cañons which cut it, will hesitate to assent to the assertion that an unbroken table-land once stretched from the base of the Sierra de la Plata all the way across to the mountain chains west of the Colorado, and that from this plateau, grain by grain, the sedimentary materials which once filled the broad and deep valleys of the Colorado and San Juan have been removed by the currents of these streams. The mind is awestruck in the contemplation of the magnitude of the element of time which enters into the analysis of the process by which these stupendous monuments of erosion have been produced; but if the numerical faculty is baffled in the effort to count the years or ages which must have been consumed in the erosion of the valleys and cañons to which I have referred, even the imagination itself is lost when called upon to estimate the cycles on cycles during which the much grander features of the high table-lands were wrought from a plateau which once overspread most of the area of the Colorado Basin, burying the present Sage-plain 2,000 feet beneath its upper surface.

As I have before said, the Great Sage-plain is everywhere floored by the Lower Cretaceous sandstones; massive resistent strata, 300 to 500 feet in thickness. These are succeeded in the ascending series, where the upper members of the formation are present, by the Middle Cretaceous shales, principally soft argillaceous beds, from 1,200 to 1,500 feet in thickness. Above these belong the Upper Cretaceous sandstones and marls, occupying an equal vertical space. Now, over the great plateau, floored and protected by the Lower Cretaceous sandstones, are everywhere scattered mounds of greater or less elevation, composed of the Middle Cretaceous shales, and in the interval between these mounds are scattered thousands and millions of the fossils characteristic of these shale-beds, washed, like pebbles, from their soft envelope. Here we have conclusive evidence that the Middle Cretaceous shales once completely covered the sandstone-floor of the Sage-plain from which they have been nearly removed by aqueous action. As we approach the margin of the sandstone plateau, we find the mounds of overlying shale becoming more numerous and higher, until, reaching the edge of the high mesa, they blend in solid escarpments more than 1,000 feet in altitude, crowned by the massive, but soft, sandstones which form the third and upper division of the Cretaceous series.

Such are some of the facts which may be observed about the base of the Mesa

Verde, facts of which the significance will be readily appreciated; but these are not all the things that may be seen from the vicinity of our present standpoint. The Mesa Verde is, geologically, but a portion of the high table-lands which border the Upper San Juan; the northern margin of which is followed by our route from the ford of the Chama to the Mancos. Here this plateau terminates abruptly in a bold and most picturesque wall, of which the general course, though varied by many salient and re-entering angles, is nearly north and south from the Sierra de la Plata to the San Juan. This mesa we completely encircled; examined it at a thousand points, and can speak of its structure and extent with confidence. To obtain a just conception of the enormous denudation which the Colorado Plateau has suffered, no better point of view could possibly be selected than that of the summit of the Mesa Verde. The geologist here has, as it seems to me, satisfactory proof of the proposition I have before made, that, from the greater portion of the Colorado Plateau, strata more than 2,000 feet in thickness have been removed by erosion. He here has a view toward the west, limited only by the powers of human vision. Directly west the Sage-plain stretches out nearly horizontal, unmarked by any prominent feature, to the distance of a hundred miles. There the island-like mountains, the Sierra Abajo and Sierra La Sal, rise from its surface. South of these is the little doubled-peaked mountain, called by the Mexicans *Las Orejas del Oso*—the bear's ears; beyond these his vision could not reach, but our explorations enable us to tell him there lies the broad eroded valley of the Colorado, bounded by two steps, of over 1,000 feet each, below the level of the Sage-plain, and in the bottom of that valley, the chasm of the Colorado Cañon, whose perpendicular walls are 1,500 feet in height; beyond the trough of the Colorado, a plateau corresponding to the Sage-plain, and beyond this a representative of the Mesa Verde. Looking southwest, he would see the Sage-plain terminated in that direction by the excavated valley of the San Juan; beyond this its representatives of similar character and elevation; higher and more distant than these, the long perspective lines of the lofty mesas north and west of the Moqui villages; the precise counterpart of that on which he is supposed to stand.

On the northern margin of the plateau, we are assured by those who have been there that the constituent rocks of the Mesa Verde are exposed, holding the same positions as here. Are we not then driven by these facts to conclude that, over all this area of undisturbed sedimentary rocks, surrounded by table-lands composed of like strata, presenting corresponding, but now widely separated faces, these strata once stretched in unbroken connection; and that, from the great interval, where now wanting, they have been removed by the same all-potent influence which has left such grand and so similar records in the cañons of the Colorado and its tributaries.

The geology of the country lying between the Sierra La Plata and Sierra Abajo is so monotonous as to require no lengthy description; all that need be said of it is in brief notes of our different days' marches contained in my journal. From these I make the following extracts:

"*August 10th, Camp 21, on Rio Dolores.*—The Rio de los Mancos is a clear mountain stream, formed by two branches, which unite just below our camp, and which rise in the foot-hills of the Sierra de la Plata, on its western side. Each of the two branches is about the size of the La Plata; they flow through a pretty valley, and are bordered by thickets of willow and alder, and groves of pine and cottonwood. As usual, at such high elevation, the cottonwood is all of the narrow-leaved species—*Populus angustifolia*. The immediate banks of the Mancos are at this point composed of the black shales, which overlie the Lower Cretaceous sandstones, containing *Ostrea congesta*, *Inoceramus problematicus*, &c. Very near camp (19) is a clear, cold spring, of which the water is highly charged with sulphuretted hydrogen; another of the mineral springs flowing from the dark Cretaceous shales, so common in New Mexico, where they are known as *Ojos heriondos*. Soon after leaving the Mancos, we came upon the Lower Cretaceous sandstones, which form the surface-rock to the Dolores. These sandstones are covered in places by detached hills of overlying shales and light-blue limestone, as usual, crowded with their characteristic fossils. The sandstones below are exposed in all the ravines which we crossed, and in nearly every locality where I examined them, I found in them impressions of angiospermous leaves, *Populus*, *Salix*, *Quercus*, &c. After traveling 15 miles, we descended into a narrow valley of erosion, traversed by a small clear stream, a tributary of the Dolores. The walls of the valley are in places nearly perpendicular, and are composed of the Lower Cretaceous sandstones, of which some 200 feet are exposed. These are generally yellow and coarse, but alternate with laminated, greenish, ripple-marked layers, beds of greenish and gray shales, and occasional bands of lignite. Nearly all contain the impressions of the stems of plants and dicotyledonous leaves, similar to those so frequently before seen in the same formation. The lowest stratum visible at this point, is a fine-grained compact sandstone, very uniform in texture, and as white as loaf-sugar; a most beautiful building material."

The country lying between the Mancos and Dolores is generally dry and sterile, yet is everywhere covered with fragments of broken pottery, showing its former occupation by a considerable number of inhabitants; it is now utterly deserted. Near the mountains it is pretty well timbered; further west, trees become more scattered and smaller, the pines confined to the narrow valleys, the uplands dotted with groves of piñon and cedar, with wide intervals covered with sage-bushes and soap-plant, *Yucca angustifolia*. The Dolores rises on the west side of the Sierra de la Plata, many miles north of our route, and is here a clear, rapid stream, as large as the San Juan at the Pagosa. It runs through a beautiful but narrow valley, several hundred feet below the surface of the surrounding country. This is a valley of excavation, cut in the Lower Cretaceous rocks, which form bluffs on either side over 200 feet high, in many places perpendicular. The bottom-lands are nearly level, half a mile wide, and very fertile, covered with fine grass, with groves of cottonwood and willow, and scattered trees of yellow pine. Near the river the thickets are overgrown with virgin's bower and hop, which form almost impenetrable jungles. Great numbers of flowers ornament the open grounds, generally of the species so common in the valleys before passed through.

The bluffs bounding the river below our camp show the following section:

1. Soil with rolled gravel and bowlders, drift from the Sierra de la Plata, principally white and black porphyry like that on the Mancos and La Plata.

Capt. J.N. Macomb, Exp. in New Mexico & Utah.

RIO DOLORES & SIERRA DE LA PLATA
FROM NEAR CAMP 21.

Plate V.

2. Dark-blue calcareous shales with bands of dove-colored limestone, weathering light-ash, with thinner layers of brown sandy limestone.

In the shales are imbedded great numbers of *Gryphæa Pitcheri*, generally of small size but beautifully perfect. They exhibit a great variety of form, some being very high and narrow; others broader, like the typical *G. Pitcheri;* others nearly orbicular, like *G. dilatata* of the Oxford clay; others still broader, with a transverse diameter considerably greater than the antero-posterior. Between these various forms are connecting links which seem to prove that all belong to one species. The dove-colored limestones, here as on the Chama and Canadian, contain almost exclusively *Inoceramus problematicus*, and also exhibit the peculiar fracture noticed in the localities mentioned above, and others, on exposure, cracking horizontally into concavo-convex chip-like fragments, having sharp edges.

The ferruginous layers represent the fish-bed of the Pagosa, the Chama, the Canadian, &c., a clearly defined geological horizon throughout all the Cretaceous area of New Mexico; they contain here *Ostrea lugubris* and many fragments of *Inoceramus I. problematicus* and a much larger species probably not described.

3. Coarse yellow sandstone, often a conglomerate, containing impressions of dicotyledonous leaves, *Salix*, &c., and thin bands of lignite.

4. Greenish or light-brown soft calcareous sandstone, with local layers of blue clay-shale and thin seams of lignite; no fossils observed.

5. Thick-bedded light-yellow or white sandstone, locally coarse or fine, sometimes a conglomerate containing quartz pebbles, generally fine-grained and nearly white; no fossils.

6. Green or purple clay stones and shales.

7. Soft greenish sandstone.

Most of the strata enumerated above are exposed in the cliffs bordering the valley; for several miles are entirely unbroken, conformable throughout, and have a gentle dip to the west. The facts here observed are of special interest as deciding beyond all appeal the question of the relative age of the sandstone group containing angiospermous leaves, so marked a feature in the geology of New Mexico. This is but one of the great number of cases where these sandstones were found overlaid by strata containing well known Cretaceous fossils. It is to be hoped that this mooted question will now be considered settled, since it must be so in the mind of every honest investigator.

From the summit of the hill from which the preceding section was taken, we obtained a magnificent view of a wide extent of country lying on every side of us. In the east the Sierra de la Plata rose as a high and unbroken wall, presenting a more varied outline than when seen from the other side; south of the Sierra, the *puerta* through which we had passed; beyond this, stretching far off southward, the green slopes and lofty battlements of the Mesa Verde beetling over the plain like some high and rock-bound coast above the level ocean; south, and near us, the miniature peak and chain of La Late; far more distant, the Sierras Carriso and Tunecha in the Navajo country; occupying the whole western horizon the monotonous expanse of the Sage-plain, beyond which rose the low summits of the Orejas del Oso, Sierra Abajo, and

Sierra la Sal. In the north appeared a new and grand topographical feature. From N. 10° W. to N. E. magnetic stretched a chain of great mountains, higher and more picturesque than any we had seen. These have no common name, but one of the peaks is called, from the stream which washes its base, Sierra San Miguel.

Whether these mountains form a single chain or several, and what is their prevailing trend cannot be said with certainty without closer inspection; the overlapping lines of their bases, which would decide that question, being concealed by intervening highlands. I should infer, however, from the view we had of them, that they represent several distinct ranges, with a trend nearly north and south, set *en échelon*. Between the most easterly of these mountains and the Sierra de la Plata is a low gap, in which stands a remarkable pinnacle of rock; even at a distance of seventy or eighty miles a striking object. One of the mountains in this group bears a large surface of snow, and its height cannot be less than 13,000 feet. Several others are nearly as lofty, and are cones of great beauty.

The hill from which we obtained this view is crowned with an extensive series of very ancient ruins. The principal one is a pueblo, nearly 100 feet square, once substantially built of dressed stone, now a shapeless heap, in which the plan of the original structure can, however, be traced. Like most of the ruined pueblos of New Mexico, it consisted of a series of small rooms clustered together, like cells in a beehive. Near the principal edifice are mounds of stone, representing subordinate buildings. Among these are numerous large depressions marking the places of cisterns or *estuffas*. Quantities of broken pottery, similar to that so commonly seen in like circumstances, but bearing the marks of great age, strew the ground about these ruins.

A mile or two up the river are several other stone houses built high up in the cliffs, 150 feet above the stream; they are usually placed on ledges covered by projecting rocks, which act as roofs. These houses are not large, and were probably only occupied by the guardians of the fields once in cultivation below. All of these, as well as the more extensive ruins before mentioned, are admirably located for defense, and would be easily held by a handful of determined men against any number of assailants armed only with the weapons of savage warfare.

Between our camp on the Dolores and Surouara no new geological feature was noticed. The Lower Cretaceous sandstones everywhere form the rocky substratum, here and there covered with patches of the overlying shale. From these shale-beds millions of Gryphæas have washed out, covering the surface and rattling under the mule's feet like gravel-stones. Sage is the predominant vegetation, and no water is found in the interval; yet we passed several ruined buildings, and broken pottery is scattered everywhere.

Surouaro is the name of a ruined town which must once have contained a population of several thousands. The name is said to be of Indian (Utah) origin, and to signify desolation, and certainly no better could have been selected. The surrounding country is hopelessly sterile; and, whatever it once may have been, Surouaro is now desolate enough. Here are two cañons, cut in the sandstone by two former streams. These unite nearly a mile below camp. All the interval of mesa between them is covered with ruins. The houses are, many of them, large, and all built of stone, hammer-dressed on the exposed faces. Fragments of pottery are exceedingly common, though, like the buildings, showing great age. There is every evidence that a large population resided here for many years, perhaps centuries, and that they deserted it several hundred years ago; that they were Pueblo Indians, and hence peaceful, industrious, and agricultural. How they managed to exist here, and how their town was depopulated, are questions that suggest themselves at once, but certainly the former is the more puzzling. They may have been exterminated by the Navajos and Utahs, warlike and aggressive tribes who occupy the adjacent region; but where a population of many thousands once existed, now as many hundreds could not be sustained, either by agriculture or the chase. The surrounding country contains very little animal life, and almost none of it is now cultivable. It is 7,000 feet in altitude, intensely cold in winter, and very dry throughout the year. The want of water alone would forbid the residence of any considerable number of persons at Surouaro if everything else were furnished them. The arroyos, through which streams seem to have once flowed, are now dry, and it was only with great difficulty that sufficient water was obtained for the supply of our train. The remains of *metates* (corn-mills) are abundant about the ruins, and corn was doubtless the staple article of their existence, but none could now be raised here. The ruins of several large reservoirs, built of masonry, may be seen at Surouaro, and there are traces of *acequias*, which led to these, through which water was brought perhaps from a great distance. At first sight the difficulties in the way of obtaining a supply of water for any considerable population at this point would seem insurmountable, and the readiest solution of the problem would be to infer a change of climate, by which this region was made uninhabitable. Such a conclusion is not *necessary*, however, for the skill and industry of the ancient inhabitants of the arid table-lands of New Mexico and Arizona achieved wonders in the way of procuring a supply of water. Sometimes this was done by carefully collecting, in cisterns of masonry, every drop of a trickling spring; sometimes by canals, through which water was brought from long distances. The Moqui villages are now supplied, though rather scantily, by such means, where, if the cisterns were to fall into ruins, a single traveler could hardly find water enough for himself and horse.

From Surouaro to the base of the Sierra Abajo our experience was exceedingly monotonous. The physical aspects of the country are everywhere the same, and its geological structure equally unvaried. The Lower Cretaceous sandstones here lie nearly level, but are exposed in all the ravines, generally dry, which we crossed, while low mounds of the overlying shales were almost constantly in sight; their characteristic fossils lying about in such profusion that thousands of tons of them might have been collected.

After leaving the immediate vicinity of the mountains, no beds of drift or transported materials of any kind were met with, and it is evident that the denudation which the strata once covering the Sage-plain have suffered has not been effected by any deep and wide-spread currents by which this country has been swept, but by the quiet and long-continued action of atmospheric influences—rains, frosts, &c. No flowing stream was met with in all this part of our route, and we were compelled to depend for our supply of water upon the springs or pools to which we were led by the trail we were following. At the Tierra Blanca we encamped at the finest of these springs which we saw. Here the water issues from the base of a low cliff of sandstone, of which the surfaces are whitened by a saline efflorescence, consisting in a great degree of chloride of sodium; a phenomenon which has given to the locality the name it bears.

Our next stopping place was at the Guajolotes, a large pool of bad surface-water; a natural reservoir in the sandstone rocks, containing great numbers of water-lizards—*Siredon*—called by the Mexicans guajolotes.

The Ojo del Cuerbo is a small spring similar to that of the Tierra Blanca, except that the water is less abundant and is sulphurous.

We had here approached comparatively near to the Sierras Abajo and La Sal, the one being twenty, the other forty miles distant. Of isolated mountain groups the La Sal is considerably the higher and more extensive; both are, however, of insignificant dimensions as compared with the lofty ranges of the Sierra San Miguel.

Up to this point we had constantly met with fragments of broken pottery scattered over the surface, and had frequently seen traces of ruined buildings.

CAÑON PINTADO.

Between the Sierras Abajo and La Sal passes a natural line of drainage, marked above by a formidable cañon, which furrows the Sage-plain many miles up toward the Sierra San Miguel. North of the Sierra Abajo this cañon terminates, or rather it opens to the right and left, its walls extending to the bases of the two groups of mountains I have mentioned, forming here the western terminus of the Sage-plain. To reach the second and lower plateau it is necessary to descend the cliffs which are formed by the cut edge of the first; this we did, following the Spanish trail, at a point about fifteen miles northeast of the Sierra Abajo, where a lateral cañon enters the great one I have described a few miles above its mouth. Here we descended at once more than 1,000 feet, leaving behind us the plateau of the Sage-plain, with its unvarying topography and monotonous Cretaceous geology, to enter the great eroded valley of the Colorado; a region of which the geology is all Triassic or Jurassic, and where the scenery exhibits all the brilliant colors which characterize the rocks of these formations in the West, combined with all the variety of form which erosion can produce. From the vivid colors of the walls of the cañon where we entered it, it was named by our party Cañon Pintado. Its walls are precipitous, generally almost perpendicular, the lower half composed of strata which are bright red, green, yellow or white; soft but massive beds weathering, as such materials are so prone to do in this region, into arches, domes, spires, towers, and a thousand other imitations of human architecture, all on a colossal scale. The bottom is smooth and nearly level, in many places covered with the finest gama grass, in others with the salt-bush (*Sarcobatus*).

A section of the rocks exposed in the cañon is as follows, the thickness of the strata being estimated:

Section of the cliffs of Cañon Pintado.

		Feet.
1.	Coarse yellow sandstone, floor of Sage-plain	200
2.	Gray and green shales, interstratified with coarse gray sandstones and yellow conglomerate	250
3.	Red and green shales, with bands of whitish and greenish sandstone, with silicified wood and Saurian bones	350
4.	Yellow and red massive calcareous sandstones	200

In the foregoing section No. 1 is the Lower Cretaceous sandstone forming the surface-rock over all the country lying between the Sierra La Plata and Sierra Abajo. A short distance back from the cañon it is overlaid by patches of shale with Gryphæas, and therefore represents the surface of the Lower Cretaceous group. No. 2 is probably also Cretaceous, though here containing no fossils by which this question could be determined with certainty. A group of rocks, having similar lithological characters, at the Moqui villages, lies between the red beds below and the massive leaf-bearing sandstones above, and there contains *Ammonites percarinatus* and other Lower Cretaceous fossils. As will be seen in the progress of our geological narrative, at intermediate points on the San Juan a thickness of several hundred feet of soft green sandstones and green sandy shales separates the coarse yellow sandstones (the floor of the Sage-plain) from the red gypsiferous rocks below. Until fossils shall be discovered in these beds, it will be impossible to draw any sharply defined line marking the base of the Cretaceous formation; and since the strata are here everywhere conformable, it is extremely doubtful whether any such line of demarcation exists in nature.

Saurian bones.—On the north side of the cañon just opposite our camp (26), in the face of the cliff, about 250 feet above its base, I discovered the bones of a large Saurian. Probably the greater part of the skeleton is still imbedded in the rock, as, although I spent two days, with several assistants, in excavating at this point, the tools at our command were too light for such heavy work as it proved to be, and we were compelled to leave many bones, which we could see, but had not the means to extricate from their envelopes. The special object of our efforts, the head, was not reached, but still remains to reward some future geologist who shall visit this interesting locality, with more time at his command and more adequate implements for rock excavation than we possessed. The bones we obtained were mainly those of the extremities: a femur entire; the greater part of a humerus; several of the phalanges of the toes; portions of the ribs, and other large and, to me, quite incomprehensible bones. All of these have been placed in the hands of the distinguished anatomist, Professor Leidy, who will make them the subject of a special report. The size of the animal, as indicated by these bones, must have been very large. The femur taken out measured 30 inches in length, by 4 in diameter, at its smallest part, the articulations being much thicker. A portion of the scapula which was taken out was 22 inches long and 16 wide at the broadest part, and this but a fragment.

Near the locality where the larger skeleton was found a part of a rib of a smaller individual was picked up, and on the opposite side of the valley a shapeless fragment of a large bone was found at the foot of the cliff. From these facts it is evident that the Gypsum formation, usually so entirely barren of fossils, would here well repay labor spent in its examination; and it is greatly to be desired that future explorers of this far-off region will make an earnest effort to obtain what is, perhaps, here alone obtainable, the means of settling the vexed question of the parallelism of the Gypsum formation with deposits whose age has been accurately determined elsewhere.

In the same stratum with the Saurian bones I discovered the only fossil shells I have ever seen from that group of rocks in New Mexico. These have the form of *Natica*, but are probably not susceptible of accurate classification.

Three miles below our "Saurian camp" (26), we reached the mouth of the Cañon Pintado, which here opens out on to the second step of the table-lands in the descent to the Colorado. The surface-rock of this plateau is everywhere the soft, massive, calcareous sandstone or indurated marl which forms the base of the section in Cañon Pintado. It is a comparatively soft rock, and contains a great deal of gypsum, very uniformly disseminated. It lies in thick beds, scarcely separated by any distinct partings, and yet exhibits the most striking examples of oblique stratification which have ever come under my observation; the inclined layers, which compose some of the beds, forming an angle of 30° and 40° with the primary planes of stratification, which are horizontal. The slopes of the inclined layers are often 50 or 60 feet in length, with a rise of 20 or 30, showing that they were deposited from water, at times very much agitated. The colors of this rock are always very decided, but, in the same stratum, or on the same horizon, they are exceedingly local; a lemon or orange yellow being succeeded quite abruptly by rose-red, and this again by white. The prevailing shade is, however, a red, deep blood-red, or some lighter tint, such as brick-red, rose-tint, or flesh-color. It is a rather remarkable fact, that with such inclined and contorted layers of deposition this rock should include so little coarse material, and it is impossible to resist the conclusion that it is far more a chemical than mechanical precipitate, and that the period of its deposition was the commencement of a great epoch, during which peculiar physical conditions prevailed over not only the greater part of our continent, but of the world, so peculiar and so widespread that we may almost call them cosmical.

Everywhere over the second plateau are scattered buttes and pinnacles, wrought, from the massive calcareous sandstone and the overlying Saurian beds, by the erosion which has swept from this surface all traces but these of the immense mass of sedimentary rocks which once covered it. Of these one of the most striking seen from our route is the Casa Colorado, represented on Plate VI. It is a detached butte, some 300 feet in height, composed of red sandstone covered with the harder layers of the Saurian beds. Another symmetrical and beautiful dome, composed of the same materials, is lemon-yellow, with a base of red.

Our camps 27 and 28 were on what I have called the second plateau. Of these the first was at La Tenejal, a deep excavation in the red sandstone, which retains so large a quantity of surface-water, and for so long a time, as to become an important watering-place on the Spanish trail. These natural reservoirs are frequently met with in this region, and during the dry season are of vital importance not only to such travelers as may be passing through it, but also to the small number of animals which here make their home. It is not at all uncommon to meet with them even on the summits

CASA COLORADO & LA SAL-MOUNTAINS.
LOOKING NORTHERLY.

of the sandstone buttes, which I have described, and it has often happened to me, after a fatiguing climb to the top of some high cliff or pinnacle, to find its smooth-washed summit-rock scooped out in cavities from 2 to 20 feet in diameter, holding sometimes many barrels of the clearest rain-water, and affording me the two rarest possible luxuries in this arid region—a drink of pure water and a cleansing and refreshing bath.

The Ojo Verde is a copious spring in a cañon cut out of the red sandstone, ten miles west of La Tencja. The surrounding country is very sterile, sparsely set with sage bushes and small cedars, but about the spring the bottom of the cañon is covered with the greenest and most luxuriant grass. The La Sal Mountain shows very finely from this point, distant twenty miles. It is seen to be composed of several short ranges, separated by narrow valleys, having a trend several degrees north of east, but these are set somewhat *en échelon*, and the direction of the longest diameter of the mountain mass is north-northwest and south-southeast; such, at least, seems to be the structure of this sierra as seen from a distance. Perhaps closer inspection would show that the view obtained from this point was in some respects deceptive. Of the composition of the Sierra La Sal we know nothing except what was taught by the drifted materials brought down in the cañons through which the drainage from it flows. Of this transported material we saw but little, but that consisted mainly of trachytes and porphyry, indicating that it is composed of erupted rocks similar to those which form the Sierra Abajo, of which it is in fact almost an exact counterpart. From the cliffs over Ojo Verde we could see the strata composing both the upper and second plateaus, rising from the east, south, and southwest on to the base of the Sierra La Sal, each conspicuous stratum being distinctly traceable in the walls of the cañons and valleys which head in the sierra. It is evident, therefore, that the rocks composing the Colorado Plateau are there locally upheaved, precisely as around the Sierra Abajo and the other isolated mountains which I have already before enumerated, and to which I shall have occasion again to refer.

VALLEY OF THE COLORADO.

The general features of the trough of the Colorado, at the junction of Grand and Green Rivers, have been already sketched, but the detailed description of our explorations of this remarkable region yet remains to be given. From the difficulties in the way of such exploration, reported by our scouts, it was not thought advisable to attempt to reach the river with our entire party. A depot camp was therefore established at Ojo Verde, where most of the men and animals remained, while a small detachment, with which I was connected, made the desired reconnoissance of this part of our route. Of this excursion I find in my journal the following descriptive notes:

August 22.—Started this morning for the junction of Grand and Green Rivers, Captain Macomb, Lieutenant Cogswell, Mr. Dimmock, Mr. Campeau, myself, and three servants forming the party. On leaving camp we struck southwest, gradually ascending for six miles, when we reached the brink of a magnificent cañon twelve hundred feet in depth, called, from the prevailing color of its walls, Cañon Colorado, into which with great difficulty we descended. The summits of the cliffs are here nearly five hundred feet above the Ojo Verde, composed of the same rock exposed there, the base of the section in Cañon Pintado. The sandstone is here yellow or straw-color, very massive, without fossils, and very remarkably cross-stratified. About four hundred feet of this stratum are here exposed.

Below this succeed one hundred and fifty feet of red, foliated sandstone, with some bands of red shale, precisely like the red sandstones of New Jersey and the Connecticut River Valley. Below this two hundred and seventy feet of reddish-brown sandstone, very massive, forming perpendicular faces. Still below, a series of green and red thin-bedded sandstones and red and purple shales, three hundred and fifty feet in thickness. The strata here rise gently to the westward, till, at a point ten miles from Camp 28, a low anticlinal crosses our route. From thence to the river the dip is westward. This part of the cañon is exceedingly grand and beautiful, both from the form and coloring of its walls. A few piñons and cedars cling to the sides and crown the summits of the walls, while scattered cottonwoods and thickets of willow, with here and there a small tree of a new and peculiar species of ash, form a narrow thread of vegetation along its bottom. This, and many similar gorges, form the channels through which the drainage of the western slope of the Sierra Abajo reaches the Colorado. Twelve miles west from the Ojo Verde the several cañons unite by the elimination of their dividing walls, and debouch into a comparatively open country. Descending the cañon we, therefore, at its mouth come out upon a third distinct plateau, from which the mesa cut by the Cañon Colorado has been removed; its edges receding in magnificent broken walls south and northwest. From this point the view swept westward over a wide extent of country, in its general aspects a plain, but everywhere deeply cut by a tangled maze of cañons, and thickly set with towers, castles, and spires of most varied and striking forms; the most wonderful monuments of erosion which our eyes, already experienced in objects of this kind, had beheld. Near the mesa we were leaving stand detached portions of it of every possible form, from broad, flat tables to slender cones crowned with pinnacles of the massive sandstone which forms the perpendicular faces of the walls of the Cañon Colorado. These castellated buttes are from one thousand to fifteen hundred feet in height, and no language is adequate to convey a just idea of the strange and impressive scenery formed by their grand and varied outlines. Toward the west the view reached some thirty miles, there bounded by long lines and bold angles of mesa walls similar to those behind us, while in the intervening space the surface was diversified by columns, spires, castles, and battlemented towers of colossal but often beautiful proportions, closely resembling elaborate structures of art, but in effect far surpassing the most imposing monuments of human skill. In the southwest was a long line of spires of white stone, standing on red bases, thousands in number, but so slender as to recall the most delicate carving in ivory or the fairy architecture of some Gothic cathedral; yet many, perhaps most, were over five hundred feet in height, and thickly set in a narrow belt or series some miles in length. Their appearance was so strange and beautiful as to call out exclamations of delight from all our party.

Next to the pinnacles the most striking objects in our view were buttes of dark, chocolate-colored rock, which had weathered into exact imitation of some of the feudal castles of the Old World; yet, like all the other features in the scene, they were on a

LONG BRIDGE OF HOUSES ON CAPRI, LABYRINTH ROUTE.

gigantic scale. These buttes are composed of the liver-colored sandstones and chocolate shales of the walls of the Cañon Colorado, which consist of a great number of alternations of thinner or thicker layers of sandstone with those of shale. This structure in erosion gives rise to many curious and beautiful results, such as a beaded appearance in columns, while harder or thicker layers form their capitals and bases. It also produces what seem to be walls of masonry, with frieze and cornice.

Soon after issuing from the mouth of Cañon Colorado, the little intermittent stream which traverses it begins to cut the floor of the rocky plain that borders the Colorado River, and, following that stream as the only possible avenue through which we could reach our destination, we were soon buried in a deep and narrow gorge, which is thence continuous till it joins the greater cañon of Grand River. This cañon, from its many windings and the many branches which open into it, we designated by the name of Labyrinth Cañon. Its walls are from one to two hundred feet in height, so that there is no egress from it for many miles. The bottom is occupied with cotton-woods, and thickets of narrow-leaved willow, cane, and salt-bush; all of which, with fallen rocks, quicksands, and deep water-holes, made the passage through it almost impossible. Some two miles below the head of Labyrinth Cañon we came upon the ruins of a large number of houses of stone, evidently built by the Pueblo Indians, as they are similar to those on the Dolores, and the pottery scattered about is identical with that before found in so many places. It is very old but of excellent quality, made of red clay coated with white, and handsomely figured. Here the houses are built in the sides of the cliffs. A mile or two below we saw others crowning the inaccessible summits—inaccessible except by ladders—of picturesque detached buttes of red sandstone, which rise to the height of one hundred and fifty feet above the bottom of the cañon. Similar buildings were found lower down, and broken pottery was picked up upon the summits of the cliffs overhanging Grand River; evidence that these dreadful cañons were once the homes of families belonging to that great people formerly spread over all this region now so utterly sterile, solitary, and desolate.

At the ruined pueblos we reached the surface of the Carboniferous formation; having passed through the entire thickness of the Gypsum series since leaving the Sage-plain.

The complete section of the walls of the Cañon Colorado continued to this point, is as follows:

		Feet.
1.	Yellow massive calcareous sandstone, base of preceding section	400
2.	Red micaceous sandstones, interstratified with red shales	150
3.	Red and brown massive sandstone	270
4.	Green and red shelly sandstones, and red shales, softer than No. 2	350
5.	Greenish-gray micaceous conglomerate	15
6.	Red and purple shale	60
7.	Grayish sandstone	18
8.	Chocolate and purple soft sandstones and shales in thin bands	275
9.	Soft liver-colored and white sandstone	75
10.	Brick-colored massive, calcareous sandstone, weathering into towers and bottle-shaped buttes	80

	Feet.
11. Liver-colored sandstone	15
12. Gray limestone	2
13. Brick-red sandstone, like No. 10	25
14. Chocolate sandstone, like Nos. 8 and 11	12
15. Blue limestone, containing *Athyris subtilita*, *Spirifer cameratus*, &c., and other Carboniferous fossils.	

Descending the cañon till night came upon us, we made our camp under the overhanging cliffs on the north side, where some pot-holes in the rocky bottom promised us a supply of water.

August 23, *Camp* 29 *to Grand River.*—Leaving servants and packs in camp, we to-day descended the Cañon of Labyrinth Creek, to its junction with Grand River. Until within a mile of the junction, the character of the cañon remains the same; a narrow gorge, with vertical sides, from 150 to 300 feet in height, its bottom thickly grown with bushes and obstructed with fallen rocks and timber, passable but with infinite difficulty. At the place mentioned above, however, our progress was arrested by a perpendicular fall, some 200 feet in height, occupying the whole breadth of the cañon, and to reach Grand River it was necessary to scale the walls which shut us in. This we accomplished with some difficulty on the south side, to find ourselves upon the level of the rocky plain into which we sunk when entering the cañon. The view we here obtained was most interesting, yet too limited to satisfy us. Looking down into the cañon we had been following, we could see it deepening by successive falls until, a mile below, it opened into the greater Cañon of Grand River, a dark yawning chasm, with vertical sides, in which we caught glimpses of the river 1,500 feet below where we stood. On every side we were surrounded by columns, pinnacles, and castles of fantastic shapes, which limited our view, and by impassable cañons, which restricted our movements. South of us, about a mile distant, rose one of the castle-like buttes, which I have already mentioned, and to which, though with difficulty, we made our way. This butte was composed of alternate layers of chocolate-colored sandstone and shale, about 1,000 feet in height; its sides nearly perpendicular, but most curiously ornamented with columns and pilasters, porticos and colonnades, cornices and battlements, flanked here and there with tall outstanding towers, and crowned with spires so slender that it seemed as though a breath of air would suffice to topple them from their foundations. To accomplish the object for which we had come so far, it seemed necessary that we should ascend this butte. The day was perfectly clear and intensely hot; the mercury standing at 92° in the shade, and the red sandstone, out of which the landscape was carved, glowed in the heat of the burning sunshine. Stripping off nearly all our clothing, we made the attempt, and after two hours of most arduous labor succeeded in reaching the summit. The view which there burst upon us was such as amply repaid us for all our toil. It baffles description, however, and I can only hope that our sketches will give some faint idea of its strange and unearthly character.

The great cañon of the Lower Colorado, with its cliffs a mile in height, affords grander and more impressive scenes, but those having far less variety and beauty of detail than this. From the pinnacle on which we stood the eye swept over an area some fifty miles in diameter, everywhere marked by features of more than ordinary

Capt. J. N. Macomb. Exp. in New Mexico & Utah.

Plate VII.

HEAD OF LABYRINTH CREEK, LOOKING SOUTH-EASTERLY

interest; lofty lines of massive mesas rising in successive steps to form the frame of the picture; the interval between them more than 2,000 feet below their summits. A great basin or sunken plain lay stretched out before us as on a map. Not a particle of vegetation was anywhere discernible; nothing but bare and barren rocks of rich and varied colors shimmering in the sunlight. Scattered over the plain were thousands of the fantastically formed buttes to which I have so often referred in my notes; pyramids, domes, towers, columns, spires, of every conceivable form and size. Among these by far the most remarkable was the forest of Gothic spires, first and imperfectly seen as we issued from the mouth of the Cañon Colorado. Nothing I can say will give an adequate idea of the singular and surprising appearance which they presented from this new and advantageous point of view. Singly, or in groups, they extend like a belt of timber for a distance of several miles. Nothing in nature or in art offers a parallel to these singular objects, but some idea of their appearance may be gained by imagining the island of New York thickly set with spires like that of Trinity church, but many of them full twice its height. Scarcely less striking features in the landscape were the innumerable cañons by which the plain is cut. In every direction they ran and ramified deep, dark, and ragged, impassable to everything but the winged bird. Of these the most stupendous was that of Grand River, which washes two sides of the base of the pinnacle on which we stood, a narrow chasm, as we estimated, full 1,500 feet in depth, into which the sun scarcely seemed to penetrate. At the bottom the whole breadth of this cañon is occupied by the turbid waters of Grand River, here a sluggish stream, at least with no current visible to us who were more than 2,000 feet above it. In this great artery a thousand lateral tributaries terminate, flowing through channels precisely like that of Labyrinth Creek; underground passages by which intermittent floods from the distant highlands are conducted through this country, producing upon it no other effect than constantly to deepen their own beds. Toward the south the cañon of Grand River was easily traced. Perhaps four miles below our position it is joined by another great chasm coming in from the northwest, said by the Indians to be that of Green River. From the point where we were it was inaccessible, but we had every reason to credit their report in reference to it.

After reaching the elevated point from which we obtained this view, I neglected to take the rest I so much needed, but spent the little time at my command in endeavoring to put on paper some of the more striking features of the scene before us. Standing on the highest point, I made a hasty panoramic sketch of the entire landscape. The effort had, however, nearly cost me dear; for before I had completed the circle of the horizon I was seized with dreadful headache, giddiness, and nausea, and, alone as I then was, had the greatest difficulty in rejoining my companions.

The greater part of the walls of the cañon of Grand River are formed of Carboniferous rocks; the summits of the cliffs are, however, composed of Triassic red sandstone, the equivalent of those resting on the Carboniferous limestone on the Little Colorado and in the valley of the Pecos. The Carboniferous cannot, therefore, be said to be the surface formation anywhere in this region, as it is nowhere exposed except in the trough of the Colorado, and there in the cañons. The composition of that portion of this formation to which I had access in the cañon of Labyrinth Creek is as follows; the Triassic sandstone resting on the upper member of the section:

13 s f

Section of Carboniferous rocks in Labyrinth Cañon.

	Feet.
1. Blue slaty argillaceous limestone, with nodules of chert, and containing crinoidal columns in great numbers, *Athyris subtilita, Bellerophon, Productus, &c.*	20
2. Massive blue limestone, portions of which are quite sandy, generally variable in color and composition	50
3. Slaty blue argillaceous limestone, somewhat cherty, crowded with fossils, among which are *Athyris subtilita, Spirifer cameratus, Productus semireticulatus, P. scabriculus, P. Rogersi, P. punctatus, P. nodosus, Orthisina umbraculum, Myalina ampla, Pleurotomaria excelsa*—a large and fine new species—*Allorisma subcuneata*, &c	40
4. Red shale, no fossils	6
5. Bluish-white, red or mottled sandy limestone, no fossils	35
6. Red calcareous shale, no fossils	7
7. Red or bluish-white, mottled sandy limestone, massive, no fossils	25
8. Coarse blood-red sandstone, in some localities becoming red shale, no fossils	22
9. Hard blue cherty limestone, with a few fossils of the same species found in No. 3	36

The last number of the series forms the fall or precipice which stopped our progress down the cañon. The remainder of the section was inaccessible to us; as seen from above it seemed to consist of alternations of strata, similar to those already enumerated. If we may judge of the thickness of the Carboniferous formation in this vicinity by what it is lower down on the Colorado, we cannot suppose that the base of the series is reached in the cañon of Grand River.

On comparing this exposure of the Carboniferous strata with that at Santa Fé, described in Chapter II of this report, and those of the banks of the Colorado below the mouth of the Little Colorado, noticed in my report to Lieutenant Ives, Chapter VI, pp. 60 and 62, it will be seen that the fossils are generally identical; that, while two or three new species were added in each locality to the Carboniferous fauna of the Mississippi Valley, most of them are the same with the most common and characteristic fossils of our Coal-Measures in Illinois, Ohio, and Pennsylvania.

In lithological characters there is a general correspondence between all the localities in New Mexico where the Carboniferous rocks are fully exposed, but at Santa Fé there is a greater proportion of coarse material, sandstones and conglomerates, than at the more western localities. At Santa Fé, too, we find land-plants, characteristic Coal-Measure forms, and even a thin bed of coal; all of which indicate the immediate proximity of dry land.

Too little was learned of the lower part of the series on Grand River to enable me to institute a fair comparison between the Carboniferous rocks at this locality and those on Cataract Creek, 150 miles below. In the upper part of the formation we find, however, here as there, cherty limestones with similar fossils, but the great beds of gypsum of Cataract Creek are certainly wanting here.

Combining the sections exposed at different points along our route in our descent, step by step, from the summit of the Mesa Verde to the cañon of Grand River, we have the following *résumé* of the strata and formations passed through:

HEAD OF CAÑON, COLORADO
EROSION OF TRIASSIC SERIES.

General section of the Valley of the Colorado.

No.	Strata.	Feet.	Formation.	Locality.
1	Soft, yellow sandstone, alternating with gray, purple, and greenish marls, containing silicified coniferous wood................	600	Cretaceous.	Mesa Verde.
2	Dark bitumino-calcareous shales, with concretions and thin bands of compact blue limestone weathering yellow. Fossils in the upper part, immediately beneath No. 1, *Ammonites placenta, Baculites anceps, Aporrhais Newberryi*, &c.; toward the lower part, *Inoceramus, Nautilus, Ostrea congesta*, fish-scales	1,200	.... do	Do.
3	Gray or dark-brown shales, with bands of dove-colored limestone weathering white, and thin layers of brown sandy limestone. Fossils: *Gryphæa Pitcheri, Inoceramus problematicus, I. fragilis, Ammonites percarinatus, A. Macombi, Ostrea lugubris, O. uniformis, Ptychodus Whipplei, Lamna Texana*, &c.......................	150	.... do	Sage-plain.
4	Coarse, yellow sandstone, sometimes interstratified with beds of shale and lignite. Fossils: Leaves of angiospermous plants, *Salix, Quercus*, &c..	250	.... do	Do.
5	Green and gray shales, and soft green or yellowish sandstones or conglomerate	200	.... do	Edge of Sage-plain.
6	Red and green shales, with bands of soft, white, red or greenish micaceous sandstones. Fossils: Saurian bones and silicified wood	350	Jurassic ?	Cañon Pintado.
7	Red, yellow, or white massive calcareous sandstone. No fossils....	550	Triassic.	Do.
8	Red, thin-bedded sandstones; with red shales. No fossils..........	150	.... do	Do.
9	Red and brown massive sandstone, fine-grained, not hard. No fossils	270	.... do	Colorado Cañon.
10	Soft red sandstone, in thin layers, separated by beds of red or dark brown shales	350	.... do	Do.
11	Greenish-gray micaceous conglomerate and gray sandstone, separated by red and purple shales...	92	.... do	Do.
12	Soft, liver-colored sandstones, becoming, suddenly and locally, nearly white, with partings of shale	350	.... do	Do.
13	Brick-red massive calcareous sandstones, with some like the last....	164	.... do	Do.
14	Blue limestone, somewhat cherty. Fossils: *Spirifer camuratus, Athyris subtilita, Productus semireticulatus*	110	Carboniferous.	Cañon of Grand River.
15	Bluish-white, red, or mottled sandy limestone, with partings of red shale	95	.... do	Do.
16	Hard blue cherty limestone. Fossils same as No. 14................	36	.... do	Do.
17	Alternations of blue limestone, red and gray sandstone, to bottom of cañon	1,000	.... do	Do.

Finding it impossible to pass down in the vicinity of the Colorado to its junction with the San Juan, we were compelled to retrace our steps, and again ascending to the Sage-plain, crossed southwardly over its western extremity, along the eastern base of the Sierra Abajo, to the San Juan Valley. This part of our route afforded us little that was new in any department, and need not, therefore, long detain us. We found the structure of this portion of the Sage-plain precisely like that before passed over. The Lower Cretaceous sandstones everywhere form the surface-rock, except where covered with the overlying shales. The fossils of these shale-beds are often thickly scattered over the surface, as in many localities enumerated on the preceding pages. The plateau is here, as farther eastward, more or less broken by the cañons of the draining streams. These head in the Sierra Abajo and progressively deepen until they terminate in the eroded valley of the San Juan. At various points along this part of our route we saw ruins of ancient buildings, similar in character to those on the Dolores; and fragments of broken pottery, an equally characteristic record of the Pueblo race, were everywhere met with.

Sierra Abajo.—Our near approach to the Sierra Abajo, while skirting its northern and eastern bases, gave us a better knowledge of its extent and structure than we had before obtained. The impressions we then received of it are given in the following extract from my notes: "August 30, Camp 31, Mormon Spring. Our last camp was at the eastern base of the Sierra Abajo. Within the last few weeks we have been on three sides of this sierra, and have learned its structure quite definitely. It is a mountain group of no great elevation, its highest point rising some 2,000 feet above the Sage-plain, or perhaps 9,000 feet above the sea. It is composed of several distinct ranges, of which the most westerly one is quite detached from the others. All these ranges, of which there are apparently four, have a trend of about 25° east of north, but being arranged somewhat *en echelon*, the most westerly range reaching farthest north, the principal axis of the group has a northwest and southeast direction. The sierra is composed geologically of an erupted nucleus, mainly a gray or bluish-white trachyte, sometimes becoming a porphyry, surrounded by the upheaved, partially eroded, sedimentary rocks. The Lower Cretaceous sandstones and Middle Cretaceous shales are cut and exposed in all the ravines leading down from it, while nearly the entire thickness of the Cretaceous series is shown in spurs which, in some localities, project from its sides; apparently the remnants of a plateau corresponding to, and once connected with, the Mesa Verde. Whether the Paleozoic rocks are anywhere exposed upon the flanks of the Sierra Abajo I cannot certainly say, though we discovered no traces of them. It is, however, probable that they will be found in some of the deeper ravines, where, as in most of these isolated mountains composed mainly of erupted material, they are doubtless but little disturbed, but are buried beneath the ejected matter which has been thrown up through them.

The relations of the Cretaceous rocks to the igneous nucleus of the Sierra Abajo are very peculiar, for, although we did not make the entire circuit of the mountain mass, and I can, therefore, not speak definitely in regard to the western side. As far as our observations extended we found the sedimentary strata rising on to the trachyte core, as though it had been pushed up through them.

CHAPTER VI.

GEOLOGY OF THE BANKS OF THE SAN JUAN.

GENERAL FEATURES OF THE COUNTRY BORDERING THE SAN JUAN—SECTION OF LOWER CRE-
TACEOUS STRATA SOUTH OF SIERRA ABAJO—BIRD'S-EYE VIEW OF COUNTRY BORDERING
SAN JUAN—HIGH MESAS OF THE NAVAJO COUNTRY—TRIASSIC ROCKS OF LOWER SAN
JUAN—LOWER CRETACEOUS STRATA OF CAMP 37—MIDDLE CRETACEOUS BEDS AND FOS-
SILS SOUTH OF LE LATE—THE NEEDLES—THE CRESTON—UPPER CRETACEOUS STRATA
AT MOUTH OF THE ANIMAS—RUINS IN THE SAN JUAN VALLEY—CAÑON LARGO—SECTIONS
OF UPPER CRETACEOUS STRATA—PLATEAU COUNTRY BORDERING CAÑON LARGO—BUTTES
OF MARLS AND SANDSTONES, HIGHEST MEMBERS OF THE SERIES OF SEDIMENTARY ROCKS
COMPOSING COLORADO PLATEAU—GENERAL SECTION OF UPPER CRETACEOUS STRATA—
NACIMIENTO MOUNTAIN, ITS STRUCTURE AND RELATIONS—NOTES ON THE DIFFERENT FOR-
MATIONS EXPOSED ON ITS SIDES—JOURNEY THROUGH COUNTRY BORDERING WESTERN BASE
OF NACIMIENTO MOUNTAIN—DIVIDE BETWEEN SAN JUAN AND RIO GRANDE—MOUNT TAY-
LOR—CABEZON—TERTIARY STRATA AT JEMEZ—THE VALLES—TRAP PLATEAUS.

The great features in the structure of the country traversed by the San Juan River have been given in a preceding chapter, and there now remains for the completion of the picture only the presentation of the more local details upon which the generalizations before advanced were based.

Anticipating in some degree the progress of our geological narrative, to render the subject more readily comprehensible, the following outline sketch of the geology of the immediate banks of the San Juan is here given:

Taking their rise in the valleys dividing the parallel ranges of the Rocky Mountains, Sierra de la Plata, Sierra de los Pinos, Sierra San Juan, &c., the tributaries of the San Juan unite in the open country lying south of these mountain ranges to form a channel of drainage, having nearly an east and west course, to the Colorado. In addition to the tributaries of the San Juan which have been enumerated, far less important ones flow from the east and south. These are the rivulet traversing Cañon Largo, rising at the north end of the Nacimiento Mountain, the Chaco, Gothic Creek, and the Chelly, which drain the arid mesas of the Navajo country and the slopes of the Tunecha and Carrizo.

The country traversed by the northern and more important branches of the San Juan, bordering our outward-bound trail, has been fully described in the preceding chapters. That bordering Cañon Largo and the course of the Chaco opens to us a new geological field, and one which includes the exposures of the highest portion of the series forming the table-lands of the Colorado Plateau. This interesting region requires for its full illustration the detailed description to be hereafter given.

Its general character is, however, as follows:

The Nacimiento Mountain here bursts up through the table-lands in an unbroken wall forty miles in length, with a nearly north and south trend. On its western flank the various stratified rocks composing the Colorado Plateau lie inclined at a high angle with the horizon. Of these the Carboniferous series and the overlying Triassic formation stand nearly vertical. Upon these the Lower and Middle Cretaceous groups rest with a gentler inclination, while the Upper Cretaceous sandstones, and perhaps Tertiary strata, are represented in detached buttes and mesillas, the remnants of continuous sheets mostly removed by erosion. A few miles westward the disturbing influence of the elevation of the Nacimiento range ceases to be visible, and the different stratified rocks, which I have enumerated, hold a nearly horizontal position, which they maintain thence westward, with little variation, to and beyond the Colorado. Through the table-lands which they here form, Cañon Largo is excavated, gradually deepening till it joins the valley of the San Juan, where its walls have an altitude of 700 to 800 feet. At the eastern terminus of Cañon Largo, and along the base of the Nacimiento Mountain, are scattered the insulated buttes to which I have before referred as representing the summit of the series of conformable strata composing the Colorado Plateau; a group of purple, white, and gray marls, interstratified with soft, yellow calcareous sandstones, the latter predominating as we descend, and forming what has been described in the preceding pages as the Upper Cretaceous group, containing, near its base, the fossils collected on the Rio de la Plata, *Ammonites placenta*, *Baculites anceps*, &c.; a horizon probably corresponding to No. IV of Meek and Hayden's Nebraska section. From the perfect conformability throughout this group of rocks, their general lithological similarity from summit to base, where they contain Cretaceous fossils; in short, from absence of proof to the contrary, I have been driven to include them all provisionally in the Cretaceous formation. It is by no means certain, however, that this classification is rigidly correct, for it is not impossible that future investigations will prove that the upper part of this group should be regarded as Eocene Tertiary. That no Miocene beds occur here, is, I think, certain, as all the information obtained of the geology of the Rocky Mountain region goes to show that, between the time of the deposition of the Upper Cretaceous strata and the Miocene epoch, important changes occurred in the physical geography of the central portion of our continent—changes of level by which the conformability prevailing throughout the sedimentary strata, from the Silurian up, was finally interrupted. The only reasons we yet have for suspecting that the upper portion of the series on the San Juan is Tertiary, are the inordinate thickness—(if all Cretaceous) 3,000 to 4,000 feet—of the rocks which are more recent than the Triassic formation; and the more suggestive fact that, in Texas, the Eocene beds exhibit a marked lithological similarity to those forming the summit of the series at the head of Cañon Largo, and follow the Cretaceous strata in perfect conformability. We can only say, therefore, that, with the evidence now before us, while it is possible, and perhaps probable, that the uppermost members of the Colorado series are Eocene Tertiary, we have as yet no proof that such is the case.

LOWER SAN JUAN, LOOKING WEST FROM NEAR CAMP 35.

The area occupied by the most recent strata found in the San Juan country is but limited. The detached buttes which they form, and to which reference has before been made, stretch southwesterly from the north end of Nacimiento Mountain toward San Mateo, along the line of the divide between the Chaco and the Chelly; in other words, between the waters of the Rio Grande and those of the San Juan. Westward from this summit the table-land, which I have described in the preceding chapters as the plateau of the Upper San Juan, extends to the distance of one hundred miles or more, terminating in the mural faces of the Mesa Verde. Through this plateau Cañon Largo and its continuation, the valley of the San Juan, are cut to the meridian of the Sierra de la Plata; thence, westward, the lower plateau of the Sage-plain stretches to the margin of the valley of the Colorado. In this lower plateau the trough of the San Juan is also deeply sunk; cutting through the Lower Cretaceous group, and exposing, especially toward its mouth, many hundred feet of the underlying Triassic formation. Throughout the whole of its course through the table-lands the valley of the San Juan is a narrow trough, bounded by abrupt, often perpendicular, rocky sides; its rich and verdant bottom-lands forming a thread of fertility which traverses a region elsewhere arid and barren.

On our way south from the Sierra Abajo we struck the San Juan at a point some fifty miles or more above its mouth. Before descending from the plateau of the Sage-plain into the valley of the river, we obtained from several points views which swept over all the country bordering the lower part of its course. Of these that from the vicinity of Camp 33 was peculiarly comprehensive and grand; revealing features so novel and striking that I regarded them as worthy of somewhat detailed description in my note-book. That description is as follows:

"Soon after leaving camp (33) we obtained a beautiful view of all the country bordering the Lower San Juan, of which nearly 10,000 square miles were at once visible. From this point the eye swept a great semicircle from the Sierra de la Plata in the east around southward to the Bear's Ears in the west. From the Sierra de la Plata the long line of the lofty Mesa Verde stretched southward to the valley of the San Juan, there terminating in high and abrupt cliffs. In the open valley of the river stood the isolated pinnacles of the Needles, a peculiar and picturesque feature even at this great distance. In the southeast the bold front of the northern end of the Sierra del Carrizo rose frowningly from the immediate borders of the valley, and stretched away southward in a succession of peaks till lost in the distance.

"Directly south the view was bounded by the high and distant mesas of the Navajo country, succeeded in the southwest by the still more lofty battlements of the great white mesa formerly seen by us from the Moqui Villages, and described in my report to Lieutenant Ives. Of these high table-lands the outlines were not only distinctly visible, but grand and impressive at the distance of a hundred miles. Nearly west from us a great gap opened in the high table-lands which limit the view in that direction; that through which the San Juan flows to its junction with the Colorado. The features presented by this remarkable gate-way are among the most striking and impressive of any included in the scenery of the Colorado country. The distance between the mesa walls on the north and south is perhaps ten miles, and scattered over the interval are many castle-like buttes and slender towers, none of which can be less than 1,000 feet in height, their sides absolutely perpendicular, their forms wonderful imitations of the structures of human art. Illuminated by the setting sun, the outlines of these singular objects came out sharp and distinct, with such exact similitude of art, and contrast with nature as usually displayed, that we could hardly resist the conviction that we beheld the walls and towers of some Cyclopean city hitherto undiscovered in this far-off region. Within the great area inclosed by the grander features I have enumerated, the country is set with numberless buttes and isolated mesas, which give to the scene in a high degree the peculiar character I have so often referred to as exhibited by the eroded districts of the great central plateau. Here and there we caught glimpses of the vivid green of the wooded bottom-lands of the river, generally concealed by the intermediate and overhanging cliffs."

The general geological structure of the wide area then seen was nearly as intelligible and apparent as it could have been upon closer inspection; the higher mesas everywhere composed of the Upper Cretaceous strata—isolated portions of a once continuous sheet; the plateau on which we stood the massive sandstones and conglomerates of the Lower Cretaceous group; while the bottom of the trough of the San Juan, where exposed, showed the blood-red tint of the Triassic rocks.

Near Camp 34 we descended from the plateau of the Sage-plain and encamped in the valley of the Rito del Sierra Abajo, a few miles above its junction with the San Juan. In this descent we passed over the cut edges of all the members of the Lower Cretaceous group, which afforded me the following section:

Section of Lower Cretaceous strata at Camp 34.

		Feet.
1.	Dove-colored calcareous shale, with *Gryphæa Pitcheri*, in knolls on No. 2.	
2.	Yellow, coarse sandstone, often a conglomerate, with pebbles of black and white flint	25
3.	Gray shale, with lignite and silicified wood	12
4.	Yellowish, coarse sand-rock, with pebbles of flint (locally), sometimes massive, nearly white, quartzose	50
5.	Green shale	2
6.	Massive, nearly white sand-rock; the same noticed on the Dolores at Tierra Blanca, &c	16
7.	Yellowish-white sand-rock, with pebbles of flint	12
8.	Soft greenish-yellow sandstone, massive, but easily decomposed	10
9.	Verdigris-green concretionary, hard calcareous sandstone	2
10.	Green and chocolate shales, with bands of fine argillaceous and calcareous sandstone of several colors	30
11.	Soft greenish-yellow sandstone	29
12.	Green, chocolate, purple, pink, and white marls, with concretionary bands of similar colors of hard, fine argillo-silicious rock	110
13.	Greenish-yellow sandstone, like No. 11	85
14.	Soft greenish sandstone, decomposing like No. 8	8

		Feet.
15.	Soft greenish sandstones and shales, alternating with and replacing each other. Locally, this group is very massive, hard, almost quartzose, like No. 4; in other places, almost replaced by greenish shales. This is probably the base of the Cretaceous system. Continuing the section down the valley of the Rito to the San Juan, we have—	140
16.	Red, white, and greenish thin-bedded micaceous sandstones, alternating with red shales—the Saurian beds of Camp 26, No. 2 of section on page 91	130
17.	Red, massive, cross-stratified calcareous sandstones—No. 3 of section of Camp 26; No. 1 of section—(p. 95,) to river-bottoms	160

The last two members of the section evidently represent the upper portion of the Gypsum formation (Trias.) They form the cliffs immediately bordering the valley of the river at Camp 35, and the trough in which it flows from Camp 36 to its mouth.

The second bench, or higher cliffs bordering the valley at Camp 35, composed of the Lower Cretaceous rocks, contain conglomerates—the equivalents of the upper members of the preceding section—much coarser than those observed farther north; the pebbles being frequently as large as the fist, with only sufficient paste to cement them. Among these pebbles I noticed several composed of silicified wood, probably derived from the erosion of the Triassic rocks.

In the trough of the San Juan, at this point, are extensive beds and terraces, composed of coarse gravel and bowlders, evidently brought down by the river from the mountain-ranges which it drains, and, in some instances, the bowlders must have been rolled by the stream fully two hundred miles from their place of origin.

The structure of the country about Camp 37 is quite fully given in my journal. My notes are as follows: "That portion of the valley of the San Juan passed through to-day is, in its general aspects, similar to that before described, but the cliffs bordering it are less continuous and abrupt. In many places they are 300 or 400 feet high, perfect cañon walls, but oftener they recede from the river, leaving open areas; the mouths of lateral valleys cutting up through the mesas toward the mountains.

"Geologically as physically, we have ascended considerably, and have just sunk the 'Saurian rocks' (Upper Triassic?), leaving the cliffs bordering the valley composed exclusively of Lower Cretaceous strata. During the greater part of to-day's march thin-bedded Triassic sandstones and shales formed the base of the wall along which we passed. These rocks are here more argillaceous than farther north, contain much saline matter, but no beds of gypsum, and no fossils so far as observed." By reference to my report on the geology of the Colorado expedition, it will be seen that further south they are still less sandy; at the Moqui Villages, consisting mostly of soft red and green marls.

The Lower Cretaceous strata are here more fully exposed, and have a greater thickness than where examined farther north and east; approaching more nearly the character exhibited by this group at the Moqui Villages. The cliffs near camp are composed of—

	Feet.
1. Yellow, coarse sandstones and conglomerates; floor of Sage-plain	200
2. Greenish shales and sandstones	175
3. Greenish-yellow sandstones and greenish shales	250

14 S F

The character of the subdivisions will be better seen by the following analysis:

1st. Yellow sandstone group; here less coarse and containing less conglomerate than at camps 33, 34, and 35. As at those localities, on the Cimarron, in Kansas and Nebraska a portion of this group is here an exceedingly hard, whitish, quartzose sandstone. Beds of lignite and silicified wood are common.

2d. Greenish shales and sandstones; the same group described in my notes on the geology of the vicinity of Camp 34, Nos. 10, 11, 12 of section, page 104, here much less highly colored, consisting of thick beds of greenish shale, locally pink or purple, with bands of yellowish, greenish or purple concretionary silicious rock; no fossils.

3d. Greenish sandstones and shales; the same group exposed in the lower part of the section at Camp 34. The shales and sandstones frequently replace each other; the group at Camp 37 being nearly all massive, yellowish-green sandstone, while, a few miles below, the shales greatly predominate; no fossils discoverable.

"*Mouth of the Mancos.*—Camp 38, thirteen miles. We have to-day ascended in the geological scale, have nearly submerged the lowest member of the section at Camp 37, and the mesas back from the river on the north side run far up into the Middle and Upper Cretaceous group. On the south side the mesas are not as high; the Lower Cretaceous rocks forming the surface almost to the Sierra Carrizo, near which the Upper Cretaceous beds appear again. The mesas north of our camp, composed of the Middle Cretaceous strata, extend north and east to the base of the Sierra Le Late, and, if not cut off by the valley of the Mancos, would connect with the Mesa Verde. As usual in all this region, the shales contain great numbers of *Gryphœa Pitcheri.*

"In the Lower Cretaceous sandstones, I here find impressions of dicotyledonous leaves, similar to those found on the Dolores and elsewhere.

"As in other parts of the valley of the San Juan which we have passed through, the ruins of ancient buildings are here very frequently met with; some in the open ground of the valley, some in or on the cliffs; all built of stone, surrounded by broken pottery, evidently the remains of that great Pueblo race which once occupied all this region, but which is now without an inhabitant.

"*Camp 38, 39, 15 miles.*—In our march of to-day, a marked change has taken place in the valley of the San Juan, which has become more open, is bounded by less high and abrupt walls; the bluffs, like the bottom, being covered with fine grass. This change is dependent, mainly, upon the fact that we have ascended from the Lower to the Middle Cretaceous strata, and have passed from a region of coarse massive sandstones to one where almost nothing but soft-blue shales are visible.

"Before leaving the Lower Cretaceous sandstones, some interesting local peculiarities were noticed in that group. The lignite, which in greater or less quantity they always contain, about and above the mouth of the Mancos becomes a very conspicuous feature in their structure. Of one cliff which we passed, not more than 100 feet in height, full one-half was composed of carbonaceous matter. The dip, as before, is gently eastward, and at Camp 39 the Lower Cretaceous sandstones had entirely disappeared beneath the overlying rocks.

"Here the cliffs near the river are composed of the dark shales of the Middle Cre-

THE NEEDLES, LOOKING SOUTH-WESTERLY.

taceous series, quite rich in fossils. Perhaps a hundred feet above the sandstones is a band of brown, shelly, sandy limestone, which forms a projecting ledge in the face of the cliffs, giving cornices and capitals to the castles and palaces into which they have been worn. This ferruginous stratum marks a distinct horizon, and may be traced over an immense area in New Mexico. It is the same that I have before referred to in my notes on the banks of the Dolores, Camp 21, the Pagosa, the ford of the Chama, Galisteo, and the banks of the Canadian. This stratum is characterized by the following fossils: *Inoceramus problematicus, Ostrea lugubris, Scaphites larviformis, Ptychodus Whipplei*, &c. Several undescribed species of *Inoceramus, Ostrea, Ammonites*, &c., are also found in it; one of the *Inocerami*, abundant at Camp 39, being 2–3 feet in diameter. The place of *Gryphæa Pitcheri* is just beneath this stratum; while the overlying shales are filled with fragments of a large *Inoceramus*, covered with the closely-set shells of *Ostrea congesta*.

"A few miles north of Camp 39 is the southwestern corner of the Mesa Verde, which stretches from this point northward to our former trail, and, eastward, forms the north bank of the San Juan as far as the eye can reach. It has an altitude of 2,000 feet above camp, and presents, with its many detached buttes and pinnacles, its long and lofty walls, a most grand and imposing object. On the south side of the river, now quite near to us, stand out in strong relief the picturesque basaltic pinnacles of 'The Needles,' while further south the view is bounded by the high ridges of the Carisso and Tunecha Mountains."

From Camp 40 we obtained a nearer and still better view of "The Needles," which is represented in the accompanying lithograph plate.

This is a mass of erupted rock, rising with perpendicular sides from the middle of the valley. From all points, where seen by us, it has the appearance of an immense cathedral, of rich umber-brown color, terminating in two spires. Its altitude is about 1,700 feet above its base; above the river 2,262 feet. It is everywhere surrounded by stratified rocks, and its isolated position and peculiar form render its origin a matter of some little doubt. My conviction, however, is very decided that its remarkable relief is due to the washing away of the sediments which once surrounded it, and which formed the mold in which it was cast. In no other way can I imagine its vertical faces of 1,000 feet to have been formed.

For ten miles after leaving Camp 40 we were traveling along the trough of the river excavated in the Middle Cretaceous shales; the Upper Cretaceous sandstones capping the bluffs on either side. We here reached what seemed to be, in the distance, a mesa wall crossing the river. This proved, however, to be a mass of dislocated and ruptured strata, forming a huge broken wall, similar to that described in the Geology of the Colorado Expedition, page 95, called by the Mexicans the Creston. This wall marks a great line of fracture which traverses the country in a zigzag course from the Sierra de la Plata southward toward the Tunecha Mountains. It crosses the river nearly at right angles, with a trend N. 20° W. magnetic, forming a wall several hundred feet high, cut by the river in a narrow passage, through which we worked our way with extreme difficulty.

The Creston evidently once formed a dam across the valley of the San Juan, over which its waters poured in a cascade. This is shown by the gravel terrace which, east of it, rises to the height of 300 feet above the present bed of the stream. The strata composing it are set at an angle of about 35°, and are the equivalents of those which form the greater part of the Mesa Verde. As affording a more complete section of the Upper Cretaceous rocks in this region than any I had before observed, I examined them with some care, and found them to consist of the following elements:

Section of rocks composing the Creston.

Feet.
1. Yellowish-brown calcareous sandstone, generally thick-bedded............ 260
2. Yellowish-brown sandy shale, with thin bands of sandstone and beds of lignite.. 150
3. Yellow sandy limestone, with strata of hard blue limestone............:..... 70
4. Dove-colored and purplish shales, with beds of impure lignite............ 175
5. Gray and purple shales, with bands of sandy limestone, and lines of concretions of umber-colored and purple iron-stones........................ 200
6. Brown calcareous sandstones... 20
7. Gray and purplish shales, with bands of ferruginous sandy limestone...... 170
8. Yellowish-brown sandstones, whitish above.................................... 150
9. Gray and blue shales, continuous with those of Camps 39 and 40.

In this section, No. 1 is geologically the highest, and forms the most elevated portion of the Creston.

The shales of No. 9 immediately overlie the ferruginous limestone of Camp 39, which contains so many *Inocerami*, fish-teeth, &c.

The interval between these two groups represents the middle and upper portions of the great group of shales which form the middle division of the Cretaceous system, so often referred to in the preceding pages.

As in the sections observed on the northern route, the bands of sandstone and ferruginous sandy limestone are shown to be only local phenomena; since they sometimes expand and assume great local importance, and again disappear and give place to a nearly homogeneous mass of calcareous shales, 1,300 to 1,500 in thickness.

Among the strata forming the Creston are several beds of lignite, of which one, six feet thick, visible for many miles along the river, is unusually compact and pure; in its general appearance precisely resembling some of the coal strata of the Carboniferous series.

No fossils were discovered in any of the rocks here exposed above the *Inoceramus* limestone, but probably impressions of plants would be obtained from the shales over the lignite beds, if time were given to search for them.

From the Creston to the mouth of Cañon Largo the banks of the San Juan are composed throughout of the strata which have just been enumerated, lying in unbroken sheets, with a gentle easterly dip. In these strata the valleys of the San Juan, La Plata, and Animas have been deeply cut, and are bounded by abrupt, frequently perpendicular walls, the edges of table-lands, many hundred feet in height. The bottom-lands of these valleys, though narrow, are fertile; sustaining a vigorous growth of grass, and along the margin of the streams groves of cottonwood, and thickets of willow and buffalo-berry (*Eleagnus argenteus?*).

Though now entirely deserted, these valleys were once occupied by a dense population, as is shown by the extensive ruins with which they are thickly set. Those on the Animas, twenty miles above its mouth, have already been noticed.

At the junction of this stream with the San Juan the remains of a large, but very ancient, town are visible, the foundations of many buildings of considerable size still remaining, and traces of an acequia through which water was brought from a point some miles above on the Animas.

Near Camp 43 also are the ruins of several large structures, of which portions of the walls of stone are still standing, twenty or more feet in height. Indeed, it may be said that from the time we struck the San Juan we were never out of sight of ruins, while we were following up its valley.

CAÑON LARGO.

At Camp 44 we left the valley of the San Juan and entered the mouth of Cañon Largo, which we followed up in an easterly direction until, at its head, near the western base of the Nacimiento Mountain, we came out on to the surface of the great plateau of the Upper San Juan, *through* which we had been so long passing, sunk far below its surface in the excavated valleys which intersect it. Of these valleys Cañon Largo may be taken as a type. It differs in nothing from that of the San Juan or Animas, except that, instead of a large perennial stream, a small, generally dry, arroyo traverses its bottom, and its bounding cliffs, composed of the upper strata of the table-lands, exhibit geological features not met with in other portions of our route.

By the easterly dip of the rocks and the rapidity of the fall of the stream, we were constantly ascending in the series from the Creston to the head of Cañon Largo. At the mouth of the Animas we had nearly sunk the whole of the Middle Cretaceous group, its upper members (gray shales and marls) forming the base of the high cliffs, composed mainly of the Upper Cretaceous sandstones, here very massive, and showing a thickness of 600 to 700 feet. At the mouth of Cañon Largo we had risen still higher in the series, the Middle Cretaceous shales having entirely disappeared; the lofty cliffs which bound the valley at this point being formed entirely of the Upper Cretaceous rocks, alternations of soft yellow sandstones and white, gray, or purple marls. The lowest member of this series here is the same with that which forms the summit of the Creston section, and more fully exposed at the mouth of the Animas, where it presents perpendicular faces of 300 to 400 feet of massive, homogeneous, soft, yellow, calcareous sandstone. A few miles farther north, on the La Plata, this rock contains at its base *Ammonites placenta*, *Baculites ovatus*, &c., which serve to mark very satisfactorily its place in the geological scale, viz: Upper Cretaceous, No. IV or V, of Meek and Hayden's Nebraska section. This is surmounted by some ten alternations of marls and sandstones in the cliffs bordering Cañon Largo, the series being entirely conformable and similar in lithological character throughout. At the head of Cañon Largo, as we shall see further on, these strata are succeeded by others, several hundred feet in thickness, also conformable, but, lithologically, showing a preponderance of marls over the sandstones. Whether all this great group belongs, like its base, to the Cretaceous system, we have at present no means of determining; the only fossils found being such as do not suffice to solve the problem. These are, so far as observed, silicified trunks of large coniferous trees, and abundant, though rather obscure, impressions of angiospermous leaves of species different from any found elsewhere in the Tertiary or Cretaceous strata.

The character of the marls of this series is very well given in my notes upon the lowest bed exposed at Camp 43, a few miles below the mouth of Cañon Largo. These notes are as follows:

"The hills which bound the valley opposite camp are about 250 feet high, composed of greenish-gray and yellowish-white marls, generally very soft, but occasionally containing lenticular masses of coarse sandstone and conglomerate. Dispersed through the marls are many spherical concretions of ferruginous sandstone which decompose on exposure; plates of selenite, in places covering the slopes, and masses of water-worn, silicified, carbonized, calcified, or gypsumized wood. All the beds contain much saline matter (mostly sulphates) which effloresces on the exposed surfaces. The prevailing color of these marls is whitish, and in their general aspect the hills which they form closely resemble the chalk-hills of Southern England."

At Camp 44, I made the following entry in my journal:

"To-day we reached the mouth of the Cañon Largo, and the crossing of the San Juan. The valley is here, as below, moderately fertile, bounded by rounded hills of chalky strata, with terraces of gravel near the river; all covered with good grass. The soil of the bottom-lands is alkaline, often covered with salt-bush (*Sarcobatus*), but sustaining extensive groves of cottonwood and thickets of buffalo-berry; the latter loaded with fruit. In geology little change is noticeable; the dip of the rocks continues easterly, and we have the chalky marls mentioned in yesterday's notes, succeeded by a stratum some 50 feet in thickness of yellowish, soft, oölitic, coarse-grained, calcareous sandstone, so friable as to be scarcely transportable, but very massive, and standing in perpendicular faces in the cliffs. In this stratum is a band of gray clay-shale, in which I find abundant impressions of leaves, but have been unable to obtain any specimens sufficiently perfect for determination.

"Above this sandstone is a bed of greenish-white and purple marl, weathering like the marls of the Trias, and closely resembling them in all things. Above the marl is another bed of sandstone similar to that below; then another bed of marl, &c."

At Camp 45, my journal says: "Cañon Largo is bounded by high and precipitous walls on either side, composed of soft yellow sandstones, and white and variegated marls. The cliffs are not absolutely perpendicular, but ascend in grades; the sandstone forming vertical faces, the marl, slopes."

"The alternations in this series present very little variety; the sandstones, some ten in number, being very like each other; the marls, of about equal force, showing no marked differences. They often form rounded but furrowed hills, of which the surfaces are whitened by a saline efflorescence or are covered with fragments of ferruginous concretions and fossil wood. This silicified wood is very abundant and seems to be all coniferous."

"Since leaving the surface of the great sandstone-bed, the base of the Upper Cretaceous series, so fully exposed at the mouth of the Animas, we have passed up through three strata of soft calcareous sandstone with an equal number of marl-beds; the average thickness of the sandstone being about 50 feet, of the marl, 75."

At Camp 46 I ascended the cliff on the south side of the cañon and found it to be 674 feet in height. The section of the strata composing it is as follows:

		Feet.
1.	Coarse soft yellow sandstone, partially conglomerate	55
2.	Greenish-white marl, with silicified wood	50
3.	Soft yellowish sandstone, partly conglomerate, with small quartz pebbles containing obscure impressions of plants	120
4.	Greenish argillo-silicious rock, breaking into irregular masses above, shaly below, shading into purple marl	50
5.	Soft, white, massive, calcareous sandstone, in places traversed by veins of gypsum	20
6.	Gray or greenish-white marl, with bands of hard bluish-gray limestone, containing fucoids and silicified wood	80
7.	Yellowish soft sandstone	50
8.	Greenish-white and purple marl, with selenite, bands of concretionary limestone and large trunks of silicified wood	80
9.	Soft yellowish, coarse sandstone	60
10.	Greenish and purple marls, with concretionary limestone	109

From the summit of this cliff I was able to overlook most of the country bordering Cañon Largo, and could see that it was occupied by broad mesas extending east to the Nacimiento Mountain, and north to the bases of the Sierra de la Plata, Sierra San Juan, Navajo, &c., all of which were in full view. South and west higher portions of the plateau limited my vision.

On this plain I noticed islands of higher strata than those on which I stood. These are 300 or 400 feet in thickness, and of the same general character as the walls of Cañon Largo. Adding these to the strata exposed in Cañon Largo, and those noticed in the San Juan above the mouth of the Animas, and we have an aggregate thickness of about 1,500 feet for this upper series alone.

In my notes made at Camp 47, I find the following memoranda: "In the exposures I have now examined of the Upper Cretaceous (?) strata, I have enumerated eleven beds of sandstone, with an equal number of marl-beds. The aggregate force of these two groups is nearly the same, though each stratum is liable to great local variation; the section at one point being considerably different from that at others. The sandstones are quite variable in thickness, both as regards the same stratum at different places, and comparing the different beds with each other. The summit of the cliffs along Cañon Largo is formed of a group of sandstones of unusual thickness, in places full 200 feet, with only thin partings of marl. This stratum has protected the beds below and produced the abruptness of the walls. It forms the floor of the adjacent Sage-plain, from which the upper layers, being softer, have been removed by erosion."

At Camp 48 I write: "To-day left Cañon Largo and came out on the plateau before mentioned. A sage-plain with rolling surface, fashioned by erosion, on which rise the extreme Upper Cretaceous (?) strata in buttes and detached mesas."

One of these buttes at Camp 48 afforded me the following section:

	Feet.
1. Soft yellow sandstone	60
2. Greenish-white marl	70
3. Soft yellow sandstone with large concretions, weathering brown	50
4. Marl, greenish-white above, purple below	75
5. Soft white sandstone with hard concretions	20
6. Marls, greenish-white above, purple below, with concretions of silicious limestone	50
7. Coarse, soft, whitish sandstone	30
8. Greenish-white and purple marls	90

This series should be added to that of the cliff at Camp 46.

Just before reaching the base of the Nacimiento Mountain, we crossed the divide between the Pacific and Atlantic, and reached the highest point, geologically, attained on any part of our route. The immediate base of the mountain is swept by a line of drainage which flows south along its western side, around its southern extremity passes into the Puerco, and thence into the Rio Grande. The line of divide diverges from the north end of the Nacimiento Mountain, running southwesterly to San Mateo and the Sierra Madre. For at least a hundred miles it stretches across the table-lands unmarked by any disruption of the strata or line of upheaval.

The crest of the water-shed is here formed of series of buttes and mesas composed of soft, marly strata; the extreme summit of the great group, which, on negative rather than positive evidence, I have designated as Upper Cretaceous.

BUTTES WEST OF THE NACIMIENTO MOUNTAIN (EOCENE TERTIARY (?).

These buttes include about 400 feet of strata not included in the sections before given. They are as follows:

	Feet.
1. Soft yellow sandstone	40
2. Purple, yellow, and greenish soft marls	60
3. Soft yellow sandstone	35
4. Green, purple, yellow, and white marls, with thin layers of white sandstone	70
5. White sandstone	25
6. Green and purple marls	80
7. Coarse, white sandstone	20
8. White and purple marls	50
9. Soft yellow sandstone, summit of cliff in section at Camp 48.	

These strata are all conformable among themselves and to those below; lying nearly or quite horizontal. The marls of this series are darker than those of the preceding sections, having a purplish-green appearance at a distance. The sandstones are very soft, and being thinner than the marls they form but a slight interruption to the uniformity of the slope of the sides of the buttes, and are scarcely noticeable, except

THE CABAZON
FROM NEAR CAMP 54.

when quite near. No fossils were found in any part of this section, and the abundance of selenite and the profuse efflorescence of the sulphates of alumina, magnesia, &c., seem to indicate the prevalence of conditions unfavorable to life during the deposition of these strata, as well as in the similar non-fossilliferous marls of the Trias. Combining the sections observed at various points between the mouth of the Animas and the Nacimiento Mountain, we have, for the aggregate thickness of the conformable and generally similar strata resting upon the Middle Cretaceous shales, 2,000 feet, made up as follows:

		Feet.
1.	Marls and sandstone forming buttes of divide	380
2.	Marls and sandstone section at Camp 48	445
3.	Marls and sandstone section at Camp 46	674
4.	Marls and sandstone in valley of San Juan	500
	Total	1,999

It may be suspected, from the many alternations of similar strata in the preceding sections, that there has been in some cases a repetition, but that is quite certainly not the case. Although no fossils were found which might serve as criteria for the identification of strata, the geological exposures are so full that all the more important beds may be traced without break or interruption, and the order of superposition accurately determined by simple inspection of the interlocking of the different sections. In measuring altitudes the barometer was constantly used, and the heights of inaccessible points frequently obtained by triangulation. By these means, and the use of Locke's level where necessary, all the generalities of the thickness of strata were determined with a good degree of accuracy.

As regards the question of the precise geological age of this great group of sandstones and marls, as I have stated in the earlier part of this chapter, we have not, as yet, the means of arriving at a perfectly satisfactory conclusion. The lower part of the series is, we know, Cretaceous; as it contains characteristic fossils of No. IV of Meek and Hayden's Nebraska section. The most natural inference, therefore, is, that a portion at least of the overlying beds represent the upper part of No. IV and No. V of the Nebraska section. Since there are no fossils in the upper beds, and since they are apparently conformable to the lower, and generally similar to them in lithological characters, we have evidence that they were deposited while the physical conditions of this portion of the continent remained essentially the same. In one sense, therefore, they do all belong to one great geological epoch, and, without evidence to the contrary, should be classed together.

This argument, however, has little force, for, as we have seen, all the sedimentary strata of the Colorado plateau are conformable, and there is unusual similarity of lithological character among those which we know, by their fossils, belong to different formations. That none of these strata are Miocene may be safely affirmed, as previous to that epoch great and radical changes were effected in the physical geography of our continent, and the uniformity which had characterized the deposition of the sediments forming the great central plateau was entirely broken up; the sea retreating from the central portion of the continent, throwing down its sediments only along the shores and up the valley of the Mississippi; the inland Miocene-Tertiary having been deposited in bodies of fresh water. It is possible, however, that some portion of this series is of Eocene age, though of this we have as yet no proof.

It is true that, in Texas, the Eocene beds, distinctly marked by their fossils, are lithologically similar to some of those under consideration, and they are there entirely conformable to the Cretaceous strata, of which they seem but a continuation; the two formations blending and not separable by any sharp lines of demarcation.

NACIMIENTO MOUNTAIN.

Though not a lofty or extensive mountain range, this is perhaps the most instructive and interesting of all those which I had an opportunity of examining in the western country. Its extreme altitude is about 10,000 feet; its length something like 50 miles. Throughout this distance it forms a single simple ridge of nearly uniform height, with no peaks nor depressions. At either end it gradually falls off, and is lost in the level of the plateau country which nearly surrounds it. Although its physical features are so unpretending, its geological structure is in the highest degree interesting and suggestive; such indeed that it seems to me it not only furnishes a key to the mode of formation of all the great ranges of the Rocky Mountain system to which it belongs, but that, if properly studied, it would serve to explain nearly all the difficulties of that now much-mooted subject, the origin of mountain chains. What its structure is may be very briefly told.

The central core or axis of the Nacimiento Mountain is composed of massive red granite, similar to that so common in the other ranges of the Rocky Mountain system. This forms its summit and the greater part of its mass. Upon the slope of the granite axis rests the Carboniferous formation, for the most part limestone, in many places nearly vertical, yet but slightly metamorphosed. Outside of the Carboniferous are the white and red sandstones, marls, and gypsums of the Trias; many of these beds also standing quite vertical, but wholly unchanged. Outside of the Trias the Lower Cretaceous rocks form another distinct circle; beyond these, the Middle Cretaceous shales; still beyond, the great group of Upper Cretaceous sandstones and marls, which I have just described.

When we stood on the summit of the mountain all these different formations were spread out before us as on a geological map, each distinguishable by its color or texture, and as readily recognized as though traced on a diagram for a lecture-room.

The impression produced upon my mind by our first ascent of the Sierra de Nacimiento may be gathered from the following extracts from my notes:

"After arriving in camp (50) I went over with Mr. Fisher to the Nacimiento Mountain, which we ascended. Our approach was up a beautiful but narrow valley, through which a clear, cold stream flows for some distance, then sinks and rises at intervals, forming a series of fine springs. The vegetation of this valley is almost identical with that of the valleys of our northern route; the elevation being nearly the same—7,500 feet. The timber is yellow pine, piñon, cedar, (two species,) bitter and sweet cotton-wood, Gambell's oak, and the narrow-leaved willow.* On the summit of

---
* *Pinus ponderosa, P. edulis, Juniperus tetragona, J. virginiana, Populus angustifolia, P. monilifera, Quercus Gambelli, Salix angustifolia.*

the mountain, Douglas' spruce, yellow pine, the western balsam-fir, with thickets of aspen, oak, maple, and red-flowered locust.* As we progressed we passed in succession over the upturned edges of all the sedimentary rocks seen on our route.

1. The Upper Cretaceous sandstones and marls, but slightly inclined, and not reaching within two or three miles of the mountain.

2. The Middle Cretaceous shales, forming a broad belt of clay-soil, from which project here and there ledges of the harder strata, filled with the fossils characteristic of this formation—*Inoceramus problematicus, Gryphœa Pitcheri, Ostrea congesta,* &c.

3. The Lower Cretaceous sandstones, from their hard and massive character, having resisted erosion, are now forming hills and cliffs of considerable height.

4. The Triassic formation; its soft red marls, forming bare surfaces of blood-red color, its sandstones standing out in strong relief, forming walls and palisades, often nearly vertical, sometimes 40 or 50 feet in height, and only 5 or 6 feet in thickness.

5. The Carboniferous series, mostly massive gray or whitish limestone, reaching far up on the mountain sides, scarcely at all metamorphosed, and filled with fossils.

6. A central core or axis of red granite forming the great mass of the range.

Our view from the summit was particularly fine. Immediately below us the different formations which I have enumerated were distinctly visible, running in parallel bands along the mountain side. Some five miles north of our position the range falls off and disappears in the plain, but the line of upheaval is distinctly marked by an arching of the unbroken sedimentary rocks. The upper part of the arch is removed, and the surface-rock is a pure white sandstone, probably Triassic, beneath which the "red beds" appear, forming on the east side of the mountain a beautiful rose-red valley.

On the north we had a complete panorama of the mountains passed on our outward route, a view sweeping from the Santa Fé and Taos Mountains to the Sierra de la Plata.

Toward the west stretched a vast plain, deeply scored by many lines of erosion, of which Cañon Largo may be taken as a type. This plateau—the San Juan division of the great Colorado Plateau—filled all the horizon, from the Sierra la Plata around to San Mateo, the distant summits of the Carrizo and Chusca being just perceptible above its surface. This great Cretaceous plain sweeps up with nearly horizontal strata to the base of the Nacimiento; the series being most complete, the strata still horizontal, six miles west of the mountain. At this point all the formations begin to rise toward the east; their angles of elevation becoming greater as they approach the granitic axis, where they are frequently quite vertical. The Nacimiento axis is here and farther north the great divide between the waters of the Pacific and Atlantic, though, as before stated, the drainage of most of its western slope passes around the south end into the Puerco; the crest of the water-shed being formed by a line of high table-lands, which passes southwesterly between the head-waters of the Chaco and the Puerco toward Mount Taylor (San Mateo). The line of upheaval which forms the divide at Campbell's Pass, is widely different from the Nacimiento axis, being indeed no other than that of the Sierra Madre, which is entirely lost northward, as we saw no indication of it on the San Juan.

After leaving Camp 50, we made several days' marches southward, skirting the

---

* *Populus tremuloides, Quercus Gambelli, Acer.* sp. *Robinia Neo Mexicana.*

western base of the Nacimiento Mountain, until, reaching a practicable pass near its southern extremity, we crossed over to the peublo of Jemez. The country traversed in this part of our route we found to be much like the foot-hill region bordering the northern mountains, very picturesque, well watered, covered with fine timber, the valleys rich and productive, but from their great elevation early touched with frost and doubtless very cold in midwinter. Here, as almost everywhere else on our route, we found numerous ruins of stone-built structures, evidence of the presence in ancient time of a large population, where now neither Indian nor white man dwells.

In geology our experience was for the most part but a repetition of that already described, as we were passing in review all the strata before so fully examined in the valley of the San Juan.

The exposures were here, however, exceedingly full and satisfactory, and I had constantly recurring opportunities of testing the accuracy of the classification previously adopted.

That the evidence furnished by our observations in this interesting region may be consulted in the solution of any question that may be raised in regard to the geological structure of this portion of New Mexico, I transcribe from my note-book some of the records made from day to day as we progressed on our journey.

"*September 21, Camp* 50 *to* 51.—To-day we followed south along the western base of the Nacimiento Mountain, over a rolling surface, crossing many wooded hills and pretty valleys formed by the erosion of the Cretaceous strata. This formation, as we can see, occupies all the country southeast from us as far as Mount Taylor; there, as I learned on a former expedition, it is cut through by the valley of the San José, but beyond that extends, we know not how far, southward. At Camp 51 we have precisely the same section as that described at Camp 50; all the formations, from the Carboniferous to the Upper Cretaceous, lying in sheets, with edges upturned, along the base of the mountain. There is, however, here a distinct valley worn out between the Cretaceous table-land and the mountain. Near our camp are buttes and mesas several hundred feet in height, composed of the yellow sandstones of Cañon Largo, of which the summits are thickly strewn with bowlders of red granite and limestone, evidently washed down from the neighboring mountain before the intervening valley had been cut out by the stream which now flows through it. The amount of erosion indicated by the presence of this local drift where it is now found is enormous. I previously noticed the same phenomena in many localities among the foot-hills of the northern mountains. We find here everywhere in the sandstones great numbers of silicified trees, many of them of very large size, apparently all coniferous. Fragments of these trunks are strewed so abundantly over the surface that they have been used very generally as building-stones in the construction of the ancient pueblos.

"In seams and pockets of fine clay in the sandstones I find abundant impressions of angiospermous leaves, apparently of those of sycamore, alder, oak, &c., but the material inclosing them is so friable that they cannot be taken out entire, nor can the fragments be transported for determination. Among these impressions are some coniferous leaves and stems of a conifer or cycad, very much like the *Ulodendron* of the Coal-Measures; a scaly trunk with elliptical disks three inches in diameter. I also obtained fragments of fern leaves, but too imperfect for determination.

"*September* 22.—To-day we ascended the mountain in search of a pass, and found the base and flanks covered by the upturned sedimentary series, just as at Camp 50; the Trias here, as at Laguna, 50 miles south, containing immense masses of snowy gypsum, a thing rarely seen on the San Juan or Grand River."

In the coarse yellow sandstones and conglomerates overlying the red beds of the Trias I find large quantities of the sulphide of copper, replacing trunks and branches of trees, just as at the "Cobre," near Abiquiu.

The summit of the mountain where we ascended is over 9,000 feet above the sea; it is covered with forests of yellow and sugar pine, Douglass spruce, and the western balsam-fir,[*] interspersed with areas occupied by oak, maple, and aspen bushes, with here and there poison-oak[†] and red-flowered locust.

"*September* 23, *Camp* 51–52.—Failing to find a pass across the mountain, we to-day resumed our course southward, camping as before on a tributary of the Puerco. The country is generally similar to that seen yesterday, but, as we descend, the forests of yellow pine are gradually succeeded by scattered clumps of piñon, and red and white cedar on the hills, the valleys grassy as before. We have also descended somewhat in the geological scale, our present camp being surrounded by mesas of the great sandstone of the Animas—the base of the Upper Cretaceous group—with an exposure of several hundred feet of the underlying strata given in the section of the Creston, viz, gray shales, with bands of concretionary iron-ore, strata of yellow or brown sandstone and beds of lignite, all Middle Cretaceous; in the shale beds is much crystallized gypsum.

"*September* 24, *Camp* 52 *to* 53.—To-day our course has been southeasterly, approaching the southern end of the Nacimiento, through a region much like that of yesterday, except that, as we have now penetrated deeply into the Middle Cretaceous shales, the surface is less broken, the hills being rounded, with long, gentle slopes; the timber has become more sparse, the country less picturesque and inviting. We have here a fine view of all the interval between the Nacimiento and San Mateo. This was apparently once occupied by an unbroken sheet of Cretaceous rocks, now for the most part removed through the agency of the tributaries of the Puerco. In the west and northwest, high mesas fill the horizon, forming the line of divide to which I have before referred. Around the base of Mount Taylor, extending many miles in every direction, is a plateau of trap, which has apparently flowed from this great extinct volcano, covering all the sedimentary rocks in its vicinity. In the open valley of the Puerco stand many picturesque trap buttes, having a general resemblance to the Needles of the San Juan. Of these the most conspicuous, called by the Mexicans the Cabazon, resembles in its outline a Spanish sombrero, but is of gigantic dimensions, being at least 1,500 feet in height.

"South from the Cabazon is a high level mesa, composed of Cretaceous rock, which forms the divide between the Puerco and the San José. This I have seen from the other side on a former expedition.

"*September* 25, *Camp* 53–54.—To-day we crossed over the south end of the Nacimiento Mountain to the pueblo of Jemez. The first part of our route was over the

---
[*] *Pinus ponderos, P. Lambertiana, Abies Douglasi*, and *Abies grandis*.
[†] *Rhus diversiloba* and *Robinia Neo Mexicana*.

upturned edges of the Cretaceous and Triassic rocks; the angle of inclination becoming greater as we approached the mountain. Our march afforded us many wild and picturesque views, made so both by the ragged outlines of the hills and the bright colors of the materials composing them; some consisting of blood-red sandstone; others of snow-white gypsum; others still of the two intermingled.

"After winding through a labyrinth of such hills, we reached the Carboniferous strata, resting directly on the granite. The rocks of this formation are here more calcareous than at Santa Fé, and abound in fossils, among which I saw most of those enumerated in the Santa Fé section, and, in addition to these, collected a coral and a crinoid, which are apparently new. On descending the eastern slope of the mountain, we found the sedimentary rocks succeeding each other precisely as before. Near the pueblo of Jemez, however, the Cretaceous strata have been entirely removed, but they are visible a few miles farther north. As on the western side, copper occurs here near the junction of the Trias with the Cretaceous. In the valley of Jemez River are a number of buttes of white tufaceous rock, representing a geological element of which we had seen no traces in all our explorations of the San Juan country. These buttes are undoubtedly Tertiary, and, as I have stated in my notes on the geology of the vicinity of Abiquiu, doubtless belong to the great series of fresh-water deposits of Miocene and Pliocene age which skirt the eastern bases of the Rocky Mountains. Here, as elsewhere, they are of local origin and limited extent; having been deposited in and partially filling an old eroded valley running north and south along the eastern base of Nacimiento Mountain. By the action of Jemez River this valley has again been washed out, leaving only here and there a mass of Tertiary rock standing isolated or adhering unconformably to the sides of the trough composed of the older strata.

"*September 26, Jemez to Santo Domingo.*—In this part of our route we were almost constantly upon the trap mesas which skirt the southern end of the Valles, and extend on the east side of the Rio Grande to the Cerillos. This great overflow of trap, though deeply eroded by the Rio Grande, is geologically quite modern, presenting the same appearance, in all respects, as the trap plateaus which surround the San Francisco Mountain, Mount Taylor, the Raton, &c.; all of which I have before described."

The Valles.—No one has yet penetrated the Valles to study their geological structure, but there can be little doubt of its general character. This mountain group is composed of a number of parallel ranges, of but limited extent, having the general trend of all the chains of the Rocky Mountain system of this vicinity, separated by several well-marked, picturesque, and fertile valleys, from which, rather paradoxically, the mountains take their name. While we know that the sedimentary rocks are visible in many places in the Valles, and that the principal axes are granitic, still the presence of immense sheets and masses of trap give an aspect to the scenery and a character to the geology somewhat different from those of most of the mountain regions visited on the present expedition. On the eastern side of the Valles, to and beyond the Rio Grande, nothing but trap is visible; and we here re-entered the region so fully described in a preceding chapter.

DESCRIPTIONS

OF THE

CRETACEOUS FOSSILS

COLLECTED ON THE

SAN JUAN EXPLORING EXPEDITION UNDER CAPT. J. N. MACOMB, U. S. ENGINEERS.

BY

F. B. MEEK.

A REPORT ON THE CRETACEOUS FOSSILS CONTAINED IN THE COLLECTIONS BROUGHT FROM NEW MEXICO BY THE EXPLORING EXPEDITION UNDER THE COMMAND OF CAPT. J. N. MACOMB, OF THE UNITED STATES TOPOGRAPHICAL ENGINEERS.

BY F. B. MEEK.[*]

The following pages and the accompanying plates contain descriptions and illustrations of eleven new species of Cretaceous fossils. Figures and descriptions have also been added of a few previously known forms, of special interest as guides in identifying the several formations, and in determining their relations to established horizons in the same system elsewhere.

By reference to the able report of Dr. Newberry, the geologist of the expedition, it will be seen that he divides the Cretaceous rocks of New Mexico into three groups, as follows:

1. THE UPPER DIVISION, consisting of gray, white, and purple marls, alternating with soft, yellow, calcareous sandstone, altogether 1,500 feet in thickness. In this group, a portion of which he thinks may possibly prove to be of Tertiary age, he observed numerous silicified trunks of trees, together with leaves of *Alnus*, *Platanus*, &c. At the base of the whole, he found a thin bed containing *Placenticeras placenta*,[†] *Baculites anceps*, var., *Anchura*, *Inoceramus*, &c.

2. THE MIDDLE DIVISION is composed of dove-colored and ferruginous limestones, shales, &c., altogether from 1,200 to 1,500 feet in thickness, and containing *Prionocyclus*, *Mucombi*, *Scaphites larvæformis*, *Inoceramus problematicus*, *Ostrea congesta*, &c.

3. THE LOWER DIVISION, consisting of yellow or brown sandstone and green shales, 250 to 400 feet in thickness, containing *Ammonites*, *Exogyra*, *Plicatula*, and leaves of *Salix*, *Platanus*, *Quercus*, &c.

After a careful examination of the specimens from these rocks, I fully concur with Dr. Newberry in the opinion that all of those of the Lower Division, with possibly

---

[*] This report was prepared in 1860, and has remained unpublished until this time (November, 1875). I have at this latter date given it as careful a revision as numerous other engagements would permit; and, in doing this, several changes of nomenclature were found to be necessary, in order to bring the whole up to the present more advanced state of palæontological science. Such changes as refer to other publications issued at any date after that first above mentioned, were of course made in the revision of the MS. at the latter date.—F. B. M.

[†] The name *Placenticeras* was first proposed by me in the Proceedings of the Philosophical Society of Philadelphia, 1870; and again used in Hayden's Second Annual Report of the United States Geological Survey of the Territories, 297, 1872; also in Upper Missouri Palæontology, now in the press (November, 1875). *Ammonites placenta*, DeKay, is the type of the group.

the exception of a portion of its upper beds, represent the Dakota group (No. 1) of Upper Missouri Cretaceous series; also that his Middle Division occupies the same horizon as the Fort Benton and Niobrara groups (Nos. 2 and 3) of the Upper Missouri section; while the lower bed at least, of his Upper Division, represents apparently a blending of the Fort Pierre group and Fox Hills beds, Nos. 4 and 5 of the same.

The relations between the two sections will be more clearly understood by placing the names of the several groups of each side by side; thus:

NEW MEXICAN CRETACEOUS SECTION.	UPPER MISSOURI CRETACEOUS SECTION.
Upper Division (lowest bed at least)............	{ Fox Hills Beds, No. 5. { Fort Pierre Group, No. 4.
Middle Division...........................	{ Niobrara Division, No. 3. { Fort Union Group, No. 2.
Lower Division	Dakota Group, No. 1.

The vegetable remains from the Lower Division of the New Mexican section (as well as those from the others) have been investigated by Dr. Newberry, in whose report the reader will find them fully described and illustrated. The molluscan remains from the Lower Division are, *Exogyra columbella*, M.; *Plicatula arenaria*, M., *Pinna* (fragments), *Gervillia?* (fragments), *Gryphæa* (undetermined fragments), and *Prionotropis Woolgari** (=*Ammonites percarinatus*, H. & M.).

The following is a list of the species described and identified from the Middle Division, each of those followed by the letter M. being new, and described by the writer from these collections, viz: *Ostrea congesta*, Conrad, *O. lugubris*, Conrad, *O. uniformis*, M., *Gryphæa Pitcheri*, Morton, *Exogyra arietina*, Roemer, *E. lævisculu*, Roemer, *E. columbella*, M., *Anomia nitida*, M., *Caprotina bicornis*, M., *Inoceramus fragilis*, Hall & Meek, *I. problematicus*, Schlotheim (sp.), *I. latus*, Mantell?, *Crassatella Shumardi*, M., *Cyprimera? crassa*, M., *Turritella Leonensis*, Roemer, *Prionocyclus? Macombi*,† M., *Prionotropis Woolgari*, and *Scaphites larvæformis*, M. & H.

Of these eighteen species, the following are common to the rocks of this horizon in New Mexico, Kansas and Nebraska, viz., *Ostrea congesta*, *Inoceramus problematicus*, *I. fragilis*, *I. latus ?*, *Scaphites larvæformis*, and *Prionotropis Woolgari*. None of them, however, are known to occur in New Jersey, or at other localities east of the Mississippi, in the United States; though *Inoceramus problematicus*, *I. latus*, and *Prionotropis Woolgari* occur in Europe.

From the lowest bed of the Upper Division, the collection contains specimens of *Avicula Nebrascana*, Evans & Shumard, *Callista Deweyi*, Meek & Hayden, *Cardium bellulum*, M., *Anchura? Newberryi*, M., *Baculites anceps*, Lamarck ?, and *Placenticeras placenta*, Dekay (sp.).

Avicula Nebrascana, *Callista Deweyi*, *Baculites anceps ?*, and *Placenticeras placenta* are common to this lowest bed of the Upper Division in New Mexico and the corresponding horizon on the Upper Missouri; and *Placenticeras placenta* also occurs in the same position in New Jersey and Alabama, while *Baculites anceps* also occurs in New

---
* The name *Prionotropis* proposed by me in the Palæontology of the Upper Missouri, now (November, 1875) in the press; the American form there referred to *Prionotropis Woolgari*, Mantell, being the type.

† This generic name was proposed by me in Hayden's Report of the Geological Survey of the Territories in 1872-208 (foot-note), and the genus is more fully described in the Palæontology of the Upper Missouri, now in the press.

Jersey and in the Upper Chalk of Europe; as well as on the North Platte, in the Fox Hills Group of the Upper Missouri Cretaceous section.

Although it has been found convenient, throughout considerable areas on the Upper Missouri, to subdivide the equivalents of the Middle and Upper Divisions of the New Mexican section each into two groups, this is not everywhere the case, and Dr. Newberry did not find any well-marked physical breaks in either of these divisions in New Mexico.

It is worthy of note that, as on the Upper Missouri, the strongest palæontological break is just where Dr. Newberry draws the line between his Middle and Upper Divisions. Up to this time, not a single species is known to cross this line, either on the Upper Missouri, in Kansas, Nebraska, Texas, or in New Mexico.

A careful study of extensive collections of these fossils, brought by Dr. Hayden from these rocks on the Upper Missouri, has satisfied me that the beds above this horizon represent the Upper or White Chalk of Europe (= *"Étage Sénonien,"* d'Orbigny); while those below (from which we have yet obtained fossils) represent the Lower or Gray Chalk, and probably the Upper Greensand of Europe (= the *Turonien* and *Cénomanien*, d'Orbigny).* The evidence, so far as it goes, to be derived from the New Mexican collections under consideration, warrants the same conclusion in regard to the rocks from which they were obtained.

LAMELLIBRANCHIATA.

Genus OSTREA, Linn.

OSTREA LUGUBRIS, Conrad.

Plate 1, figs. 1 a, b, c, d.

Ostrea lugubris, Conrad (1857), U. S. and Mex. Bound. Report, vol. 1, p. 156, plate 10, fig. 5 a, b.

Shell small, thin, oval, or subcircular. Lower valve attached by most of its under surface; while its lateral and ventral margins rise abruptly, usually for a short distance, above the base of attachment, becoming at the same time ornamented by small regular plications, which are sometimes rendered slightly rugose by marks of growth; beak small, obtusely angular, usually turned a little to the left, and attached by its whole under side; area short, triangular; muscular scar transversely ovate-reniform, and placed near the left or anterior side. Upper valve flat, or sometimes a little convex near the umbo, and slightly concave in the middle; marked by small regular plications, which rarely extend to the umbo, and are often confined to the free margins.

Length of a large specimen, 0.95 inch; breadth of same, 0.65 inch; depth varying from 0.12 to 0.28 inch.

This seems to be a common and characteristic species in the lower portions of the Middle Cretaceous of New Mexico. The specimens usually have a proportionally larger scar of attachment than that figured by Mr. Conrad. Where they are attached by the whole under side of the lower valve, the plicated margins rise little above the base of attachment; but where the scar of adhesion is small, the free plicated margins are more produced; though it seems never to be a very deep shell. It was not gregarious to the

---

* Proceedings of the Academy of Natural Sciences of Philadelphia, January, 1862.

same extent as *O. congesta* of Conrad; the specimens being usually found scattered about on the surfaces of calcareous and sandy slabs, to which, in most instances, they were evidently attached during the life of the animal.

Locality and position.—Banks of the Canadian, Vado del Chama, Galisteo, Pagosa, Middle Cretaceous of Dr. Newberry's section.

OSTREA (GRYPHÆA?) UNIFORMIS, Meek.

Plate I, figs. 2 *a*, *b*, *c*.

Shell small, rather thin, trigonal-ovate or subcircular in form, not oblique; under valve rather deep, subcarinate along the middle, and arched beneath from the beak to the opposite margin; beak curved upward, but truncated by the area so as to rise little above the margins; area small; margins on each side of the area sometimes faintly marked by fine crenulations along the groove for the reception of the edge of the upper valve; surface marked by about three or four rather regular plications on each side of the larger mesial fold or carina; lines of growth obscure; muscular scar transversely oval, moderately distinct; upper valve unknown.

Length from the beak to the opposite extremity, 1.16 inches; antero-posterior diameter, about 1 inch; convexity or depth of the under valve, 0.65 inch.

This is a very peculiar shell, and cannot be confounded with any other species with which I am acquainted. Its large, prominent, mesial fold, extending from near the beak of the under valve to the opposite extremity, with three or four smaller plications on each side, give it much the appearance of some of the plicated *Brachiapoda* when viewed on the under side. The folds, or plications, vary somewhat on different specimens; but usually they are remarkably uniform for a species of this genus, and impart to the free margin opposite the beak a zigzag character, very similar to the front of some species of *Spirifer*. No specimens of the upper valve were obtained; but it will probably be found to have a large mesial sinus corresponding to the elevation of the other valve, and must possess a projection, curving down at the middle of the free margin opposite the beaks, to fill the deep notch in the margin of the other valve.

Thinking this species might be identical with one or the other of two peculiar oysters described by Dr. Shumard, from the Cretaceous rocks of Texas, under the names *O. bellaplicata* and *O. quadriplicata*, I sent him sketches of our shell, and he wrote that it is most nearly like his *O. bellaplicata*, though, he thinks, clearly distinct. The *O. bellaplicata* attains a much larger size, some of the specimens being as much as three inches in diameter, while its hinge-line is proportionally much longer, and its surface distinctly ornamented with concentric markings.

Locality and position.—Pagosa; Middle Cretaceous of the New Mexican section.

Genus EXOGYRA, Say.

EXOGYRA COLUMBELLA, Meek.

Plate I, figs. 3 *a*, *b*, *c*, *d*.

Shell small, rather thin, ovate; posterior side forming a semi-oval curve from the umbo to the ventral edge; anterior side rounded below the beak; ventral margin rounded. Lower valve convex, the most gibbous part sometimes forming an obtuse umbonal prominence, which is not separated from the front by a sulcus; beak slender, pointed, and distinctly coiled to the left; surface ornamented by small, but distinct, rather regular, radiating costæ, which bifurcate along the umbonal ridge; marks of growth rather obscure. Upper valve flat, oval, apparently smooth or only having obscure lines of growth.

Length from the most prominent part of the umbo to the ventral margin, 1 inch; transverse breadth, 0.72 inch; depth or convexity, about 0.42 inch.

It is possible that this shell may be identical with *E. læviuscula* of Roemer (Kreid. von Texas, plate ix, fig. 3 *a*, *b*, *c*); but with the means of comparison now within my reach, I can but regard it as distinct. All the specimens of it that I have yet seen are more oval in form and have a less distinctly spiral beak than the form described by Roemer. They also differ in having the under valve always marked by regular radiating costæ, while that of *E. læviuscula* is generally quite smooth, or rarely presents traces of nearly obsolete, rather broad, plications, as represented by fig. 3 *c* of Roemer's plate ix (Kreid. von Texas). It seems likewise to be a thinner and less robust shell than Roemer's species, and holds a lower stratigraphical position. In surface-markings as well as in general form, it closely resembles young specimens of *E. columba* of Lamarck (Anim. sans Vert., vi, 198) as figured by Goldfuss in his Petrefact. Germ. and by d'Orbigny in the Paléont. Français. It never attains more than one-eighth the size of adult individuals of that species, however, and differs in having an oval instead of a circular upper valve.

Locality and position.—Covero, Lower Cretaceous; also at Sierra Abajo, from the base of Middle Cretaceous, and at Galisteo, from the same member of Dr. Newberry's section.

Genus ANOMIA, Linn.

ANOMIA NITIDA, Meek.

Plate I, figs. 4 *a*, *b*.

Upper valve subcircular or a little oval transversely, very thin and brilliantly pearly, depressed-convex, the most prominent part being near the middle; lateral margins nearly equally rounded, ventral border forming a semi-oval curve; cardinal margin arched, or apparently presenting a similar outline to the ventral side; beak small, much compressed, nearly or quite marginal, and located at the middle of the dorsal side; surface marked by fine, rather regular, obscure, concentric striæ. (Under valve unknown.)

Transverse diameter, 1.07 inches; diameter from the cardinal to the ventral margin, 0.89 inch.

It is possible that some of the species referred to the genus *Anomia* from the Cretaceous and older rocks would be found to present fundamental differences from the typical forms of this group if we could see the under valve and the hinge and muscular impressions. Some six or seven species are now known from the Cretaceous rocks of this country, of nearly all of which, I believe, only upper valves have been found.

Locality and position.—Pope's Well; top of Middle Cretaceous.

Genus CAPROTINA, d'Orbigny.

CAPROTINA (REQUIENIA?) BICORNIS, Meek.

Plate I, figs. 7 a, b.

Shell apparently nearly equivalve; valves produced in the form of two oblique spiral horns; beaks greatly elevated, distinctly spiral, and directed obliquely forward and outward, the turns of each being widely disconnected; aperture of the valves comparatively small, ovate-subtrigonal in form, being a little higher than wide, and nearly straight on the basal and anterior sides, which range at right angles to each other; umbonal ridges rather prominent, spiral, and curving down to the anterio-basal margin. In front of these ridges, the valves are flat, and behind them convex. Surface ornamented by moderately distinct marks of growth.

Height, 2.43 inches; antero-posterior diameter, 1.74 inches; transverse diameter between the extremities of the beaks, nearly 2.75 inches; height of aperture of the valves, 1.38 inches; antero-posterior diameter of same, 1.22 inches.

The only specimen of this curious fossil I have seen is imperfect, the beak of its right valve being partly broken away. As near as can be determined, its valves seem to have been nearly equal, which, together with the greatly-produced and spiral character of its beaks, give it much the appearance of a *Diceras*. Still, as it shows no traces of an external ligament, while its shell-structure and surface-marking are like those of *Caprotina*, I do not feel warranted in placing it in the genus *Diceras*, though its generic relations must remain doubtful until specimens showing the hinge and interior can be seen.

The substance of the shell is of moderate thickness, and composed of two layers, which readily separate. The inner layer seems to be compact, and presents a distinctly-striated surface, the striæ being parallel to each other and ranging at right angles to the marks of growth. The outer layer appears to be more laminated, and breaks readily at right angles to the surface. Where portions of the shell have been removed, a distinct groove is seen extending from the posterior side of each valve spirally toward the beak. These grooves appear to have been left by a ridge or lamina on the inner side of each valve, and curve around the beak so as to be visible in an anterior view, as represented at a, fig. 7 b, plate 1.

In form and general appearance, this shell is evidently rather closely allied to *Requienia Archiaciana*, d'Orbigny (Pal. Français, Terr. Crét., iv, 363, plate 597). The grooves left upon the cast of its interior by the spiral ridge, or lamina, extending from the posterior side of each valve, are also exactly as in that species. It differs, however, in having much less prominent and angular umbonal ridges, while its valves seem to be more nearly equal, and its beaks are more produced and more widely separated.

Locality and position.—Fort Lancaster, Texas; from the middle portion of Dr. Newberry's section.

Genus PLICATULA, Lam.

PLICATULA ARENARIA, Meek.

Plate I, figs. 5 a, b, c.

Shell small, broad-ovate, usually a little oblique; ventral margin rounded; sides converging to the beaks at an angle of about 70° to 80°; beaks more or less angular. Under valve moderately convex. Upper valve nearly or quite flat. Surface of each valve ornamented by eighteen to twenty small, rather sharply-elevated, plications, only about half of which extend to the beaks, while the intermediate ones usually extend from one-third to one-half way from the free margins; concentric markings rather obscure.

Length from beak to the most prominent part of ventral margin, 0.50 inch; transverse diameter, 0.43 inch; convexity, 0.11 inch.

Resembles in size and form *P. incongrua*, Conrad (United States and Mexican Boundary Report, vol. 1, plate 6, fig. 10, 1857), but differs in not having squamose concentric markings as well as in having shorter plications intercalated between those that extend to the umbo. The substance of the shell must be thin, since the plications are rather distinctly marked on internal casts.

Locality and position.—Covero; Lower Cretaceous of Dr. Newberry's section.

Genus INOCERAMUS, Sowerby.

INOCERAMUS FRAGILIS, Hall and Meek.

Plate I, fig. 6.

Inoceramus fragilis, Hall and Meek, Mem. American Acad. Arts and Sci., vol. 5, new series, plate 2, fig. 6.

The specimens of this species in the collection are larger than that first figured and described by Professor Hall and the writer, which is evidently a young shell. They agree, however, so nearly in all other respects as to leave no doubts in regard to their identity. In comparing the figure here given with that first published in the Memoirs of the American Academy, it should be borne in mind that the anterior side of the latter was mistaken for the cardinal margin, both in the description and in the arrangement of the figure on the plate. The figure given on the accompanying plate is correctly arranged, with the hinge-margin upward.

This species has a wide geographical distribution in the far west, having been collected at several distantly-separated localities between Fort Benton on the Upper Missouri and New Mexico in the far southwest. I have no knowledge of its occurrence anywhere east of the Mississippi.

Locality and position.—Vado del Chamo; base of the Middle Cretaceous of Dr. Newberry's section.

Genus CRASSATELLA, Lam.

CRASSATELLA SHUMARDI, Meek.

Plate II, figs. 7 a, b, c.

Shell under medium size, very thick, oval-subtrigonal, moderately convex; extremities narrowly rounded; base forming a semi-oval curve; dorsal outline sloping from the beaks at an angle of about 100°; beaks moderately prominent, rather obtuse, located slightly in advance of the middle; surface marked by fine lines of growth, and small, regular, concentric ridges; escutcheon lanceolate; lunule lance-oval, rather deep; muscular scars strongly impressed.

Length, 0.78 inch; height, 0.72 inch; convexity, 0.40 inch.

I have not seen very satisfactorily the hinge of this shell; but, as near as can be determined from impressions left in the matrix, it appears to present the characters of the genus *Crassatella*. It is chiefly remarkable for thickness of the valves in proportion to the size of the shell.

Locality and position.—Pope's Well; top of Middle Cretaceous of New Mexican section.

Genus CYPRIMERIA, Conrad.

CYPRIMERIA ? CRASSA, Meek.

Plate I, figs. 8 *a, b, c, d.*

Shell lenticular, rather thick, moderately convex; beaks distinctly compressed, and projecting very slightly beyond the regular curve of the cardinal margin; anterior muscular impression narrow-subovate and acute above; posterior broader, and rhombic-subquadrate; pallial line distinct, with a very faint sinuosity, or mere truncation, immediately under the posterior muscular impression; surface merely marked by concentric striæ.

Height, 1.93 inches; length, or antero-posterior diameter, 2 inches.

I am not altogether sure that this species will be found to agree *exactly* in its generic characters with Mr. Conrad's genus *Cyprimeria*, as its hinge-teeth do not seem to agree in some slight details with that of the type of that genus. Indeed, on first preparing a description of it for this report, I had proposed a provisional subgeneric name for it; but, on revising the MS., and comparing the figure, I find it resembles *Cyprimeria* at least so nearly that I have concluded to refer it to that genus. This has, however, been done partly because I am unwilling to propose a new name without having the type-specimen at hand for further study, it being in New York, and the circumstances being such that I have to revise the MS. in great haste.*

The hinge of this shell may be described as follows: hinge-plate broad and flat; anterior teeth compressed, the two in the right valve close together, and receiving that of the left between them, ranging very obliquely forward and downward; posterior tooth of right valve thicker, ranging obliquely backward and downward, grooved along the middle, and fitting between the posterior teeth of the left valve.

Locality and position.—Pope's Well; top of the Middle Division of the New Mexican Cretaceous section.

Genus CARDIUM, Linn.

CARDIUM BELLULUM, Meek.

Plate II, figs. 6 *a, b.*

Shell small, thin, ovate, a little oblique, gibbous, the most convex part of the valves being somewhat above the middle; beaks elevated, rather slender, incurved, slightly oblique, and located a little in advance of the middle; hinge very short, anterior and antero-basal margins forming together a semi-oval or nearly semicircular curve; postero-basal border prominent, and somewhat narrowly rounded; anal margin obliquely truncated above, so as to form with the slope in front of the beaks an angle of nearly

---

* Since writing the above, I have again examined the type-species, and find that it agrees so nearly with *Cyprimeria* that, so far as they show, there would seem to be no satisfactory reason for separating it.

90°; surface ornamented by about thirty small, simple, radiating costæ, all of which appear to be continued to the beaks.

Height, 0.27 inch; breadth, 0.23 inch; convexity, 0.22 inch.

There may be fine concentric markings on well-preserved specimens of this species, though none are visible on that from which the above description is made out. The radiating costæ are small, regular, and about equal to the grooves between. They are moderately well defined, but seem to become gradually obsolete toward the anterior and posterior dorsal margins. It is a neat little shell, presenting a regular cordate outline as seen from the anterior or posterior side.

Locality and position.—Rio de la Plata; base of upper member of the New Mexican Cretaceous series.

GASTEROPODA.

Genus ACTÆON, Montft.

ACTÆON INTERCALARIS, Meek.

Plate II, figs. 4 a, b, c.

Shell small, narrow-subovate, or subfusiform; spire rather elevated; volutions five to five and a half, compressed-convex, increasing gradually in breadth, and more rapidly in height; last one a little produced below, and forming about half the entire length; suture well defined; aperture narrow-subovate, very acutely angular above; surface marked by fine, slightly-impressed, punctured striæ, about twelve of which may be counted on the second turn.

Length, about 0.40 inch; breadth, 0.21 inch; apical angle nearly regular or a little convex, divergence about 35°.

The only specimen of this species in the collection has the lower part of the aperture and a portion of the columella broken away. The aperture, however, was evidently quite narrow, and the columella somewhat tortuous, with apparently one oblique fold below the middle. The fine, punctate, revolving grooves are not more than from one-third to one-half as wide as the spaces between on the second whorl, and can scarcely be seen without the aid of a magnifier.

This shell is more nearly allied to *A. subelliptica* (Meek and Hayden), from the Fort Pierre Group (=Cretaceous formation No. 4) of the Upper Missouri section, than any other with which I am acquainted. It may be readily distinguished from that species, however, by the much greater elevation of its spire in proportion to the length of its body-whorl, being in this respect about intermediate between *A. subelliptica* and *A. attenuata* (M. & H.), but quite distinct from them both.

Locality and position.—Same as last.

Genus ANCHURA, Conrad.

ANCHURA ? NEWBERRYI, Meek.

Plate II, fig. 5.

Shell of medium size, thin, fusiform; spire moderately elevated; volutions six, distinctly convex, increasing rather rapidly in size; suture well defined. Surface ornamented by revolving lines, two of which, on the body-whorl, become so much larger than the others as to form small carinæ. Of these two carinæ, the upper only is seen on the second turn, where it is much reduced in size; and, on those above, it is not distinguishable from the other revolving lines. Marks of growth obscure; aperture unknown; lip extended into a long appendage, the form of which cannot be determined from the specimen examined.

Length, exclusive of the beak, 0.65 inch; breadth of body-whorl, exclusive of the lip, 0.37 inch; apical angle slightly convex, divergence about 40°.

The collection contains but a single specimen of this species, and it is unfortunately so firmly imbedded in the hard matrix that it is impossible to work out the labial appendage. It evidently extends out, however, at least as much as 0.55 inch from the axis of the shell; and as its lower margin (which is thickened and a little reflexed) is seen to curve downward, it is probable that there are two salient points to the lip, one of which curves a little downward and the other upward. The lower margin of the lip can be seen to extend out to f of fig. 5, plate 2.

The body-whorl contracts into the beak below, but the latter is broken from the specimen, so that its form and length cannot be determined. Some eight or nine of the revolving lines may be counted on the upper turns, and about twenty (including the two carinæ) on the body-whorl. Half of those on the under side of the body-volution are larger than any of those above the carinæ, while between each two of them there are one or two smaller lines.

In size and general appearance, this species (at least as seen with the lip concealed in the matrix) bears some resemblance to *A. Americana*, Evans & Shumard (sp.), but has a less-elevated spire, and differs in being destitute of vertical costæ. In the latter character, it is more nearly like *A. sublævis*, Meek & Hayden, from which it may be readily distinguished by its two revolving carinæ on the body-whorl. It may be an *Aporrhais*, and have to be called *Aporrhais Newberryi*.

Locality and position.—Same as last.

CEPHALOPODA.

Genus BACULITES, Lam.

BACULITES ANCEPS, *var.* OBTUSUS.*

Plate II, figs. 1 *a, b, c, d, e, f, g, h.*

Baculites anceps, Lamarck (1822), An. Sans Vert., vii, 648.—D'Orbigny (1835), Tab. des Céph., 75; and (1840) Paléont. Fr. Terr. Crét., i, 565, plate 139, figs. 1, 7.—Roemer, Texas, 416; and (1852) Kreid. von Texas, 30, Inf. ii, figs. 3 *a, b, c,* &c.; and of many others.
Baculites vertebralis, Defrance (1816), Dict. Sci. Nat., Supp., iii, 168; and of some others, but not of Lamarck.

The collection under examination contains a number of specimens agreeing almost exactly in size, form, and surface-undulations with those figured under the name of *B. anceps* by Dr. F. Roemer, in his beautiful work on the Cretaceous rocks and fossils of Texas. As Dr. Roemer gives no enlarged figures showing the details of the septa of the Texas specimens, however, we have no means of determining whether or

---
* Originally I had not used the variety-name *obtusus* in connection with this shell; but I have applied that name to this form in the Upper Missouri Palæontology, now in the press (November 2, 1875), and add it here in revising the MS. of this report.

not they agree with those of the forms under consideration, though it is probable they will be found to present essentially the same characters. It is, therefore, chiefly owing to the probable identity of our specimens with those investigated by this distinguished author (who doubtless had an opportunity to make direct comparisons with authentic European examples of Lamark's species) that those under examination are here referred provisionally to *B. anceps*.

As I have had an opportunity to examine but two authentic specimens of *B. anceps* from foreign localities, and these were mere fragments, I have no means of knowing to what extent that species varies in form and internal characters. It is worthy of remark, however, that the two fragments of *B. anceps* here alluded to, as well as the figures of that species given by Professor Bronn in his *Lethæa Geognostica*, and those given by d'Orbigny in his *Paléontologie française*, although agreeing very nearly in form and surface-undulations, all differ from our New Mexican specimens, as well as from those figured by Dr. Roemer, in being rather distinctly carinated on the dorsal side. Again, on comparing the septa of the two European specimens of *B. anceps* mentioned above with d'Orbigny's enlarged figure of the same, it was found that they agree quite nearly in all their essential characters, while they both present rather marked differences from those of the New Mexican forms.

These differences consist not merely in the greater obtuseness of all the smaller divisions of the septa-lobes of the specimens under examination, but also in the form and mode of branching of the lobes themselves, as may be seen by reference to the figures given on plate II. I strongly suspect these differences to be of specific importance; but, without other means of comparison than those now available, it is difficult to determine whether this is the case or not.

It will be observed that the figures on plate II represent two rather marked varieties, some of the specimens being more slender and less compressed than others, and provided with obtuse, nearly circular, nodes, instead of transversely-elongated, arcuate undulations, as in the more compressed forms. A careful study of the whole series of specimens, however, shows that there are intermediate gradations between these two forms, while the septa present almost precisely the same characters throughout the entire series.

These two extremes of form bear very nearly the same relations to each other that *B. asper* of Morton does to his *B. carinatus*, which forms they also very closely resemble in their external characters, excepting that neither of them is ever carinated on the dorsal side, as in the typical *B. carinatus* of Morton. Dr. Roemer suggests that the latter is probably not distinct from *B. anceps* of Lamarck; and Mr. Gabb, who examined Dr. Morton's typical specimens, has arrived at the conclusion that not only that form (*B. carinatus*), but *B. asper* also, are merely varieties of *B. anceps*.* (See Proceedings of the Academy of Natural Sciences of Philadelphia for November, 1861.)

Without expressing any decided opinion in regard to this latter conclusion (not having seen the specimens upon which it is based), I would remark that the figures of the septa of *B. carinatus* and *B. asper* given by Mr. Gabb, seem to present some rather marked differences from those of *B. anceps*, though it is not improbable that there may

---

* Our figures 2 *a* and 2 *b*, on plate II, represent a section and a septum of *B. anceps* of Europe, for comparison.

be intermediate gradations connecting these extremes with Lamarck's species. At any rate, Mr. Gabb's figures of the septa of *B. carinatus* and *B. asper* certainly differ so materially from those of our New Mexican specimens (which, as already stated, are quite constant in their internal characters) as to make it desirable that the latter should be designated by another name (at least as a variety), until all doubts in regard to their relations can be removed by a direct comparison of a good series of specimens of all the forms alluded to.

Locality and position.—Same as preceding.

Genus PRIONOCYCLUS, Meek.

PRIONOCYCLUS ? MACOMBI, Meek.

Plate II, figs. 3 a, b, c, d.

Shell discoidal; umbilicus shallow, somewhat less than the diameter of the last whorl from the ventral to the peripheral side, and showing all the inner turns; volutions increasing gradually in size, very slightly embracing, compressed so as to be nearly flat on the sides, but rounding into the umbilicus; periphery rather narrow, nearly flat, and provided with a small mesial carina, which is very slightly waved in outline; lateral margins of the periphery each having a row of small compressed nodes, arranged one at the termination of each of the costæ, with their longer diameters nearly parallel to the peripheral keel; sides of each turn ornamented by from thirty-six to forty rather obscure, slightly flexuous costæ, only every second, third, or fourth one of which extends across to the umbilical margin, where they are usually a little swollen.

The septa are generally a little crowded in adult shells, and divided into two very unequal principal lobes on each side. Siphonal lobe slightly longer than wide, and ornamented by three branches on each side, the two terminal of which are a little larger and much less spreading than the lateral pair, and each ornamented by some five or six sharp digitations along the margins and at the extremity; while the first pair of principal lateral branches above the terminal ones are of nearly the same form as the latter, but more spreading, and the third pair are smaller, and merely provided with a few digitations; first lateral sinus (dorsal saddle of old nomenclature) as long as the siphonal lobe, but much wider, and deeply divided into two unequal parts, of which the one on the siphonal side is larger than the other; each of these principal divisions being ornamented by some four or five short, irregular branchlets, with obtusely digitate margins; first lateral lobe longer and slightly wider than the siphonal, and provided with some seven or eight short, rather unequal, merely digitate, and palmately-spreading terminal and lateral branchlets; second lateral sinus narrower, but as long as the first on the outer or siphonal side, and much shorter on the umbilical, having two short, unequal, digitate, terminal branches at the end, and some three or four short, irregular divisions along the oblique margin of the umbilical side; second lateral lobe small, or scarcely more than twice as large as the auxiliary lobe of the siphonal sinus, and somewhat irregularly bifid, the divisions being short, and, like the lateral margins, more or less digitate.

Greatest diameter of a specimen retaining only a small portion of the non-septate outer whorl, 4.40 inches; greatest convexity of same, 0.95 inch; breadth of umbilicus, 1.35 inches; breadth of last whorl from the siphonal to the umbilical side, 1.80 inches.

Young specimens of this species differ materially from the adult; those not more than an inch or an inch and a half in diameter being destitute of nodes, and provided with a continuous instead of a waved carina. Their costæ are also more crowded, more numerous, and curve distinctly forward near the peripheral margins. At this size, the shell closely resembles specimens of *Ammonites percarinatus*, Hall and Meek, of the same age; but, as it advances in growth, it assumes quite different external characters, while its septa differ at all ages.

It seems to be related to a Texas species, described by Dr. Shumard, in the Transactions of the St. Louis Academy of Sciences (vol. 1, p. 539), under the name of *A. Graysonensis*. Dr. Shumard, however, to whom I sent sketches of it, regarded it as clearly distinct. He wrote that he had seen quite a number of specimens of *A. Graysonensis*, and that none of them attain more than one-third the size of the form under consideration, while they are always destitute of nodes, and have a more distinctly-waved carnia.

I am far from being satisfied that this shell belongs to the same group as that for which I have, in one of Dr. Hayden's Reports and again in the Upper Missouri Palæontology, used the name *Prionocyclus*. It is certainly not a true *Ammonites*, however, as that genus is restricted to typical forms, but more nearly allied to *Prionocyclus*.

Named in honor of Capt. J. N. Macomb, of the United States Topographical Engineers, commander of the expedition.

Locality and position.—Banks of Canadian; lower part of Middle Cretaceous of New Mexican section.

EXPLORING EXPEDITION FROM SANTA FÉ TO JUNCTION OF GRAND AND GREEN RIVERS.

DESCRIPTIONS

OF THE

CARBONIFEROUS AND TRIASSIC FOSSILS

COLLECTED ON THE

SAN JUAN EXPLORING EXPEDITION UNDER CAPT. J. N. MACOMB, U. S. ENGINEERS.

BY

J. S. NEWBERRY,

GEOLOGIST OF THE EXPEDITION.

DESCRIPTIONS OF FOSSILS.

BY J. S. NEWBERRY.

DELTODUS MERCUREI, Newb.

Plate III, figs. 1, 1ª.

Teeth of medium size, thick and strong, cuneiform or spatulate in outline, strongly arched in both senses, broader end uniformly rounded, lateral margins thickened and rounded over, on one side depressed, on the other raised into a prominent marginal ridge, which is separated from the central portion of the crown by a relatively deep and narrow sulcus; whole surface of crown finely punctate, especially in the sulcus, and gently undulate. This is quite unlike any Coal-Measure *Deltodus* hitherto discovered. In its general proportions and appearance, it is perhaps most like *D. spatulatus*, N. & W., from the Mountain limestone of Illinois; but in the present species the marginal sulcus is much deeper and more conspicuous, and the granulation of the surface finer.

Formation and locality.—Coal-Measures; Santa Fé, New Mexico.

PTYCHODUS WHIPPLEI, Marcou.

Plate III, figs. 2–2ª.

Teeth varying in form according to their places in the mouth; largest, conical in profile; the central cone rounded above and on the lateral and posterior faces, expanded below into a flattened, subquadrate base; summit of crown marked with a few distinct, acute, transverse folds of enamel; anterior face covered with reticulate, radiating, raised lines, as in *Pt. Mortoni;* upper surface of margins of base finely and reticulately wrinkled; tuberosity of base small, subquadrate, with a broad sulcus, having an antero-posterior direction; the smaller teeth are relatively broader and lower, elliptical or subtrigonal in outline; the central cone marked with a few coarse interrupted ridges.

This is the most conical tooth of the genus, the central cone being considerably higher and narrower than in *Pt. altior*, Ag. The other known American species, *Pt. Mortoni*, has also a decidedly conical form, in that respect differing from the European species, but wants the transverse folds so characteristic of the flattened, quadrate species of the Old World.

In the specimen figured by M. Marcou, the crown is worn smooth, the folds being all gone. It is also more angular than those now figured; but the general resemblance is so strong that I do not hesitate to consider them the same.

Formation and locality.—The horizon at which the teeth of *Ptychodus Whipplei* occur in the Cretaceous rocks of New Mexico is, according to my observations, very clearly defined. It is below the middle of the series, generally within a hundred feet of the yellow Lower Cretaceous leaf-bearing sandstones.

The rock containing them is a sandy, ferruginous limestone, lying in thin bands divided by layers of dark calcareous (often bituminous) shale. The associate fossils are *Lamna Texana*, *Gryphæa Pitcheri*, *Ostrea lugubris*, *O. uniformis*, *Inoceramus problematicus*, *I. fragilis*, *Ammonites percarinatus*, *A. Macombii*, *Scaphites larviformis*, &c.

The *Ostrea* of which M. Marcou speaks as occurring with *Pt. Whipplei* is not *O. congesta*, as he supposes, but *O. lugubris* of Conrad. The place of *O. congesta* is a little higher in the series. *Gryphæa Pitcheri* is found a few feet below.

Of all these species, specimens were obtained on the banks of the Canadian at Galisteo, at the ford of the Chama, and at the Pagosa.

Athyris subtilita, Hall, sp.

Wherever we found Carboniferous rocks in the West, we were sure to meet with this wide-spread fossil. On the Colorado, west of the San Francisco Mountains, at the junction of the Grand and Green Rivers, in the Sierra la Plata, at Santa Fé, and at Pecos, it is abundant. At all these places, the most common form of the Coal-Measures in the valley of the Mississippi is most numerously represented; there, as here, varying somewhat in size, apparently accordingly as it was well or ill fed.

In the extreme upper Carboniferous or Permian beds, an *Athyris* is common which has sometimes been considered as distinct from those obtained below, for it is usually larger and more ventricose than the prevailing type of Coal-Measure specimens. It may possibly be a distinct species, but it is true that in many places in the Coal-Measures *A. subtilita* is found, assuming precisely the same form and reaching an equal size. It will, therefore, be impossible to make two species of them until some internal characters are found which can serve to distinguish them.

Spirifer cameratus, Morton.

This shell is common in the limestone of the Carboniferous series at all points in the route of our expedition where these rocks are exposed. Of the large number collected in New Mexico and Utah, and a very much larger number examined, all exhibit nearly the same character, the prevailing type as regards size and markings closely resembling that figured by Professor Hall in Captain Stansbury's Report under the name of *S. triplicatus*. Specimens collected in Eastern Kansas and others obtained from the banks of the Colorado are absolutely undistinguishable. The larger shell, considered by Mr. Davidson identical with *S. striatus* of Martin, is nowhere met with in New Mexico or Utah. It is abundant in the mountain limestone of Illinois and Missouri, but I have never seen it from the Coal-Measures. Considering the marked difference in form and position of these two shells, it is difficult to resist the conviction that if the European palæontologists could study what they regard as American representatives of *S. striatus* in great numbers as they occur in place, they would consider them as forming two distinct species.

SPIRIFER (TRIGONOTRETA?) TEXANUS, Meck.

Plate III, figs. 5, 5ᵃ, and 5ᵇ.

Spirifer (Trigonotreta?) Texanus, Meek (1871), Proceed. Acad. Nat. Sci. Phila., xviii, 179.

Shell scarcely attaining a medium size, very gibbous in the adult, varying from subquadrate or subglobose to longitudinally-subovate, the widest part being generally in advance of the middle, and the length greater than the breadth; hinge-line short, or in young individuals scarcely equaling the breadth of the valves, and in the adult often proportionally very decidedly shorter, sometimes obtusely angular at the extremities, while in the more gibbous individuals its extremities do not project beyond the lateral slopes; anterior margin often somewhat emarginate in the middle. Dorsal valve truncato-suborbicular or subquadrate, and moderately convex; beak incurved, with a narrow area, but not prominent; mesial elevation commencing as a small simple plication at the beak, but rapidly widening and becoming more prominent and angular, with on each side several small costæ, which divide so as to form altogether twelve to sixteen at the front; lateral slopes having at the beak each two or three plications or costæ, which farther forward divide so as to form as many fascicles of three each, or about nine on each side of the mesial fold. Ventral valve more gibbous than the other, and more strongly arched than the other from the beak to the front; beak very prominent in the adult, always strongly incurved over the hinge; cardinal area moderate, well defined, and extending to the extremities of the hinge without narrowing strongly laterally, rather distinctly arched with the beak; foramen slightly wider at the hinge than high, open nearly or quite to the apex, and provided with a distinct linear marginal furrow on each side; mesial sinus angular, and commencing very small at the beak, and widening and deepening rapidly to the front, where it terminates in a strongly-curved triangular projection fitting into a corresponding sinus in the margin of the other valve; surface as in the dorsal valve, the costæ within the sinus being smaller than those on the lateral slopes, and numbering about sixteen to twenty; fine, rather obscure, undulating striæ, and, near the front and lateral margins, a few stronger marks of growth traverse the valves, parallel to the free margins; while numerous small, rather scattering, but regularly-disposed granules, apparently the remaining bases of minute spines, may be seen over the whole surface of well-preserved specimens, which also sometimes show traces of very fine radiating striæ.

Length of one of the largest specimens seen, 1 inch; breadth of same, about 0.98 inch; convexity, 0.90 inch; length of hinge, 0.72 inch. Smaller specimens are proportionally less gibbous, shorter, wider, and provided with a proportionally somewhat longer hinge.

Small specimens of this species resemble a little the more gibbous varieties of *S. cameratus*, with a very short hinge; but, in the adult, the valves become proportionally more elongated anteriorly, and more gibbous, and the beak of the ventral valve is so narrow, so much produced and incurved, as to present the appearance of a *Pentamerus*. Its distinctly-granulated and minutely-striated surface, however, will always serve to distinguish, even the specimens with the most extended hinge-line, from the most gibbous varieties of *S. cameratus*, with a short hinge. Its granular surface leads me to suspect that it may possibly be a *Spiriferina*; but as I have not been able to see any certain indications of punctures, I hardly feel warranted in referring it to that group. I have not, however, given it an examination by the aid of higher power than a strong hand-magnifier. Should a more thorough examination reveal the usual punctate structure, and the internal septum of that group, it will of course have to be called *Spiriferina Texana*.

Compared with foreign forms, this shell seems to be most nearly like the extremely narrow and elongated variety of *S. duplicatus*, Phillips, as illustrated by Mr. Davidson's figure 8, Plate IV, Monogr. British Carboniferous Brachiopoda. It is much more gibbous, however, with decidedly more prominent and more angular mesial sinus; while its surface-granulations and minute striæ serve to distinguish it. Although its mesial fold has a very angular appearance, a careful examination shows it to be very slightly flattened, or sometimes even marked by a linear furrow along its crest; and there is sometimes also a slightly more prominent line along the middle of the angular sinus of the other valve.

Locality and position.—The type-specimen was found, by Mr. H. R. Roessler, associated with Coal-Measure fossils in Young County, Texas. Dr. Newberry also has specimens from the northwest corner of Jack County, west fork of Trinity River, Texas. I have never seen it from any locality north or east of Texas.—(F. B. M.)

PRODUCTUS NODOSUS, Newb.

Plate III, figs. 3-3 *d*.

This fine *Productus*, first collected on a former expedition, and described in my report to Lieutenant Ives (Colorado Expedition, Geology, p. 124, plate 1, figs. 7-7 *b*), we found in large numbers at Santa Fé, and in many localities along our route quite to the Colorado. Indeed, it is perhaps as common as any other species of the genus in Western New Mexico and Southern Utah.

The figures now given of it will convey a much better impression of its true character than those before published. From these it will be seen that, with a near approach in form and markings to *P. cora* and *P. æquicostatus*, it is distinguished from these and other species by the single line of conspicuous nodes, the bases of large spines, which mark the median line of the ventral valve. In some specimens a corresponding line of tubercles marks the dorsal valve; but they are always less distinctly marked and are often entirely wanting.

Figures 3 *c* and 3 *d* show a somewhat remarkable variation in the length of the cardinal border, but the wings are usually quite short, as in figures 3 *b* and 3 *c*.

PLEUROTOMARIA EXCELSA, Newb.

Plate III, figs. 4, 4ᵃ.

Shell large, long-conical in outline, higher than broad; whorls flattened outwardly above and below, having an angular section, the lower ones projecting considerably beyond the upper, giving the shell a shouldered appearance; surface smooth, or marked with fine lines of growth. Height, 3.2 inches. Breadth, 2.6 inches. In its large size and character of surface, this shell approaches *P. Missouriensis*, Swallow, but is apparently something smaller and more elongated in outline. In *P. Missouriensis* the width of the base is greater than the height, while in our species the reverse is true. In the Missouri specimen, which I saw in the hands of Governor Gilpin before it was described, the whorls are so fitted together as to produce smooth and somewhat concave sides; while in *P. excelsa* they are shouldered, and the outline of the sides is straight or slightly convex.

Formation and locality.—Upper part of the Carboniferous formation, in the cañon of Grand River, near its junction with Green River, Southern Utah.

LAMNA TEXANA, Roem.

Lamna Texana, Roemer, Kreide v. Texas, p. 21, taf. 1, fig. 7.

Found in company with *Ptychodus Whipplei* on the banks of the Canadian, at Galisteo, and at the Pagosa in the "fish-bed" near the base of the Middle Cretaceous series.

OXYRHINA MANTELLI, Agass.

Oxyrhina Mantelli, Ag., Roemer, Kreide v. Texas, p. 29, taf. 1, fig. 6.

This species occurs in the fish-bed of the Middle Cretaceous (No. 2 of Meek and Hayden's section) at the Pagosa. It is somewhat doubtful, however, whether it is really identical with that described by Agassiz. Probably more material will show that it is distinct.

OTOZAMITES MACOMBII, Newb.

Plate IV, figs. 1, 2; Plate VI, figs. 5, 5ª.

Frond pinnate, pinnæ opposite or subalternate, approximate or imbricated, entire, sessile; lower ones small, reniform, or circular; upper large, oblong, rounded, or truncated at the extremity; base nearly as broad as apex, very slightly auricled and rounded at upper and lower angles, attached to rachis by two-thirds to three-fourths of entire breadth; nerves numerous, fine, but distinct, equal, forked, radiating from the attached portion of the base to all parts of the lateral and apical margins; rachis slender, smooth, or finely striated longitudinally.

The outline of the entire frond is linear-lanceolate; different ones varying much in breadth and in the spacing of the pinnules. At first sight, they seem to resemble closely those of several of the Cycads of the Oolite, Wealden, and Chalk, but on more careful examination they will be found to present characters widely different. The oblong or quadrate truncated pinnules, increasing in length from the base upward, at once suggest the species of *Nilssonia* and *Pterophyllum*, to which I have alluded, such as *P. majus*, *P. minus*, *P. Schaumbergense*, *Nilssonia compta*, &c., but the nervation (fine, equal, forking nerves, radiating from the attached portion of the base to all parts of the lateral and terminal margins,) and the mode of attachment to the rachis—each pinnule being distinctly separated from the others, the base slightly auricled, with rounded lobes—exclude it from both the preceding genera as at present constituted, and associate it with that group of *Zamites* (Brong.) which form Fr. Braun's genus *Otozamites* (*Otopteris*, L. & H.). From all known species of that genus, it is, however, somewhat widely separated by its general habit; yet, if the nervation and mode of insertion on the rachis of the pinnules afford good characters for generic classification, it must be grouped with these.

By Unger and Goeppert the genus *Otozamites* is not recognized, and our fossil would be classed by them in *Zamites*. Brongniart, however, claims that the section of *Zamites* represented by *Otozamites*, Br., including species differing much among themselves, it is true, but having in common important botanical characters, may be very properly regarded as forming a natural generic group.

As this species is distinctly new, it affords no very reliable evidence by which to judge of the age of the formation in which it is found, and yet it was with very lively pleasure that I discovered this and the associate Cycad in the copper-mines of New Mexico. Extremely few fossils had been found at this horizon, although I had sought them most carefully over a large area in which the red sandstones and shales are exposed. On finding in the old copper-mine at Abiquiu great numbers of fossil plants, I was more than pleased, and when upon examination they proved to be Cycads, plants most characteristic of the Triassic and Jurassic rocks in the Old World, I felt that we had here new and important evidence that the criteria of palæontology may be trusted.

Among the Cycads of the Old World, the species most nearly allied to *Oto. Macombii* is perhaps *O. obtusa*, Lind. & Hutt. (vol. 2, p. 128), from the Lias of England, and yet it will be seen on comparison of the two species that they are quite distinctly separated.

The discovery of this species by Mr. Remond in Sonora, associated with well-marked Triassic fossils, is a fact of great scientific value, and of very special interest to me, as it proves that the entire thickness of the gypsiferous red sandstones and marls of New Mexico, on and west of the Rio Grande, is made up of strata as old as the Trias. There is no doubt of the existence of Jurassic rocks in the Rocky Mountain region; but, so far as yet known, they do not occur on any part of the route followed by M. Marcou, and where he claims to have discovered them.

The plant-beds of the Moqui villages and Abiquiu are overlain by the yellow sandstones of the Cretaceous formation, and angiospermous leaves were found by us in a number of localities within five or ten feet of the underlying red marls. On the east flank of the Rocky Mountains, in some places, as at Cold Spring, on the Santa Fé road, I found a series of calcareous strata interposed between the Gypsum formation and the Cretaceous sandstones, and these, since holding the place and having the lithological character of the beds found by Dr. Hayden a little farther north, containing Jurassic fossils, are probably of that age. It is, however, true at the present time that no Jurassic *plants* have been found on this continent.

Formation and locality.—Triassic strata: Abiquiu, New Mexico; Los Bronces, Sonora (Mr. Remond); Yaki River, Sonora (Mr. Hartley).

ZAMITES OCCIDENTALIS, Newb.

Plate V, figs. 1, 1ᵃ, 2.

Frond petioled, linear-lanceolate; pinnules springing from the rachis at an angle of about 45°, rigid, coriaceous, closely approximated, linear in outline, 6–15 lines long, rounded or subacute at extremity, very slightly constricted at base; nerves fine, parallel, scarcely visible; rachis strong, chaffy.

In the form and attachment of the pinnules, this species approaches those grouped by Fr. Braun under the name of *Pterozamites*, in which the pinnules are usually linear and obtuse, and are attached to the rachis by the entire breadth of the base, which is not constricted. In the upper pinnules of our plant, however, the bases are very distinctly narrowed, and the attachment is sensibly oblique.

There is no described species of *Zamites* for which this will be likely to be mistaken, nor does it clearly fall into any of the groups of the genus which have been established. With the lance-leaved species (*Podozamites* Fr. Braun), such as *Z. distans*, *Z. lanceolatus*, *Z. undulatus*, *Z. falcatus*, &c., it seems to have very little in common, while from the group represented by *Z. Feneonis*, *Z. pectinatus*, *Z. Taxinus*, &c. (*Pterozamites* Fr. Braun), in which the folioles are inserted by all their uncontracted bases, it is separated by the slight though distinct expansion and constriction of the bases of the leaves. It would, therefore, seem to be a sort of connecting link between the groups with auricled and those with simple folioles. It approaches, however, nearest to that group of species described by Goeppert and Dunker (*Z. Dunkerianum* Gopp, *Z. Humboldtianum*, Dunk., *Z. Lyellianum* Dunk., &c.) from the Wealden, included by these authors in Pterophyllum, but by Brongniart in *Zamites*, and perhaps nearest of all to *Pter. Saxonicum*, Reich. (Gaea, v. Saxon., p. 134, t. 4, f. 14; Gopp., "Flora des Quadersandsteins in Schlesien", in Nova Acta Acad. Leop. Carol. Cæs. Nat. Cur., Oct., 1847, p. 362, taf. xxxviii, fig. 13), from the Quadersandstone (Cretaceous) of Saxony.

Formation and locality.—Top of Triassic series; Copper-mines near Abiquiu, New Mexico.

PECOPTERIS BULLATUS, Bunbury.

Plate VI, figs. 1, 1ª.

Among the specimens collected by Mr. Remond at Los Bronces, Sonora, are several of a *Pecopteris* in fruit, which is apparently identical with that first described by Bunbury from the coal-strata of Richmond, Virginia, and subsequently found by Professor Emmons in North Carolina. This species is considered by Professor Heer as identical with *Pecopteris Stutgardtensis*, Brong., one of the most characteristic plants of the European Trias.

Without more material, it would be presumption to attempt to decide this question; but that the plant before us is identical with that found in the Triassic strata of Virginia and North Carolina there is little doubt, and it therefore becomes an important connecting link between the eastern and the western exposures of Triassic strata.

Formation and locality.—Triassic rocks; Los Bronces and on Yaki River Sonora (Messrs. Remond and Hartley).

PECOPTERIS MEXICANA, Newb.

Plate VI, figs. 2, 2ª.

Frond bi- or tripinnate, small; pinnæ elongated, narrow, linear, acute; pinnules ovate, acute or subacute, sometimes falcate; nervules delicate and few, simple or once-forked; sori from 1 to 5 on basal portion of pinnules, seated on the nerves, and apparently covered with an indusium.

This is an exceedingly neat and pretty species, quite distinct from any other with which I am familiar. The plant was evidently small, and the fronds very delicate and membranous.

In common with most of the smaller Mesozoic species of the genus, it had long, narrow, riband-like pinnæ, and pinnules more or less falcate. In the form of the pinnules, the plant resembles *Pecopteris. Whitbiensis*, but the nervation is less crowded, the pinnæ more elongated, and in size the one is but a miniature of the other.

Formation and locality.—Triassic shales; at the Coal-mines of Los Bronces, Sonora (Mr. Remond).

PECOPTERIS FALCATUS, Emmons.

Plate VI, fig. 3.

This is evidently the plant described by Professor Emmons (Geol. N. Carolina, p. 327, fig. 9) as the fertile frond of his *P. falcatus*. No specimens of the barren frond occur in the collection; but the resemblance of the plant before us to that represented in the figure to which I have referred will be apparent to any observer.

Professor Heer considers *P. falcatus* of Emmons as identical with *Laccopteris germinans* Goep. (Gatt. Foss. Pflanz. liv. 1 and 2, plate vi, fig. 8) from the Keuper of Bayreuth; and he is probably correct in that conclusion, but the want of sterile fronds in the collection made by Mr. Remond leaves this question as it was, and we are now only able to identify, by means of this and the other species common to these widely-separated localities, the plant-beds of Sonora with the Trias of North Carolina and Richmond.

Formation and locality.—Los Bronces, Sonora (Mr. Remond).

PTEROPHYLLUM FRAGILE, Newb.

Plate VI, figs. 6 and 6ª.

Plant apparently delicate and fragile; midrib of frond slender and weak; pinnules oblong on the center of the frond, quadrangular above and below; summit squarely truncated; base attached to the rachis by its entire width; nerves fine, straight, simple, parallel.

The figure now given of the central part of the frond is taken from the only specimen which shows distinctly the nervation and other diagnostic characters of the species. In this the midrib is very delicate, and the pinnules are given off at a right angle. The other figure (6ª), which represents the base of a frond, is taken from a specimen which may belong to another species, as the nervation is nearly obliterated, and the pinnules are given off at an acute angle. I have thought it probable, however, that this latter peculiarity was simply due to their position near the base of the frond. With this exception, there is no tangible difference. Should this be found to be a constant feature, however, it would make it necessary to establish a new species on the specimen represented in fig. 6.

Formation and locality.—Triassic strata; Los Bronces, Sonora, Mexico.

PTEROPHYLLUM ROBUSTUM, Newb.

Plate VI, fig. 7.

Leaf large, 6 inches or more in width; pinnæ strap-shaped, 3 inches in length; bases expanded and coalescing: summit truncated or abruptly rounded; nervation delicate; nerves simple, parallel with the border of the pinnæ.

Two specimens of this singular plant are contained in the collection made by Mr. Remond, both imperfect, but both exhibiting the same characters. These are so peculiar that, without the evidence of *two* specimens, I would have said we had here simply a frond of *Tæniopteris* torn into strips, with an accidental but striking regularity. It seems hardly probable, however, though not impossible, that we should find in this small collection two fronds torn in precisely the same way. Besides this, the curvature of the sides of the divisions, where they coalesce at the base, is almost too regular to be the result of accident. They are also too uniform in width to be the effect of mechanical force. I have thought best, therefore, to describe this provisionally as a distinct species of *Pterophyllum*.

Formation and locality.—Triassic strata; Los Broncos, Sonora.

PODOZAMITES CRASSIFOLIA, Newb.

Plate VI, fig. 10.

Plant large and strong; pinnæ long-elliptical or spatulate in form, thick and coriaceous; nervation strong, but somewhat obscured by the thickness of the parenchyma; nerves parallel with the border, converging at both extremities of the pinnæ; a more distinct nerve traverses the central line.

Only detached pinnæ of this plant are contained in the collection made by Mr. Remond, but of these there are quite a number. By their large size and thickness, they are greatly different from those of any species of *Podozamites* hitherto described, and the distinct median nerve which they show presents a feature not common, if even known, in this genus. It is, therefore, possible that more complete specimens will show it to have characters which should be given generic value.

Formation and locality.—Triassic strata; Los Broncos, Sonora.

ALETHOPTERIS WHITNEYI, Newb.

Plate VII, figs. 1, 1ª, 1ᵇ.

Frond pinnate or bipinnate; pinnules of lower portion large, 2–3 inches long, narrowed above, broad below; the lower half of the base attached to, and decurrent on, the rachis; the upper half detached and subcordate; upper pinnules shorter, becoming at last elliptical and even orbicular; nervation crowded; midrib strong; lateral nerves fine and numerous, given off at nearly a right angle, simple or once forked.

The specimens of this plant are too fragmentary and imperfect to permit a full and complete description of it. Enough remains, however, to show that it was a strongly-marked species, and one quite distinct from any before described from this horizon. That portion of the frond contained in the collection made by Mr. Remond gives the impression of a large and strong plant, much more like some species from the Coal-formation than any hitherto found in the Triassic or Jurassic rocks. The detachment of the upper half of the base of the pinnules from the rachis is a feature so peculiar that it will serve to distinguish it at a glance. At first sight, this would seem to be accidental; but each of the pinnules of the larger specimens contained in the collection before us shows it to exist in precisely the same degree, so that we must conclude it to be a constant character.

This species is named in honor of Prof. J. D. Whitney, to whom I am indebted for the opportunity of examining the Triassic plants collected by Mr. Remond.

Formation and locality.—Triassic strata; Los Bronces, Sonora (Mr. Remond).

CAMPTOPTERIS REMONDI, Newb.

Plate VII, figs. 2, 2ª.

Frond digito-pinnate or spirally discoid, from one to two feet in diameter, consisting of twenty or more pinnae radiating from a common center, and extended in the same plane. The longest pinnae are one foot in length and one and one-half to two inches wide in their central and broadest portions. By the lower fourth of their length they are united; above they are free, lanceolate in outline, with margins obtusely dentate or crenate. The central nerve of each pinna is strong and flat. From this the secondary nerves spring at a subacute angle, curve gently upward at their extremities, and terminate in the crenations of the border. The tertiary nervation is very delicate, filling all the spaces between the secondary nerves with a somewhat irregular polygonal reticulation.

This remarkable fern evidently belongs to the same genus with that figured by Schimper in his *Paléontologie Végetale* (plate xlii, fig. 4) under the name of *Camptopteris serrata*, and it seems to me highly probable to the same genus as Goeppert's *Thaumatopteris Munsteri*. It is specifically, however, quite distinct from both of these; the fronds being larger, the pinnae broader and united by a greater portion of their length, and the dentition of the margins being shallower and more rounded. The nervation of *Camptopteris serrata* is not given, but in our plant it is very distinctly shown. It consists of a series of secondary nerves springing from the midrib at an angle little less than a right angle. These are gently arched upward, and terminate in the denticles of the border. The interval between them is filled with a polygonal network of rounded or quadrangular meshes, inside of which is a finer network, having the same general character, the meshes being four-, five-, or six-angled. This is also the nervation of *Thaumatopteris*, and since one plant, as shown by its peculiar form of frond, is generically identical with the typical species of *Camptopteris*, and its nervation can hardly be distinguished from that of *Thaumatopteris*, it tends to link these two genera together. I should also mention that on one of the specimens brought by Mr. Remond from Sonora besides the expanded pinnae of *Camptopteris*, we have one spirally folded precisely like that figured by Goeppert (Gattungen, plate 1, fig. 3).

The discovery of this plant in the coal-strata of Los Bronces is a matter of no little geological interest, as no species of *Camptopteris* had been before discovered on this continent. It also adds to the strength of the evidence of the Triassic age of the

Los Bronces coal, as the two species of *Camptopteris*—*C. serrata* and *C. quercifolia*—are both from the Upper Trias of Bayreuth.

The collection of Mr. Remond contains a large number of specimens of *Camptopteris*, although these are very much broken up; two of the more complete are now figured. These show the form of the radiate, almost peltate frond, the character of the margins, and nervation of the pinnæ.

Formation and locality.—Triassic strata; Los Bronces, Sonora, Mexico.

TÆNIOPTERIS ELEGANS, Newb.

Plate VIII, fig. 1.

Frond broadly spatulate or elliptical in outline; median nerve prominent and roughened; lateral nerves remarkably strong, uniform, parallel, simple, issuing from the median nerve at an acute angle. They are straight below, but near the summit of the frond are gently arched upward.

This fern will be distinguished at a glance from any of its associates by its remarkably strong and clear nervation. Fragments only of the frond are contained in the collection, so that we are unable to indicate its exact form; but the portions seen lead to the inference that when complete it was broadly spatulate or elliptical. Among all the great group of the *Tæniopteridæ*, there is none, so far as I know, which has a nervation so distinctly-marked and exact as this one.

Formation and locality.—Triassic beds of Los Bronces, Mexico.

TÆNIOPTERIS GLOSSOPTEROIDES, Newb.

Plate VIII, figs. 2, 2ᵃ.

Frond simple, spatulate in outline, one foot or more in length, two inches in width at the broadest part. The base is long-wedge-shaped. The median nerve is very strong and smooth; the lateral nerves relatively sparse and distinct, given off at an acute angle, dividing near the base, and more or less inosculating above to form elongated and irregular meshes.

In their general aspect, the fronds of this fern bear considerable resemblance to *Tæniopteris marantacea*, so common in the Trias of Europe; but in that species the frond is supposed to be pinnate, while in this it is unquestionably simple. The nerves in our plant are also finer and anastomose much more frequently. It seems to me, however, that we have not sufficient ground for separating these plants generically, and I, therefore, for the present, consider them simply as distinct species of the same genus. Of the figures now published, fig. 2 represents the summit of the frond; fig. 2ᵃ the base.

Formation and locality.—Triassic strata of Los Bronces, Sonora, Mexico.

TÆNIOPTERIS MAGNIFOLIA, Rogers.

Plate VIII, figs. 3, 4.

This species is abundantly represented in the collection made at Los Bronces by Mr. Remond, and is perhaps the most important connecting link between the Triassic beds of Sonora and those of North Carolina and Virginia. It may be recognized at once by the remarkably fine, uniform, parallel, simple veins given off at right angles from the midrib. None of the specimens obtained in Sonora rival in size the huge fronds obtained from the coal-beds of Richmond; but it is nevertheless the largest Sonora species, and the largest specimens are fully equal to the average of those found in Virginia.

There are in the collection of Mr. Remond many simple, narrow fronds, in which the nervation is similar to that described above, and the only difference I can discover between these and the larger ones is in the greater relative width of the rachis in the narrow fronds. It is frequently as broad as in the larger ones, and is seen to be scaled or chaffy toward the base. These narrow fronds are contracted in width, and are more or less waved or ruffled. Possibly these may represent another species, but the difference between the two forms seems hardly sufficient to justify me in considering them distinct.

JEANPAULIA RADIATA, Newb.

Plate VIII, fig. 6.

Fronds radiating from a common center and apparently forming a whorl. Each subdivision has a wedge-shaped outline and is several times dichotomously branched. The *laciniæ* are nearly straight, flat, and marked by continuous parallel veins.

Detached portions of this plant could hardly be distinguished from *Jeanpaulia Munsteriana*, Ung., from the Rhætic beds of Bayreuth, as will be seen by the figure now published. The subdivisions of the fronds, or perhaps the distinct fronds, are, however, narrower and straighter than in that species.

A large number of specimens of this plant occur in Mr. Remond's collection, and some of them possibly represent the European species, being stronger and having the sub-divisions more curved than in the specimen figured.

It will be regarded as an interesting fact that a well-marked species of *Jeanpaulia* is found in the Triassic of Sonora, and I have also to add that I have in my hands specimens which indicate the existence of another species of this genus, closely allied to, if not identical with, *J. Munsteriana* in the Triassic coal-formation of China. They were collected by Prof. R. Pumpelly. I have seen, too, a large and strong species, perhaps new, from the coal-basin of Richmond, Va., whence it was brought by Prof. D. S. Martin.

PLATE I.

	Page.
FIG. 1. OSTREA LUGUBRIS	123

    1 *a*. Under valve attached to a piece of rock, and showing the inside, with the muscular impression.
    1 *b*. Outside view of an upper valve of same.
    1 *c*. Outside view of an under valve, showing the scar of attachment, which is unusually small.
    1 *d*. Inside view of another specimen.

FIG. 2. OSTREA UNIFORMIS 124
    2 *a*. Inside view of an under valve.
    2 *b*. Outside of same.
    2 *c*. Lateral view of same.

FIG. 3. EXOGYRA COLUMBELLA 124
    3 *a*. Outside of under valve, from a wax cast taken in a mould left in the matrix.
    3 *b*. An internal cast of an under valve.
    3 *c*. Side view of same.
    3 *d*. An internal cast left in the rock, of the inside of the upper valve.

FIG. 4. ANOMIA NITIDA 125
    4 *a*. View of an upper valve, with only a portion of the shell attached to the cast.
    4 *b*. An outline side view of the same.

FIG. 5. PLICATULA ARENARIA 126
    5 *a*. An internal cast of the under valve.
    5 *b*. Outside of the upper valve.
    5 *c*. A side view of same.

FIG. 6. INOCERAMUS FRAGILIS 127

FIG. 7. CAPROTINA BICORNIS 126
    7 *a*. A view of one of the valves.
    7 *b*. The two valves together.

FIG. 8. CYPRIMERIA ? CRASSA 129
    8 *a*. Outside of a right valve.
    8 *b*. An internal cast of the same valve, showing the muscular and pallial impressions and a cast of the hinge.
    8 *c*. Hinge of the right valve.
    8 *d*. An anterior view.

PALAEONTOLOGY of Capt. Macomb's Expl's.   CRETACEOUS FOSSILS.   Plate 1.

PLATE II.

	Page
FIG. 1. BACULITES ANCEPS?	130

    1 *a*. Side view.
    1 *b*. An antisiphonal view.
    1 *c*. A section of same.
    1 *d*. A septum of same.
    1 *e*. A more slender, less compressed individual, with rounded nodes instead of transverse costæ.
    1 *f*. An antisiphonal view of same.
    1 *g*. An enlarged septum of the same.
    1 *h*. Transverse section of the same.

FIG. 2. BACULITES ANCEPS, after D'Orbigny, for comparison
    2 *a*. Transverse section.
    2 *b*. A septum.

FIG. 3. PRIONOCYCLUS ? MACOMBI 132
    3 *a*. Side view.
    3 *b*. An antisiphonal view.
    3 *c*. A septum of the same, enlarged.
    3 *d*. An antisiphonal view of a very small specimen.

FIG. 4. ACTÆON INTERCALARIS 129
    4 *a*. View showing the aperture, which is imperfect in the specimen figured.
    4 *b*. A back view of the same specimen.
    4 *c*. Surface-striæ, enlarged.

FIG. 5. ANCHURA? NEWBERRYI 128

FIG. 6. CARDIUM BELLULUM 126
    6 *a*. Side view.
    6 *b*. Anterior view (the left valve being restored).

FIG. 7. CRASSATELLA SHUMARDI 127
    7 *a*. View of a specimen, with the lower part of the valves imperfect.
    7 *b*. Cardinal view of the same.
    7 *c*. An internal cast of a larger specimen.

FIG. 8. AN UNDETERMINED BIVALVE, from the same rock as fig. 7.

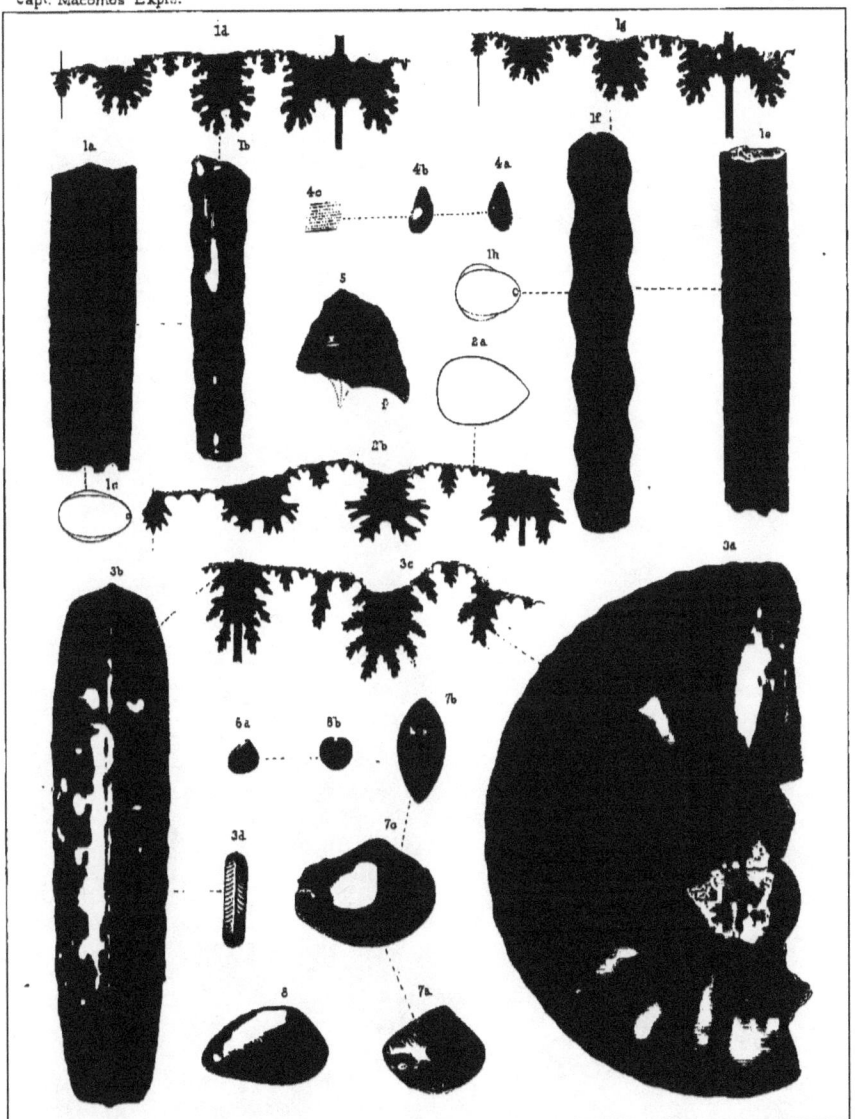

PALÆONTOLOGY of Capt. Macomb's Expln. CRETACEOUS FOSSILS. Plate II.

PLATE III.

	Page.
FIG. 1. *Deltodus Mercurii*, Newb., upper surface	137
1a. " " Newb., side view	137
Coal-Measures, Santa Fé, N. Mex.	
FIG. 2. *Ptychodus Whipplei*, Marcou, upper surface	137
2a. " " Marcou, side view	137
2b. " " Marcou, anterior face	137
2c-2f. " " Marcou, side and front view of small teeth	137
Middle Cretaceous, Pagosa, Southwestern Colorado.	
FIG. 3. *Productus nodosus*, Newb., ventral valve	140
3a. " " Newb., side view	140
3b, 3c. " " Newb., specimen with narrow hinge	140
3d. " " Newb., specimen with broad hinge	140
Coal-Measures, Santa Fé, N. Mex.	
FIG. 4. *Pleurotomaria excelsa*, Newb., side view	140
4a. " " Newb., basal aspect	140
Carboniferous strata, Cañon of Colorado River, Southeastern Utah.	
FIG. 5. *Spirifer Texanus*, Meek, side view, natural size	139
5a. A dorsal view of same specimen, showing cardinal area and foramen	139
5b. A ventral view of a larger specimen, showing the deep angular mesial sinus	139

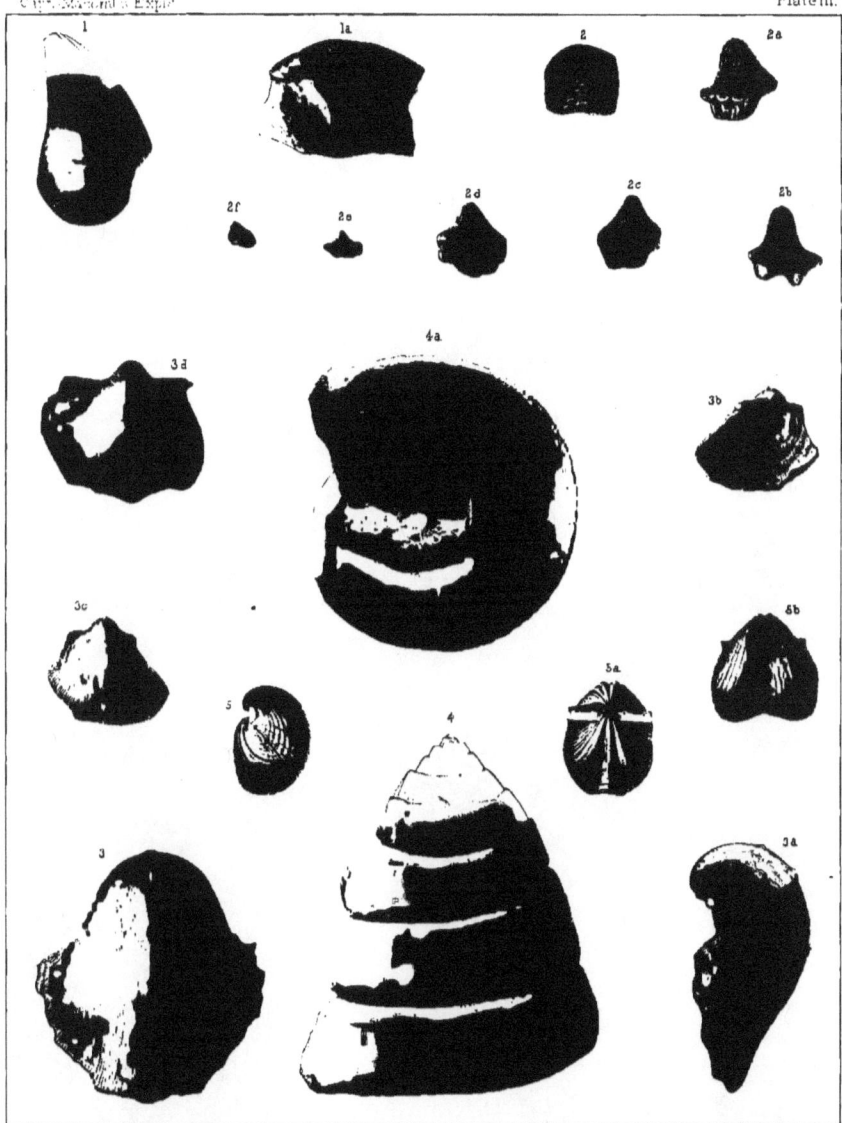

PLATE IV.

	Page.
FIG. 1, 2. *Otozamites Macombii*, Newb., Copper-mines, near Abiquin, N. Mex	141
3, 4. Branch of conifer, Copper-mines, near Abiquin, N. Mex	169
4. Branch of conifer (*Brachyphyllum?*), Copper-mines, near Abiquin, N. Mex	169

Capt. J. N. Macomb, Exp. in New Mexico & Utah. Plate IV.

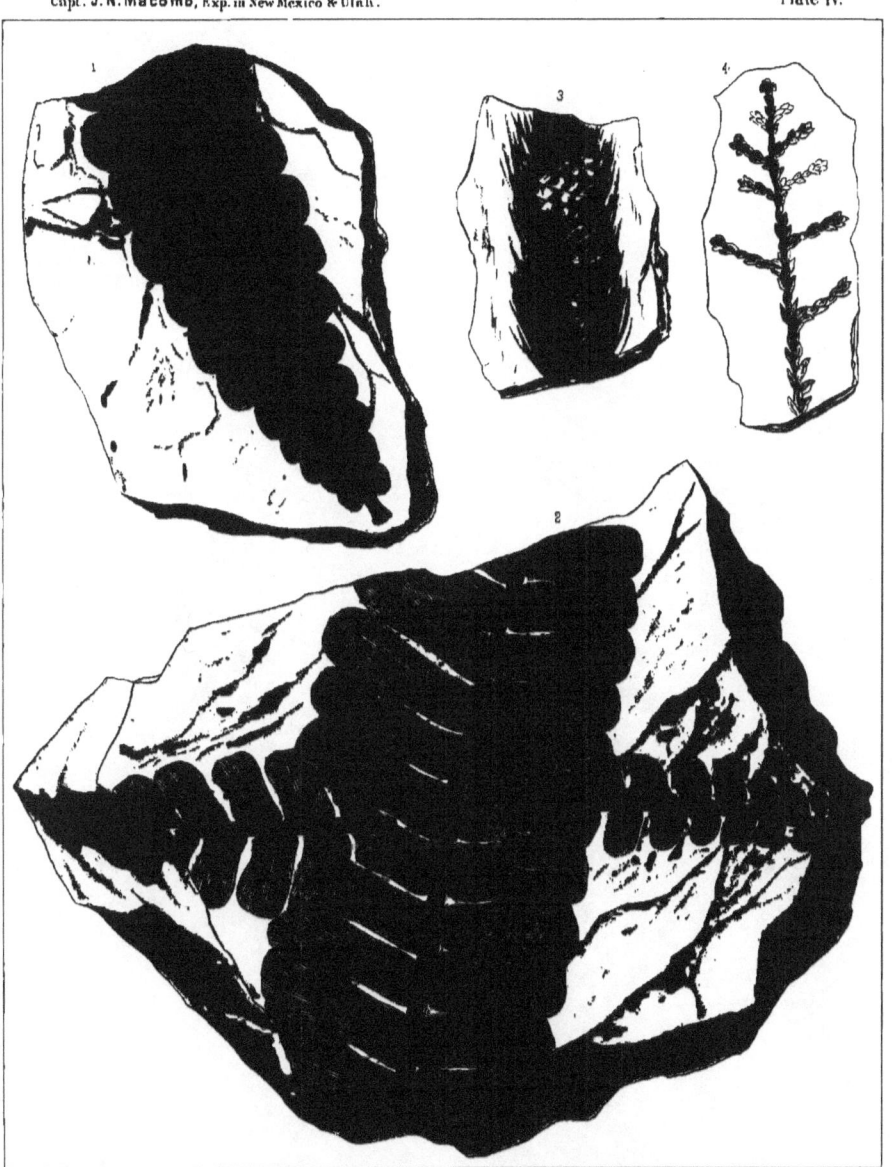

PLATE V.

	Page.
Fig. 1, 2. *Zamites occidentalis*, Newb.	142
1a. " " Newb., pinnæ enlarged, Upper Trias, Copper mines, Abiquiu, N. Mex	142
3. *Otozamites Macombii*, Newb., Upper Trias, Copper-mines, Abiquiu, N. Mex	141
4. Branch of conifer (*Pachyphyllum?*), Upper Trias, Copper-mines, Abiquiu, N. Mex	(2)
5. Cone of conifer (*Pachyphyllum?*), Upper Trias, Copper-mines, Abiquiu, N. Mex	(2)

PLATE VI.

	Page.
Fig. 1. *Pecopteris bullatus*, Bunbury	143
1a. " " Bunbury, pinnules with sori, Trias, Los Bronces, Sonora	143
2. *Alethopteris Mexicana*, Newb.	143
2a. " " Newb., pinna bearing fruit, Los Bronces, Sonora	143
3. *Pecopteris falcatus*, Emmons, in fruit, Los Bronces, Sonora	144
4. Frond of undetermined fern in fruit, Los Bronces, Sonora	
5. *Otozamites Macombii*, Newb., Los Bronces, Sonora	141
6, 6a. *Pterophyllum delicatulum*, Newb., Los Bronces, Sonora	144
7. *Pterophyllum robustum*, Newb., Los Bronces, Sonora	145
8. *Podozamites crassifolia*, Newb., Los Bronces, Sonora	
9. Branch of conifer (*Pachyphyllum?*), Copper-mines, Abiquiu, N. Mex	69
10. Branch of conifer (*Palyssia?*), Los Bronces, Sonora	145

Capt. J. N. Macomb, Exp. in New Mexico & Utah. Plate VI.

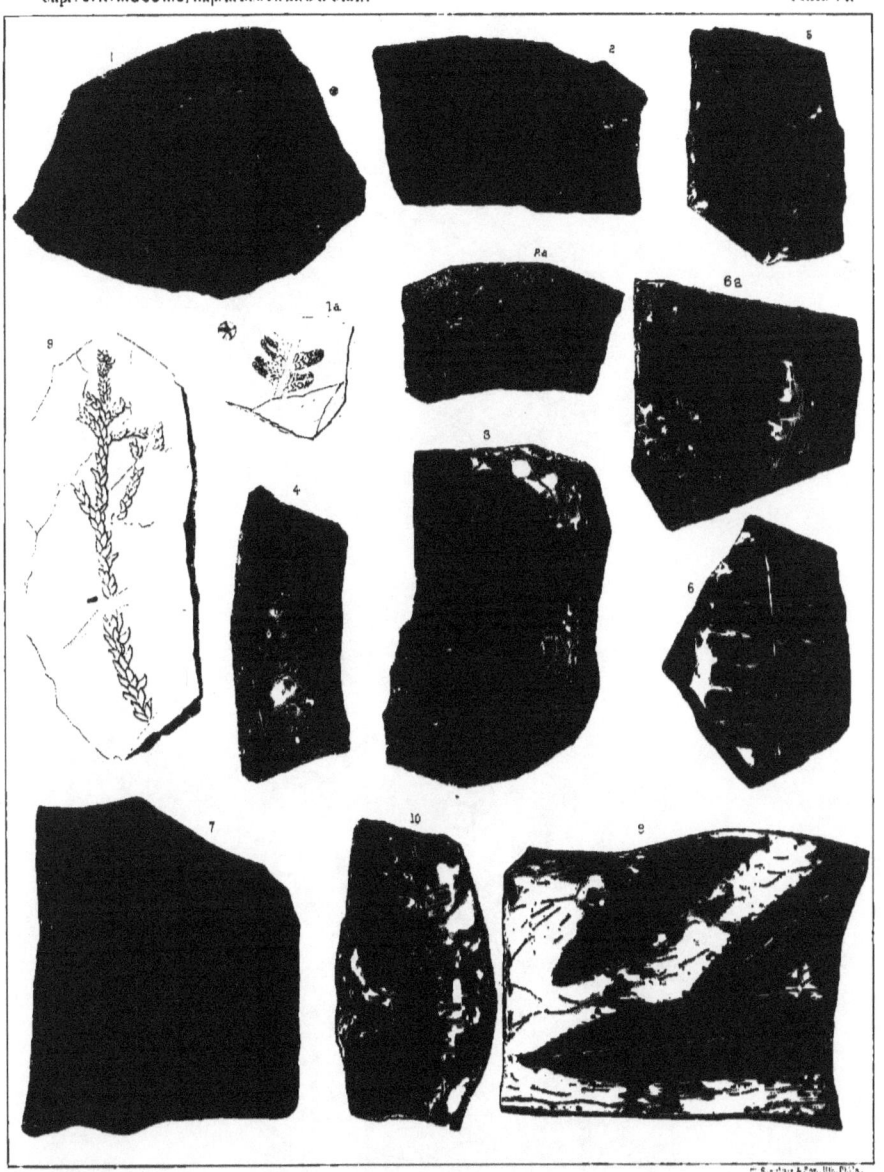

PLATE VII.

				Page
Fig. 1.	*Alethopteris Whitneyi*, Newb., upper portion of frond			145
1a.	"	"	Lower portion of frond	145
1b.	"	"	Summit of frond, Los Bronces, Sonora	145
2.	*Camptopteris Remondi*, Newb., central portion of frond			146
2a.	"	"	Portion of pinna, showing nervation, Los Bronces, Sonora	146

Capt. J. N. Macomb, Exp. in New Mexico & Utah. Plate VII.

PLATE VIII.

	Page.
FIG. 1. *Tæniopteris elegans*, Newb., Los Bronces, Sonora	147
2, 2a. *Tæniopteris glossopteroides*, Newb., Los Bronces, Sonora	147
3. *Tæniopteris magnifolia*, Rogers, Los Bronces, Sonora	147
4. *Tæniopteris magnifolia* var. ?, Los Bronces, Sonora	147
5. *Tæniopteris* sp ?, in fruit; summit of frond, Los Bronces, Sonora	
6. *Jeanpaulia radiata*, Newb., Los Bronces, Sonora	148

Capt. J. N. Macomb, Exp. in New Mexico & Utah. Plate VIII.

INDEX.

	Page.
A.	
Abiquiu	5
Abiquiu copper-mines	67
Peak	69
Actæon intercalaris	129
Alethopteris Mexicana, (Plate VI.)	
Serlii	18
Whitneyi	145
Allorisma	98
Ammonites	33, 51, 59, 77, 91, 99, 102, 107, 133
Anchura Newberryi	128
Animas	76, 80, 81
Annularia sphenophylloides	18
Anomia nitida	125
Aporrhais	99
Aquarius Mountains	55, 60
Araucaria excelsa	49
Archæocidaris	18, 21, 47
Arkansas basin	25
Arroyo Seco	69, 70
Artemesia	5
Athyris	19, 21, 43, 45, 46, 96, 98, 99, 138
Atrypha	60
Avicula	47
Axinus	19, 20, 47
Aztec Mountains	60
B.	
Baculites	72, 99, 102
anceps	130
"Bad Lands" of the Missouri	26
Nebraska	27
Bakevellia	19, 20, 21, 47
Basalt	26, 32, 52
Bear's Ears	85, 103
Bellerophon	19, 20, 21; 47
Black Hills	29, 57
Brachyphyllum	69
Buttes in Cañon Colorado	69
west of Nacimiento Mountain	112
near San Juan River	103, 104
C.	
Cabezon	1
Calamites	45, 49
Camptopteris Remondi	146
Cañon of Grand River	97
Green River	97
Largo	6, 64, 109
Piutado	90, 92
Cañons	97
Caprotina bicornis	126
Carboniferous rocks	15, 18, 63, 97, 106

	Page.
Carboniferous series	16, 22, 62
summit of	95
strata	16, 17, 19, 42, 46, 66
Cardium belinium	128
Casa Colorado	92
Cataract Creek	92
Cephalopoda	130
Cerbat Mountains	55, 59
Cerrillos, mines of the	40, 41
Cerro del Navajo	73
Chalk formation	24
Chalchuitl	41
Chama	5, 65, 70
Chonetes	19
Cimarron River	7, 24, 25
Circeopsis	52
Clay	19, 24
Coal	17, 39, 98
Coal-plants, Kansas	17
Coal-Measures, Illinois	17
Kansas	16, 17
Missouri	16
Santa Fé	46
Cobre	68
Cogswell, Lieut. M	7
Colorado River	53
basin	53, 55, 83, 93
Cañon	37, 42, 53, 93
Chiquito	56
Mountains	59, 64, 84
plateau	54, 60, 62, 94
Conglomerate	27, 29, 81
Conifers, Abiquiu copper-mines	69
Copper, old placer	40
Abiquiu	67
Los Cerrillos	41
Rocky Mountains	59
Santa Fé	37
Cottonwood Creek	18
Spring	30, 31
Cordaites	45
Crassatella Shumardi	127
Creston, the	107
Cretaceous formation	22, 25, 50, 63, 75, 77, 110
Upper	32, 50, 71, 84, 108, 121
Lower	16, 24, 32, 50, 63, 121
Middle	16, 32, 71, 121
rocks	24, 76
sandstone	23, 34
Cuchillo	66
Cyprimeria crassa	128

150 INDEX.

D.
	Page
Deltodus Mercurei	137
Dimmock, C. H	7
Divide, High	78
between Rio Grande and San Juan	74
Dorsey, Mr	7
Dragoon Creek	18, 19
Drift	81

E.
Echinoderms	18
Eighteen-Mile Ridge	27
El Vado de los Padres	6
Enchanted Spring	30
Enos, Lieut. H. M	8
Eroded buttes	92, 96, 97, 107
monuments	94
Erosion	28, 32, 37, 50, 67, 73, 112
of Colorado plateau	84
Exogyra columbella	124

F.
Fish-teeth	51, 108
Fisher, F. P	7
Fissure, volcanic	32
Foot-hills	72, 73
Fort Union	34
Fossil plants	29, 32, 33, 69
Fossils, Carboniferous	18, 19
Cretaceous	32, 33
Jurassic	29
Permian	19, 47
Fusulina	18

G.
Galisteo	38, 51
Creek	38, 48
Gallinas Mountain	34
Gasteropoda actæon	123
Gold of Galisteo Creek	39, 40
Los Cerrillos	41
Placer Mountains	39
Rocky Mountains	59
Santa Fé	37
Grand River	96
Granite	27, 81
of Santa Fé	37
Great Central Plateau	30, 50
Green River	97
Gros-bigarré	22
Gryphæa Pitcheri	33, 51, 52, 71, 88, 99, 104, 115
Guajelotes	90
Gulf of Mexico	24
Gypsum formation	21, 47, 49, 92
its parallelism	21

H.
Halymenites	77
High Divide	78
High Prairie	29

I.
Indian ornaments	41
Inoceramus	51, 52, 77, 87, 99, 107
Crispii	33
fragilis	33, 72, 127
problematicus	33, 52, 71, 72, 108, 115, 127

I.
	Page
Iron, magnetic	41
of Los Cerrillos	40
Rocky Mountains	59
old placer	40
oro	19, 31

J.
Jeanpaulia Munsteriana	148
radiata	148
Jemez	46, 67, 117
Jurassic formation	21, 28, 51, 69
fossils	16, 22, 29

L.
Labyrinth Cañon	95
Creek	98
Laguna de los Cavallos	5, 72
Lamellibranchiata	123
Lamna	33, 99, 141
Las Orejas del Oso	85, 103
Vegas	34
La Tenejal	92
Lava Plain	38
Lead	37, 39, 41
Leda	19
Lepidodendron	46
Lias	22
Limestone	26, 33
Fusulina	16
magnesian	19, 21, 22
infusorus	28
Lizards	90
Llano Estacado	48, 51
Los Cañones	69
Cerrillos	41
Lower Colorado Mountains	58
Permian formation	20

M.
Manzanita	74
Marl	21, 32, 112
variegated	48
Marnes irisées	22
McNee's Creek	31
Meek, F. B	119
Mesa	30, 48
above the Chama	69
broken	78
High	73
Great White	103
Verde	83, 85, 100, 107
Mesas of Navajo and San Juan	63, 64, 103
Mines, copper	67
gold	40
silver	41
Mogollon Mountains	55, 57, 58
Monotis Hawni	19, 21, 46
Mormon Spring	99
Mountains drained by Animas	81
Mount Taylor	55, 114
Murchisonia	19, 47
Muschelkalk	22
Myalina	19, 21, 47, 98

INDEX. 151

N.

	Page.
Nacimiento Mountain	7, 37, 56, 67, 102, 109, 112, 114
Nautilus	19, 45, 51, 77, 99
Navajo Spring	71
Needles, The	103, 107
Network of cañons	97
Neuropteris flexuosa	18
biranta	18
Newberry, Dr. J. S.	1, 7, 9, 135

O.

Ojo del Cuerbo	90
Ojo Verde	5, 93
Ojos Heriondos	86
Old placer	39, 40
Oölite	22
Orejas del Oso	85, 103
Orthis	45
Orthisina	21, 43, 45, 98
Ostrea congesta	33, 72, 77, 87, 99, 115
elegantula	33
lugubris	52, 77, 107, 123
uniformis	124
Otozamites	69, 141, 142
Macombii	141
Oxyrhina	33, 141

P.

Pachyphyllum	69
Pagosa	5, 74, 77
Palyssia	69
Pawnee Fork	22
Pecopteris arborescens	18, 49
bullatus	143
falcatus	144
Mexicana	143
Stutgardiensis	69
Pecos	49
Permo-carboniferous group	20
Pfeiffer, Albert H	5, 67, 68, 69
Piedra Parada	77
Placer Mountains	38
Plateau west of Rocky Mountains	54
Plateaus bordering Cañon Largo	109
Platyceras	45
Pleurophorous	19, 20, 47
Pleurotomaria	98, 140
Plicatula arenaria	126
Podozamites crassifolia	145
Pope's Well	51
Porphyry	26, 27, 41, 52, 76, 77, 81
Prioncyclus Macombii	132, 133
Productus	19, 21, 43, 45, 46, 58, 98, 99, 140
Pueroo	7

Q.

Quartz	26, 27, 37, 41
Quercus	99

R.

Rabbit-Ear Buttes	31
Rain-fall	40
Raton Mountains	25, 28
Red beds	47, 56
Red Fork of Canadian	31, 32

	Page.
Reservoirs	89
Retzia mormoni	43
Rhynchonella	21, 45
Rio de la Plata	81
los Mancos	85
Pinos	79
Dolores	86
Florido	79
Grande	5
Navajo	73
Piedra	77, 78
Rito Blanco	74, 76
Rock Corral	37
Rocks, jointed	77
bright-colored	68, 90, 92
Rocky Mountain system	55
Mountains, time of elevation of the	57
Ruins at Abiquin	69
Labyrinth Cañon	95
in San Juan Valley	109
on the Animas	80
Dolores	88

S.

Sago-plain	67, 83, 85, 89
Saliferous group	48
Salix Meekii	24, 31, 32, 87, 99
Sandia Mountain	56, 77
Sand-hills	27
Sandstone	24, 26, 33
San Francisco Mountains	55, 60
San Juan	5, 74, 75, 101, 106
San Juan River	106
San José Spring	7
San Mateo	55, 56, 60
Santa Fé	5, 34, 36
geology of	36, 37
minerals of	38, 39
Mountains	37, 38, 56, 65
Santo Domingo	118
Sarcobatus	99
Saurian bones	91
Scaphites Warreni	72, 121
Scoria	24, 52
Section of rocks at breaks of Red River	33
buttes west of Nacimiento Mountain	112
Cañon Colorado	95
Pintado	91
Largo	111
camp 34	104
Captain Pope's Well	52
Cedar Spring	30
Cerro Gordo	46
Colorado Valley	99
Cliffs at Moqui villages	105
Creston	108
crossing of Arkansas	27
Enchanted Spring	29
gorge of Santa Fé River	45
Labyrinth Creek	98
Middle Spring of Cimarron	28
Pawnee Fork	24

152 INDEX.

	Page.
Section of rocks at Rio Dolores	86
Santa Fé	43
San José	48
in the Valley of the Chama	71
Pecos	48
Sierra Abajo	6, 55, 62, 99, 100
de los Pinos	76, 79, 80
de la Plata	5, 56, 76, 80, 82, 84, 88
del Navajo	73, 76, 77
el Wanico	66
La Sal	55, 62, 85, 88, 89, 93
La Late	55
Madro	56, 62
San Juan	75, 76
San Miguel	56, 82, 90
Tucane	55, 62
Sigillaria Menardi	18
Silicified wood	32, 110
Silver of Los Cerrillos	41
Sierra de la Plata	81, 82
Rocky Mountains	50
Santa Fé	37
Simonson, Major	6
Siredon	90
Smoky Hill Fork	22
Smoky Hills	24
Spanish Trail	6
Spenophyllum dentatum	18
Spirifer	43, 45, 46, 60, 96, 98, 99, 138, 139
Suronam	88

T.

Table-lands skirting Rocky Mountains	34
Tæniopteris	69
elegans	147
glossopteroides	147
magnifolia	147
Tertiary basin of the Arkansas	24
fossils	25
strata	25, 26, 28, 30, 31, 36, 39, 52
at Jemez	116

	Page.
Thaumatopteris	146
Tierra Blanca	90
Maria	73, 77
Trap	27, 31, 73, 77, 81
plateaus	34, 117
buttes and mesas near Raton Mountains	31
Triassic formation	47, 63, 81, 102
rocks of Lower San Juan	103
Turquoise	41

U.

Union, Fort	7
Upper Colorado	53
Permian formation	20
magnesian limestone	21

V.

Vada del Chama	67, 71
Vail, Mr	7
Valdez, Neponocino	5
Valles, The	118
Valley of the Animas	76, 80, 81
Arkansas	22, 28
Canadian	32, 34
Cimarron	28, 30
Little Colorado	63
Pecos	48
View from High Divide	76
of country bordering San Juan	103
Volcanic action	25, 31, 34, 38, 52, 60, 61, 62
Voltzia	49, 69

W.

Walchia	48, 49
Walnut Creek	21, 22
Wasatch Mountains	55, 60
Water-supply	89, 90, 92

Z.

Zamites occidentalis	142

www.ingramcontent.com/pod-product-compliance
Lightning Source LLC
Chambersburg PA
CBHW031825230426
43669CB00009B/1230